John Wells

John Wells (1936–98) was a fou
Eye in which he wrote with
long-running political satires, *Mrs*
Dear Bill Letters. He contributed ske
Week That Was and was a columnist on *The Spectator*. His
books included *The Exploding Present*, *Masterpieces*, *Princess
Caraboo: Her True Story* and *Rude Words*, a history of the
London Library.

ʃ

SCEPTRE

Also by John Wells

The Exploding Present (1971)
Anyone for Denis? (1981)
Masterpieces (1982)
Fifty Glorious Years (1984)
Rude Words: A History of the London Library
(1991)
Princess Caraboo, Her True Story (1994)

With John Fortune
A Melon for Ecstacy (1971)

With Richard Ingrams
Mrs. Wilson's Diary 1964–70, 1974–76
The Dear Bill Letters 1980–90

Translations
The Figaro Plays (1997)

The House of Lords

From Saxon Wargods to a Modern Senate

JOHN WELLS

SCEPTRE

First published in 1997 by Hodder and Stoughton
First published in paperback in 1998 by Hodder and Stoughton
A division of Hodder Headline PLC
A Sceptre Paperback

10 9 8 7 6 5 4 3 2 1

A CIP catalogue record for this book is
available from the British Library

ISBN 0 340 64929 1

Typeset by Palimpsest Book Production Limited,
Polmont, Stirlingshire
Printed and bound in Great Britain by
Clays Ltd, St Ives plc

Hodder and Stoughton
A division of Hodder Headline PLC
338 Euston Road
London NW1 3BH

In memory of
Mark Bonham Carter
with gratitude

CONTENTS

Acknowledgements   viii
List of Illustrations   ix
Introduction: The Family Tree   xi
Chapter One   The Vacuum Behind the Throne   1
Chapter Two   The Loaf Wards   13
Chapter Three   The Gilded Tomb   25
Chapter Four   The Brains of Europe   35
Chapter Five   The Lord Chancellor's Dance   49
Chapter Six   The Barons' Beef   61
Chapter Seven   The King's Needs   69
Chapter Eight   In the Kremlin   79
Chapter Nine   The Saint with Two Heads   93
Chapter Ten   The House of Lords Abolished   103
Chapter Eleven   The Second Coming   117
Chapter Twelve   The Senate of Lilliput   129
Chapter Thirteen   A Cushion down the Trousers   141
Chapter Fourteen   Wiser Councils Prevail   153
Chapter Fifteen   Port in a Storm   167
Chapter Sixteen   A Turner Sunset   183
Chapter Seventeen   A Naked Absurdity   199
Chapter Eighteen   Incomplete Relations   217
Chapter Nineteen   A Man in Space   237
Chapter Twenty   The Theatre of Compromise   255
Postscript: Business as Usual   273
Select Bibliography   287
Index   289

ACKNOWLEDGEMENTS

As someone who has spent his life sniping at politicians in so-called satirical sketches, in *Mrs Wilson's Diary* and *The Dear Bill Letters*, I am not a historian. This is not a serious work of history, more an extended journalistic essay. I have therefore in the interests of lightness avoided footnotes and attributions. I would however like to thank, among many others, Dr Sean Kelly, Caroline Dorée, Cecily Gatacre and Benedict King for a great deal of spadework, D. L. Jones, Librarian of the House of Lords, for valuable advice at the outset, Alan Bell, the Librarian, and the staff of the London Library and Dr. Michael Evans, Assistant Curator of the Warburg Institute Library. Also to John Grigg, Hugh Montgomery-Massingberd and Sir John Sainty for reading early versions of the typescript and correcting the worst howlers. As will be apparent in the text, I am also immensely indebted to the kindness and generosity of the former Superintendent of Staff at the House of Lords, Major Peter Horsfall.

LIST OF ILLUSTRATIONS

Section I
Jacob's vision of the angels ascending and descending from heaven (Mary Evans Picture Library)
The Ladder of Virtue (Mary Evans Picture Library)
An illustration from Dante's *Paradiso* (Mary Evans Picture Library)
The Three Estates – a French scheme drawn in 1450 (Mary Evans Picture Library)
The Mediaeval House of Lords (E. T. Archive)
The Baiting of the Pope's Bull (By courtesy of the trustees of the British Museum)
Henry VIII as Head of Church and State tramples the Pope (Mary Evans Picture Library)
Seraph from the ceiling at Henry III's Painted Chamber (after 1263) (By courtesy of the trustees of the British Musuem)
The Powder Treason, 1605 (By courtesy of the trustees of the British Museum)
Queen Anne at the State Opening (Mary Evans Picture Library)
The State Opening of 1769 in the Queen's Chamber (Mary Evans Picture Library)
Queen Caroline mounts a challenge to the constitution (By courtesy of the trustees of the British Museum)

Section II
The Bright Horizon – an 1896 poster by Walter Crane (National Museum of Labour History)
The New Peerage or Fountain of Honour (By courtesy of the trustees of the British Museum)
The White Hall in 1831 (Mary Evans Picture Library)
The Rising Tide of Democracy – Brougham as Lord Chancellor proposes change (By courtesy of the trustees of the British Museum)
Destruction by Fire of Both Houses of Parliament in 1834 by H. O'Neill (E.T. Archive)
Westminster Hall (Mary Evans Picture Library)
A Punch Joke (Mary Evans Picture Library)

The Lords in their new Parliament Chamber (House of Lords Record Office)

Basing House Defended by the Cavaliers (Parliamentary Works Directorate)

Adoration of the Peerage (Mary Evans Picture Library)

'John Bull's Idol' – a cartoon in *Punch*, 1843 (Mary Evans Picture Library)

'The Lords Met for the Despatch of Business' – a cartoon in *Punch*, 1845 (Mary Evans Picture Library)

'An Appeal heard by the Lords' – a cartoon in *Punch*, 1845 (*Punch*)

'The Challenge' – a cartoon in *Punch*, 1884 (Mary Evans Picture Library)

'Will They Bell the Cat?' – a cartoon in *Punch*, 1907 (Mary Evans Picture Library)

'The Fiery Cross' – a cartoon in *Punch*, 1907 (Mary Evans Picture Library)

'The Chance of a Lifetime' – a cartoon in *Punch*, 1911 (*Punch*)

'Disagreement about the Address of the Guillotine', 1948 (Cartoons of the University of Kent/David Low/Solo Syndication)

'Kind Hearts and Coronets', 1955 (Cartoons of the University of Kent/Vicky/Daily Mail)

'If only we could get him to take a peerage', 1955 (Cartoons of the University of Kent/Cummings/Solo Syndications)

'Pay Day in the House of Lords' – a cartoon in *Punch*, 1956 (*Punch*)

'Soon we can get our demob and stand for Parliament . . .!', 1962 (Cartoons of the University of Kent/Vicky/Daily Mail)

'Kind Hearts and Coronets', 1956 (Cartoons of the University of Kent/Vicky/Daily Mail)

'It all happened so long ago', 1990 (Cartoons of the University of Kent/Garland/Daily Telegraph)

'Redundant and not a single word about retraining!', 1967 (Cartoons of the University of Kent/Garland/Daily Telegraph)

INTRODUCTION

The Family Tree

Lord Milford, ninety-one years old, sat with a shawl round his shoulders, musing in his studio in Hampstead. The walls were hung with his own paintings, bold and vaguely *fauve* in style, with blocks of vivid colour edged with strong black lines. He described himself in *Who's Who* as 'taking the Communist Whip in the House of Lords'. In fact, he was the only Communist who ever took a seat there, let alone a whip.

Stephen Spender, who knew him as a young man when he was the Hon. Wogan Philipps, claimed that Milford's political conversion dated from the time his father had seen a nude he had painted with green pubic hair, and had disinherited him. 'Given Wogan's skill as a painter in those days, it was quite clever of his father to recognize what it was meant to be, but he cut him off immediately.'

His father could not prevent him inheriting the peerage. He was the heir to a title first created in 1776 as a reward for his very remote ancestor, Richard Philipps, MP for Pembroke, for loyalty in the House of Commons during the disastrous run-up to the loss of Britain's colonies in America. The title had 'become extinct' in 1823.

But peerages move in mysterious ways. It had been revived by a cousin for ten years in the middle of the nineteenth century, he had died, and the title had disappeared into the vaults again. Then, in 1939, the honour was revived and awarded to Wogan's father for good works in Wales. Whatever Wogan thought about it, the peerage appeared to be immortal. His financial inheritance, actually for his Communist views rather than the green pubic hair, had gone to his younger brother, but as the elder son the title clung to him like a curse. In 1962, when his father died, there was legally and constitutionally nothing he could do to avoid it. With a terrible inevitability, he became Lord Milford, with a seat in the Upper House of Parliament.

Like many modern heirs to the peerage, Milford's career was far from the Wodehousian archetype. That is not to say that the creator of Blandings might not, on an inventive day, have imagined it. At the time of the Spanish Civil War, the pacifist Frances Partridge remembered him 'making signs in the air', giving the Communist salute, and fighting with the International Brigade. Since then he had lived a life of impeccable Marxist virtue.

After failing his medical exam for the Army in 1939, he spent the war organizing a trade union on a farm. He continued to paint, marrying first the novelist Rosamund Lehmann, then the former Countess of Huntingdon, whose farm in Italy he had tried to run as a workers' collective. 'It didn't' he recalled, 'really work', and finally to Tamara Rust, widow of an editor of the Daily Worker.

But he was musing more particularly about the time he had inherited his father's title and made his maiden speech in the Lords in 1963: 'When I went in, they all said, "Hello, Wogan, hello, Wogan", because they'd all known me at Eton, you see. "We must have a drink afterwards!" Then I made my speech.' He had been advised, he told the press, that his maiden speech should be uncontroversial, but he felt compelled to inform them that the House of Lords was an anachronism and should be abolished immediately. No one sitting as a hereditary peer on the red leather benches had inherited any special ability or talent that enabled them to function as a legislator. All they had inherited was money – all he'd got was a third-class railway ticket to the Soviet Union – and privilege. Money and privilege were what they shared with the new life peers, who were 'bankers, steel magnates, newspaper proprietors and industrialists of all sorts'.

If his opening remarks offended some of the derelict second- and third-generation hereditaries, who treated the House as a daycare centre for the unemployed, his crack about the life peers lost him the sympathy of several on the Labour side, down-at-heel former union bosses who had been shunted upstairs by way of a pension. But he pursued his argument, which centred on his fellow hereditary peers.

The idea of hereditary legislators was ridiculous in the age of automation and space flight. Socialism was advancing on all fronts; those in colonial lands were throwing off the hated yoke and the common people were claiming their democratic rights. He blamed the House of Lords for all the trouble in Ireland, for the suffering of British coal miners, for blocking one Bill to raise the school-leaving age between the wars and another that would have allowed a Labour government to experiment in large-scale farming. In 1956 they had even delayed the abolition of the death penalty, which had been carried in the Commons by a free vote.

It had been claimed that a second chamber was valuable because it prevented the government of the day from rushing through legislation that was harmful to the electorate. What the country needed was not a brake on democratic decisions and legislation, he told them, but an accelerator, so that democracy could play its full part in driving Britain forward.

It was, he knew, bred in their lordships' very bones to defend property and the whole capitalist system, but he appealed to them to stand aside. They must make way for a glorious future when the commanding heights of the economy would be controlled by the ordinary British people, whose skill had created the wealth of the country. Only then would the people's elected representatives in the House of Commons be the sovereign authority. Only then would the people have complete political power.

Thirty years later he still seemed bewildered by the Lords' response. 'Do you know, after I'd spoken, not one of 'em would buy me a drink? None of 'em. Not anything at all!'

Lord Milford was not alone in doubting the rights of hereditary peers to inherit a seat in Parliament with the family silver. In 1963 Michael Foot, sharing his belief that the whole thing should be abolished, had appealed to the Labour Party to 'do the job in good, clean fashion': 'Let us cut its throat. Let's make up our minds to have no further bother from the House of Lords in future.'

A. N. Wilson, stirred to consider the mystery by Lord Cranborne's defence of the hereditary system in a Lords' debate in 1996, wrote in the *Evening Standard* that the idea was outrageous. Why should a man be entitled to a vote in the Upper House because his father's name happened to be the Earl of Posh rather than Mr Smith? Such dignified bourgeois outrage was always taken with a pinch of salt by the peers and their descendants.

In June 1975, the Hon. Mrs Edith Ellen Bennard, seventy-one, daughter of the late Lord Quibell, of Scunthorpe, tried to sue the Treasury under the Sex Discrimination Act. Her finances were 'at rock bottom'. Her husband, a former bookmaker nearly twenty years her junior, was in prison, and she was living on social security. If – and this was the basis of her case – she had been a man, she would have inherited a title from her father, a former Labour MP, and would have been able to rub along on her daily expenses from the House of Lords. The Treasury Counsel, one Genevra Caws, said Mrs Bennard could only claim if she was being done out of a job, and being a member of the House of Lords was not a job. Ms Caws did not deny that the House of Lords *itself* did a good job, but being a peer of the realm entailed no contract, no obligation to provide a service, and therefore no obligation on anyone's part to provide the said peer with remuneration for any service that might be rendered.

Such attempts to catch the elusive nature of the parliamentary peerage in the butterfly net of reason have almost always failed, and despite the attractions of membership of the Upper House to Mrs Bennard, there have always been many who wanted nothing to do with it. The socialist guru R. H. Tawney, offered a peerage by Ramsay MacDonald, famously asked 'What harm have I ever done to the Labour Party?'

In the Middle Ages the Lords had to be bullied and fined to attend, and even in the late twentieth century far less than half of the hereditary peers have ever exercised their right to do so. The reasons for this are varied. Some have been actively discouraged, like the unnamed peer who interrupted during a speech on the economy with the words, 'My lords, I used to be a great French parachutist in a great French book!' (This contribution was excised from *Hansard*.) The Fourth Earl Russell, who usually took the precaution of sending his speeches in advance to the Lords for the clerks to blue-pencil the more obscene passages, held them spellbound in the 1970s with an appeal for universal nudism on the dole.

One life peer, Lord Taylor of Blackburn, an elder of the United Reformed Church and former leader of Blackburn Town Council, argued in the early 1980s that insanity should not prevent peers from attending. He himself had been detained in a psychiatric hospital, where his wife would have preferred him to stay, but he secured his release by claiming parliamentary privilege and made his way back to Westminster. There have even been times when insanity was actively welcomed, as in 1841: the opposition was seeking support for a motion of no confidence in the Government and carried in a peer, barking mad and strapped to a chair for the extra vote.

But other more conventional figures were sometimes deterred by the nature of the work when they got there, often very tedious. The second Earl of Gowrie, whose original earldom was dramatically extinguished in 1582 when his handsome ancestor was stabbed to death while trying to defend himself after dinner against the unwelcome advances of James I, then King of Scotland, was a respected minister in Mrs Thatcher's government, and later chairman of the Arts Council. He found himself, on one of his earliest visits to the Lords, having lunch next to the ninth Earl of Albemarle, born in 1882.

An impeccably dressed cartoon figure of a peer in a pepper-and-salt tweed suit with a white moustache, Albemarle owed his own seat in the House to his ancestor Arnold Van Keppel, a pretty companion of the not entirely heterosexual William of Orange, who according to *The Complete Peerage* 'had rendered no service whatsoever to his adopted country'. Gowrie risked the suggestion that he might be finding the debate a bit boring. 'Boring, my dear boy? I tell you, there are afternoons when one comes close to *fainting* for the want of a jest!'

A former clerk, Stuart Braham, tells a story about an unnamed peer in the 1960s who actually died during a debate. Given the characteristic vigour and zesty involvement of the other debaters, nobody noticed until hours later, when the Parliament Chamber cleared. At this point – and here the sceptical might question the medical evidence – it was discovered that *rigor mortis* had set in and the body was impossible to move. Doorkeepers, so the story concludes, were sent to close all the doors and rattle them as loudly as possible, while others broke the deceased peer's bones, folded him up and removed him. He would then, of course, following local logic, have been put into a taxi at the Peers' Entrance, to expire on the way to the hospital, fatalities not being encouraged in what is still officially a Royal Palace.

Even with the lure of the expenses, it was always unpaid committee work that many energetic and busy men were reluctant to do. There is even a story told of a writ of summons arriving by messenger at the front door of one unnamed peer who assumed it was a writ of another kind and legged it out of a back window.

Other peers were simply diffident. The fifth Viscount Hampden, explaining his position in the 1970s, wrote that he had never attended or voted in the House of Lords, first, because 'no legislation had been proposed that offended him or affected anything he felt particularly strongly about'; and second, because he had 'no detailed expertise' on the current subjects before the House, which made it impossible for him to contribute anything of value in the way of amendments to the Bills.

Lord Monteagle of Brandon, descended from an 'indifferent' Chancellor of the Exchequer of 1939, was a rummer cove, but none the less only an extreme case of many hereditary peers who came to the Parliament Chamber when they felt like it. He took his seat in 1947 and waited forty-five years before he felt the need to speak. This beat the previous record by Lord Glanusk, another nineteenth-century creation, who had said nothing for thirty-four. Like Hampden, Monteagle pleaded a lack of expert knowledge. 'People kept asking me, "When are you going to make your maiden speech? Surely you must be an expert on something?" I can assure you, I'm not an expert on anything. I merely thought it was better to keep my mouth shut and be thought a fool than to open it and leave no possible doubt.'

He finally addressed the historic House shortly before dinner one evening, watched by his four children and – his wife Anne having a prior engagement – by a family friend, Pauline Samuelson. He had intended to speak for ten minutes, but when he approached the Government whip's office with the news that he *meant* to break his silence, he was asked to reduce this to five. The subject he felt he 'knew more about than most' was the water shortage. Some time before, a tree had been felled at his home in Ireland, breaking a waterpipe. He had failed to notice this by reason of the boggy nature of the local soil, by which time, he said, about ten thousand gallons had gone down the drain. 'A few years ago, a plentiful supply of water was freely available to everyone and totally taken for granted. One just turned on the tap and out it came. That has now changed, with many parts of England suffering drought conditions, and it would seem to be sensible to take precautions before it is too late.' He said afterwards he thought it had gone very well, and he was glad he had taken the trouble to rehearse his lines.

It is possible to see why he enjoyed it. For someone who, unlike Lord Hampden, felt strongly about something, it would be nice to get it off one's chest. Even for a moderate exhibitionist with a limited amount of political ambition, the kind of man or woman who finds their way on to committees all over the country, there is clearly a lot of fun in being a lord.

That the qualification to be one should depend on the accident of birth or death baffles the reason. That such a system should have survived into the late twentieth century is a miracle.

Not that all life peers are without their mystery and magic. Baroness Elliot of Harwood, one of the first to be created in 1958, was the daughter of a man born, incredible as it might seem, in 1826. Her grandfather had been born before the French Revolution. Conceived when her father was well over eighty, she herself lived to a great age, walking on two sticks, bent like an angle–iron and distressing the Tory whips by sitting directly behind the government front bench. There, in the background of every ministerial statement from the Lords, she could be seen, bald except for a few sparse white hairs, lying with her head on one side, eyes closed, easily mistakable for a corpse. Alarmed that she might present a less than dynamic impression of the Party in the Upper House, Tory whips tried to persuade her to move, but she refused.

Lady Elliot was, despite appearances, entirely *compos mentis*, leaning back to listen to the Puginesque loudspeaker concealed in the bench behind. Other life peers, like Lord Wilson of Rievaulx, having no reason or inducement to retire, lost all their mental faculties without losing their seats as legislators, making the life peerage almost as irrational an institution as the hereditary.

Nor do they enjoy much greater respect. Cynics, at least, are clear that they are in the Upper House for one of two reasons: either, if they are politicians, as a booby prize for failing in the Commons, or, if they are successful industrialists, in exchange for a large sum of money.

We shall consider their role later.

A great deal of this book is devoted to examining and analysing the secret chemistry that produced the miracle of hereditary right.

It was the hereditary peers who formed the House of Lords for the first eight hundred years of its existence, who shaped its rituals and procedures, who defended its powers against the first long-delayed shocks of secular democracy, and who provided the essential mystery and the magic which has repeatedly bewildered and frustrated reformers.

This mystery and magic continues to cling to the rituals of the House of Lords. Other countries govern themselves in horseshoe-shaped arenas under bright lights in buildings of steel and glass, their elected representatives dressed in working clothes. This British senate, created by a mixture of heredity and royal favour, meets in a gilded Victorian fantasy of a medieval cathedral enriched with stained-glass windows, crests and coats-of-arms, mythical beasts rearing in wood and stone, often in fancy dress.

It is presided over by a man in a horsehair wig and knee-breeches who has only to perform a strange little dance, taking three shuffling steps to the left, to transform himself from the grave and unpartisan Speaker of the House, to all appearances the Authority of the Law Incarnate, into a committed front-bench spokesman of the government in power.

What is even eerier is that the man in the horsehair wig and knee-breeches, Lord Irvine of Lairg, is a direct successor in the office of Lord Chancellor to St Swithin, St Thomas à Becket, St Thomas More and one of the great minds of the Renaissance Francis Bacon. There is an inheritance of mind and spirit, something far older than the Victorian chamber, something as ancient and strange as Westminster Abbey, almost as old as Stonehenge.

That mystery is embedded in the hereditary system. However flawed and polluted their ancestry may be, however many cuckoos have laid and hatched their eggs higher up in the family tree, however grisly some of the legitimate offspring of the peerage have become – brothel-keepers, swindlers or drug-dealers – and however much the whole show may have been constitutionally and architecturally botched up, there is a sense of intertwining tradition, of experience and political attitudes passed on from one generation to the next that seems obscurely valuable. Priests and lawyers and members of the College of Arms have been at work for centuries, lending the tradition weight and authority.

But trying to explain the origins of these traditions is not easy.

The House of Lords was not established, like the United States Senate or the German Bundesrat, in the wake of a revolution or a war with a clearly defined role and a written constitution. Until 1544 it was not even known as the House of Lords. Royal councils, great councils, war-parties of marauding lords all figure in its early history.

Even in comparatively recent times its day-to-day working has been bewildering to foreign commentators. The printed debates of a single session fill hundreds of pages, the biographies of its leading figures whole libraries. Full records exist for nearly three centuries, and the Victoria Tower contains wooden racks full of parchment scrolls, official minutes, memoirs, letters and attendance lists that go back to the Middle Ages.

To try to write a comprehensive history of the Lords would be like trying to write a comprehensive history of Asia: to describe one landmark is to ignore a hundred others, to single out a village for attention to miss cities of far greater importance. I have tried therefore to concentrate on the central mystery of the House of Lords. How could such a blatant anachronism, a senate largely made up of unelected hereditary legislators, have survived to the end of the twentieth century?

Very little has been written in defence of the hereditary principle, and then generally under the threat of its abolition. If reason quails at the task, its champions have been forced to fall back on what Edmund Burke would have called political theology. Burke himself probably makes the best case, in his *Reflections on the French Revolution*, when he recognizes the hereditary principle at work throughout European civilization as it existed before 1789.

The tract itself is a highly coloured defence of the existing order, written in the early months of the Revolution, that reaches its climax in a description of Marie Antoinette as a Mrs Siddons-like tragic heroine being brought back as a prisoner from Versailles by a howling mob of revolutionary devils. Amusingly, he criticizes the Revolution as being 'destitute of all taste and elegance', but goes further to see the behaviour of the mob as revealing political theatre. 'Nothing in the Revolution,' he writes in his *Letters on a Regicide Peace*, 'no, not to a phrase or a gesture, not to the fashion of a hat or shoe, was left to accident.' Everything expressed a desire to disrupt continuity, to break all links with the past, to impose a 'secular messianic state'.

This in turn causes him to consider by contrast the political theatre of the old regime. He finds it in 'solemn acts, in buildings, in music, in speech, in drama, in the dignity of persons, who solemnize the natural God-given order with a modest splendour, with unassuming state, with mild majesty and sober pomp'.

Their respect for custom and the 'natural order' is rooted in the idea of heredity, in what he calls 'the patrimony of knowledge', the links of law, customs, manners and habits of life. We have inherited an ancient civil, moral and political order, and what binds society together is the fact that it is a shared inheritance.

No citizen of what Burke called the Commonwealth of Europe could 'altogether be an exile in any part of it'. When a man travelled anywhere in Europe before the Revolution 'he never felt himself quite abroad'. This was due to 'the similitude of religion, laws and manners'. He admitted that there might be different forms of religious worship, but everyone accepted a great chain that linked society together, from the 'littlest platoon' through its ranks and orders, ultimately to God. They inherited the memory of Germanic customs, of feudal institutions, 'the whole improved and digested into system and discipline by Roman law'.

Mary Wollstonecraft, when she read Burke, told him that his respect for rank had swallowed up his common feelings of humanity. Tom Paine wanted to know where the revolutionaries had learned to impale heads on pikes if not from their former rulers. Why was the suffering of the Queen worse than the suffering of a thousand ordinary women left widows by the wars of the old regime? But Burke's respect for rank, for the links of inheritance that bound one generation to the next, and therefore for hereditary nobility 'forming the chain that connects the ages of a nation', was rooted in the same belief that formed the House of Lords, and should at least be considered, if only as political theology.

Forty years after Burke wrote his *Reflections on the French Revolution*, the Great Reform Bill of 1832 looked, for a moment, likely to bring about the end of the hereditary peers in the Upper House, and Richard Trench, later Bishop of Truro, shared the same anxieties. He was then a young member of the Cambridge Conversazione Society, better known as the Apostles, and writing to a fellow Apostle he tried to put his feelings into words.

They were neither of them, like Burke, nostalgic conservatives.

Their great hero in the Society was F. D. Maurice, one of the first to call himself a Christian Socialist. Like Burke, though, they despised the French *philosophes*, Voltaire and Rousseau, whose rationalism they believed had reduced man to a machine. 'Primogeniture, heredity,' Trench wrote, 'all that rests on a *spiritual relation*, will no longer be recognised, and must be swept away before the new industrial principle.'

This book is really about the conflict of these two ideas, between the hierarchical and the egalitarian visions of society; between Burke's idea of a civilization becoming more civilized by the celebration of its past, the preening of its roots, by the maintenance of what Richard Trench called 'the spiritual relation', the kind of ancestor worship that shaped the hereditary House of Lords for the majority of its existence, and 'the secular messianic state', the 'industrial principle' that failed for so amazingly long to destroy it.

In economic terms, the survival of the English peerage was due to the rule of primongeniture, the eldest son as biological lottery-winner taking all, sisters and younger brothers fading out with a pittance to join the upper middle class. In France and in other parts of Europe, the *Code Napoleon*, insisting on a fairer division, broke up most of the old aristocratic estates within a matter of years. But the notion that the same lottery prize should include a seat in the sentate remained a mystery. The more I thought about it, the more the House of Lords seemed at the same time antique, fragile and vulnerable. It could be destroyed for ever in an afternoon by a simple majority in the House of Commons and vanish into thin air.

CHAPTER ONE

The Vacuum Behind the Throne

'During the State Opening there'll be sharpshooters on top of every building!'

The voice was quiet and reassuring, with a strong Yorkshire accent. We were looking down through leaded windows from high under the eaves of the Palace of Westminster. Below, the cars and lorries, buses and bikes were roaring and rumbling in the noisy street between us and the Abbey. Inside the Palace we were surrounded by a Victorian dream of medieval authority and authenticity: Pugin furniture, dark green wallpaper and carved Gothic doors. But the IRA could strike at ceremonial: I imagined the clatter of the Household Cavalry beneath the windows, the State Coach turning in, the jingle of harness, then the crack of high-velocity bullets chipping the paving stones and the sudden silence before the panic that would follow.

I was being shown the Works, a modern senate, in the middle of a thirty years' British civil war between Catholics and Protestants in Ulster. 'In the old days there would have been a great sucking of teeth about letting on about it, but nowadays they make a point of drawing attention to them. When Airey Neave was blown up in 1979 they said, "It's time to get the experts in, the Custodians."'

The Custodians were armed with Belgian-made rifles that could kill at two thousand yards.

Airey Neave, of course, was a member of the Commons, and nobody since Guy Fawkes had tried to blow up any member of the

House of Lords. Lord Grimond, with whom I had walked up from Westminster underground station that morning, said with a great chuckle and a wild light in his blue eyes that no self-respecting terrorist would think the Lords were worth blowing up. He suspected some of the old boys of being slightly miffed about it.

My present guide, Major Horsfall of the Coldstream Guards and Superintendent of Staff at the House of Lords, did not agree. 'In 1980 there were a hundred and sixty police and armed Custodians. How many do you think there are now? I may as well tell you, because you'll never guess. There are four hundred and sixty-two. That's three big shifts, three hundred and sixty-five days a year. We're spending something like eight million a year just on the police. Let me show you the Parliament Chamber.'

Stripped down for repairs, it looked like a film set. The great golden canopy over the Throne shone as bright as ever, the stained-glass windows filled with coats-of-arms let in a muted light, the carved heads of kings gleamed beneath the galleries, but the central heating was being mended. The bright blue gold-patterned carpet was rolled back to reveal the pipes under the back row of red-leather benches, and one of the clusters of brass lamps had been lowered to floor level for cleaning.

Each cluster of lamps, Peter Horsfall explained, had an independent electric motor that let them down on the end of a chain and then drew them up again to the painted and coffered wooden ceiling. Ten years before, a lump of rotten wood the size of a cannon-ball had fallen from the roof, very nearly killing the hundred-year-old peer 'Manny' Shinwell who had been sitting directly underneath it until a few moments before. The Tory peer 'Bertie' Denham, thinking it was a bomb, had picked it up, with insane courage, and rushed to dunk it in a pail of water. Since then, a lot more of the Victorian woodwork had been found to be unsafe, taken out and painstakingly restored at colossal expense.

Now Peter Horsfall was running his fingers along the cage of brass mesh under the clerks' table. It looked as if it had been designed, like the rest of the furniture, by Pugin. 'This only went in a couple of years back. It's to stop bombs being planted under the table.'

He pointed out the Bench of Bishops, with its lower armrest to accommodate their cassocks and surplices. It was there, according to the story, that a very old backwoodsman peer, hustled in for the Parliament Bill debate in 1911, was shortsightedly gaping at the unfamiliar surroundings when he saw the bishops, drew back in horror, and shouted, 'Good God! Women!'

But Horsfall led me on, past the Woolsack and the steps to the Throne, to an elaborately carved side door behind the gilded canopy. 'We get this checked by sniffer dogs before the State Opening. What do you think's inside? Don't worry, you'd never guess. There!'

He flung open the door to reveal a deep broom-cupboard, running the whole width of the back of the throne. Fixed into the wall was a length of floppy grey piping of enormous diameter, like an elephant's trunk. 'Vacuum. Everything goes down through a shaft. Vacuum cleaner.'

By contrast, the Throne, the Woolsack, the Bench of Bishops, the whole stage-set of the Parliament Chamber seemed even more theatrical and unreal. But what made them different from a theatre set was that they had a political purpose. They turned wishes and dreams into reality, rather like a bundle of bones, rattles and voodoo charms in a witch-doctor's hut, at the centre of a modern state.

Working on a historical film recently, I found myself in the breakfast queue next to the officer commanding a troop of Horse Guards. They had been hired by the day and put into costume to appear as the Bloody Blues harrying the workers before the Reform Bill. I said I hadn't realized that the Guards had been privatized.

He wouldn't really agree to that. He preferred to think of it as voluntary work, like shows and displays overseas: a notice went up, explaining that any money they made would be paid into regimental funds. He conceded that they might have to sign a contract, but they would never do it if they didn't feel like it. I asked him what happened if they were posted to Northern Ireland.

That was different. That wasn't a contract, that was active service for Queen and Country.

This was the purpose of the Parliament Chamber. The witchcraft turned a civil contract into a sacred obligation to die for Queen and Country. In earlier days it had turned dangerous warlords into loyal and dependable generals.

The role of the House of Commons in all this was dominant. There, the representatives of the people expressed the willingness of the nation to oppose terrorism with armed force. The House of Lords had the right to confirm or briefly delay that decision.

But it was the Commons, the Lords, the Lord Chancellor and the Queen acting together who played the sacramental role, and this, the Parliament Chamber, with its carpets rolled back and its lights let down for repair, was the set on which they played it.

Beneath its golden canopy, edged with the figures of the barons who faced King John at Runnymede, the Throne that morning was draped, as it was during ordinary sessions of Parliament, with a blue-grey dust-cover. It was a big chair and, whether or not the Queen was sitting in it in her reading glasses and a crown announcing a political party's plans for the nation, it was still no more real than any plywood throne on a stage. It was one of a pair – the other was being restored – but there had been many big chairs like it in the past that had served first as the Throne of England, then, after the Union with Scotland, as the Throne of Great Britain, and after the Union with Ireland, as the Throne of the United Kingdom. All represented in magical terms the seat of our shared national power.

In October 1460, in the middle of the Wars of the Roses, the Duke of York, soon to be Edward IV, arrived at Westminster with three hundred armed men, led them through Westminster Hall, through Westminster Palace and into the old Parliament Chamber by the river. The Upper House – what we shall call the Lords – was in session. He walked alone to the Throne, and, according to an eye-witness: 'He laid his hand on the cushion like a man about to take possession of his right, and kept his hand there for a short while. At last, drawing back, and standing still under the cloth of state, he looked attentively at the gazing assembly.' Then the senior member of the House of Lords, the Archbishop of Canterbury, stepped forward and asked him whether he wanted to see the King.

The magic had worked. The chair was not just a chair. The Duke of York had felt its force-field.

But the whole Parliament Chamber was radioactive with the dignity of the Lords. Commoners were excluded, required for centuries to stand bareheaded at the Bar of the House – a wooden barrier at the door facing the Throne – while the Lords sat in their hats. Even when a television company was filming a documentary quite recently the crew were forbidden even to stand on the carpet of the Parliament Chamber. In ritual terms, even the Throne and the Woolsack were excluded, considered to be outside the Chamber.

The Monarch could address the Lords from beneath the canopy, but if, like Charles I, in still relatively friendly days, he spoke to them from in front of the old fireplace, his words would be struck from the record, dissolved by the atmosphere of Privilege. Inside the Chamber, he had no right to speak.

The Lord Chancellor's position was even more mystical. As Speaker of the House he was presumably present, though with very little to do. But as he sat there on the Woolsack, supported by his little backrest covered in matching scarlet silk, or even stood in front of it, he was also the representative of the Monarch, and that put him technically outside the Chamber, within the force-field of the Throne.

That was why, when he performed his little dance, dressed in his full-bottomed wig and his black silk robe with the gold facings, he was magically entering the Chamber. By shuffling a few steps to the left he became another creature: partisan, biased, the spokesman of the party that had appointed him. During the committee stage of a Bill he could even walk round the table, slip off his wig and gown, take his seat on the red-leather government front bench and put his buckled shoes up on the table, revealing himself as a cabinet minister.

This separation between the Throne, the Woolsack and the House of Lords could work to the Lords' disadvantage. Early in the seventeenth century, when both Houses of Parliament were struggling to defend their rights against dictatorial demands for money from James I, the Lords decided they wanted time to discuss any Bill in private. During the committee stage, therefore, the King and his representative, the Lord Chancellor, agreed to withdraw, taking with them the Mace as the symbol of royal authority. The Lords were then free to talk in confidence, but they could do no more than talk. Constitutionally the power-pack had been removed: no decision or change to the law could be made until the Lord Chancellor returned.

The Woolsack, like the Throne, was just another piece of furniture. It was vast, scarlet and, as its name suggests, stuffed with wool, with horsehair for added bounce. As the mixture gradually turns to a hard, fibrous felt under the weight of successive Lord Chancellors' bottoms, it is regularly restuffed, most recently in 1966 with wool from sixteen Commonwealth countries including the Falkland Islands. It was, as Peter Horsfall told me, due for its next stuffing in 2006.

The Woolsack was also filled with symbolism. Wool in the Middle Ages was the country's major resource, and its theatrical purpose was to represent our shared wealth, able to lift the law above bribery, above party politics.

The electricians were now winching up the lights and laying the carpet. All that was needed to animate the scene was the cast in their costumes, the big show of the State Opening.

In *Service with a Smile*, P. G. Wodehouse's Earl of Ickenham, 'a tall, limp, drooping figure', hires his costume from Moss Bros.

> The canny peer of the realm, when duty calls him to lend his presence to the ceremony of the Opening of Parliament, hires his robes and coronet [here, Wodehouse slips up as coronets are only worn at a Coronation] from that indispensable clothing firm the Brothers Moss at Covent Garden, whose boast is that they can at any time fit anyone out as anything and have him ready to go anywhere. Only they can prevent him being caught short.

As he is returning his robes in a suitcase he runs into the Earl of Emsworth, who is intrigued by the State Opening:

> 'Were you at that thing this morning?'
> 'I was indeed,' said Lord Ickenham, 'and looking magnificent. I don't suppose there is a peer in England who presents a posher appearance when wearing the reach-me-downs and comic hat than I do. Just before the procession got under way I heard Rouge Croix whisper to Bluemantle, "Don't look now, but who's that chap over there?" and Bluemantle whispered back, "I haven't the foggiest, but evidently some terrific swell." But it's nice to get out of the fancy dress, isn't it?'

Some of the real peers, I discovered, still hired their robes; others inherited them or had them made, and they were stored all over London, in St James's Palace, in Mayfair tailors' shops and in the cellars of Ede and Ravenscroft the gents' outfitters in Chancery Lane. There they hung on rails in a windowless air-conditioned room. Their lordships' parliamentary cocked hats were kept in cases on a shelf, the robes zipped into black plastic bags labelled in white with Magic Marker.

The oldest was probably NORFOLK, DUKE OF, EARL MARSHAL, made in the eighteenth century, its smooth and faded red facecloth pocked with black-edged cigarette burns drawn together with red stitching, its greyish-yellow ermine, with a Duke's four rows of black-tipped tails, repaired and in some places replaced. Stored beside his hat was a battered black-leather case, with a Garrards' label from the turn of the century, which contained the Earl Marshal's baton. It looked like a thin piece of curtain rail made of silver-gilt, and was dented in several places. He kept his Garter at St James's Palace.

There were nineteenth-century costumes, too, the marquesses with three and a half rows of ermine tails, the earls with three, the viscounts two and a half, the barons two, all edged with a bar of shrivelled gold lace. New ones were made upstairs from bright red facecloth and boxes of yellow-gold lace. Those who could afford it had Canadian ermine, a carnivorous weasel whose white winter coat was thought to symbolize moral purity in the Middle Ages, at a cost of £6,500 each. Those who could not afford the ermine and Ede and Ravenscroft admitted that they hadn't used real ermine for years got white rabbit.

Coronets were usually kept in the bank. A duke wears a gold circlet with eight strawberry leaves, each leaf sticking up like the ace of clubs; a marquess, a silver-gilt circlet with four strawberry leaves, alternating with four silver balls raised on points; an earl, a silver-gilt circlet with eight silver balls on higher points – these stick up a long way, like a crown for the Snow Queen; and a viscount a silver-gilt circlet with sixteen silver balls set close together on the rim. Finally, a baron – the rank enjoyed by life peers – gets a silver-gilt circlet with six rather larger silver balls set on the rim.

The coronets developed over the centuries, tweaked up on occasions like the mock-medieval Coronation of George IV, their shape and ceremonial use changing slightly from age to age. When the diarist John Evelyn watched an investiture of six earls and six barons in the Banqueting House by the newly restored Charles II, he noted that once the King had crowned them, the barons 'put off their caps and circles and held them in their hands, the Earls keeping on their coronets, as cousins of the King'.

The most recent reference to a coronet in the gossip columns was shortly after the Second World War, when the eighty-three-year-old Duke of Leinster produced one he had found in the attic in a leather box with a note on saying it had been last worn for the Coronation of George III. The Duke said he had polished it up with Goddard's Polish and it looked as good as new.

The most traditional element is the costume. Early illuminated manuscripts show rows of lords kneeling before the King, already in red robes trimmed with ermine. Historians have argued about their origin, but they are thought almost certainly to have been designed, from the beginning, as a kind of fancy dress, an attempt, like Edward III's Most Noble Order of the Garter in 1348, to re-create an imaginary Arthurian golden age of order and chivalry.

The first time I saw a group of peers in their full regalia on the way to a State Opening was outside Gieves and Hawkes on the corner of Savile Row. Whether they were hiring or retrieving their own robes, they were in high spirits, climbing into a private bus. From the way they shouted and joked as they climbed the steps, I assumed that they were members of an amateur operatic society doing Gilbert and Sullivan.

The State Opening was no more than a curtain-raiser to the season of political theatre, but it was more colourful. It employed a cast of thousands and was notoriously beset by tiny disasters. Swords got caught between courtiers' legs on the way upstairs. Early in Queen Victoria's reign, the man carrying the Crown, which traditionally arrived in its own carriage on its own cushion, tripped and dropped it. It smashed. Everything was held up while officials searched for scattered diamonds.

Timing has always been complicated – and more so now under the eye of the armed Custodians on the roof. Walkie-talkies crackled to synchronize the clattering in of the Queen's carriage under the Victoria Tower with the unfurling of her standard on the high flagpole on the roof. As the Queen put on her Crown, full robes and spectacles in the Queen's Robing Room, Peter Horsfall waited outside at her request with a spare clock to reassure her that she was on time.

In the Royal Gallery, the perfumed audience waited and gossiped on gilt chairs on the raked stand, ladies in hats running in at the last minute, Sir David Frost arriving to exchange a word with his father-in-law, the Duke of Norfolk and Earl Marshal, who was cutting an impressive figure in his ancient, faded robe with the invisible cigarette burns, wielding his dented baton. He was directly descended from Hugh Bigod, a bloodthirsty and rebellious baron of the twelfth century. When he had seen his family to their seats, the Duke, now our senior Catholic peer, strolled over to the door of the Robing Room to wait for the Protestant Monarch to emerge. A former military man, he entertained his French guests and anyone else within earshot by drawing their attention to one of the patriotic wall-paintings. 'Vous voyez?' he boomed in schoolboy French. 'Agincourt! Autre victoire pour nous! Victoire des Anglais contre les Français!'

His chuckle was interrupted by a stiffening of the two doorkeepers who flanked the entrance to the Queen's Robing Room. He turned to face them, shoulder to shoulder with the Lord Great Chamberlain. The role of Lord Great Chamberlain originally belonged, in 1133, to the de Vere family, who lost it briefly to Simon de Montfort. Then, in 1781, it was left, like an unusable heirloom, to two sisters. Latterly it has been shared between their male descendants, the Carringtons and the Cholmondeleys, who swap it at the end of every reign. The Marquess of Cholmondeley, a good-looking young film director when he is not appearing as Lord Great Chamberlain, was pale from a long dose of flu but raised his staff in the traditional signal to open the doors. Nothing happened. He raised it again.

Norfolk asked him something out of the corner of his mouth, Cholmondeley muttered a reply, and the Earl Marshal said quite loudly that the doorkeepers should perhaps open the doors. They did, and the Queen appeared, looking fairly grim in her spectacles, accompanied by a debonair Duke of Edinburgh smiling to left and right, and Lord Cholmondeley began walking backwards in front of her.

Lord Hesketh, plump, youthful and rosy-faced, now appeared as Captain of the Honourable Corps of Gentlemen-at-Arms, carrying a feathered helmet and silver stick, dressed in thigh-high Wellington boots and a frock-coat. This role is always played by the Government chief whip of the day – once by a tiny Socialist life peer, Baroness Llewelyn-Davies of Hastoe, whose only concession to military costume was an even tinier brooch fastening her white blouse

– and Lord Hesketh had hesitated to buy the full outfit before the previous election. If the Tories had lost, he would never have worn it. Now he led the Queen through his Gentlemen-at-Arms, all former military men over the age of fifty-five, in plumed helmets and halberds, ready, as Hesketh himself said, 'to stab, hack or smash a helmet in defence of the Sovereign'. It was at that moment, he claimed afterwards, that his helmet began to pop out of his grasp 'like a champagne cork'. He restrained it.

Bruce Shand, Camilla Parker Bowles's father, had had a more alarming moment some years earlier when he commanded the Yeomen of the Guard, who line the rest of the processional route through the Royal Gallery. It was his duty to lower his lance as the Sovereign passed. 'I could see Willie Whitelaw behind her. He'd obviously had a very good lunch and was going very wide, so I drew back. Then as I dipped my lance I heard a most dreadful squawk behind me. I saw the Monarch smile, but it was only afterwards I realized I'd hoicked up a woman's handbag on the end of my lance.'

At the other end of the building Black Rod hammered on the door of the Commons. He was satirically heckled by Dennis Skinner – who put him off his stroke by shouting, 'Cue Black Rod!' – and symbolically sent away, acting out the symbolic truth, if he hadn't learned it from Skinner, that the Commons could not be bullied by the Monarch.

Meanwhile the royal procession entered the Parliament Chamber led by the Lord Chancellor, the Queen occupied the Throne, and the bishops and peers sharing their benches with the foreign ambassadors who had attended such State Openings for centuries. Then the Commons arrived to stand below the Bar of the Parliament Chamber, facing the Throne to listen to the Queen's Speech. One life peer lamented afterwards the undercurrent of speculation among some of his hunched and ermined fellows about who was the most fuckable of the hereditaries' wives, sitting with them in the Chamber, distinguishable by their tiaras.

No New Yorker, watching the State Opening of Parliament, would have been surprised if the processing peers had got into step at that point and sung *Iolanthe*.

> *Bow, bow, ye lower middle classes!*
> *Bow, bow, ye tradesmen, bow, ye masses!*

It looked like amateur theatricals: entirely theatrical and completely amateur.

The rituals that would follow, of course, during the rest of that session would also share an element of theatre, but at least they would have at their centre real and recognizable political business. Bills, tied with green ribbon if they came from the Commons and with red if they had begun life in the Lords, would be carried into the Parliament Chamber by clerks in wigs and gowns. Those who promoted or criticized them would refer to their opponents as 'noble Lords', to their listeners as 'their Lordships' House'. After each debate the Lord Chancellor on the Woolsack would ask them, as he had since Norman times, if they were 'Content' or 'Not Content'. Amended or ratified, the Bills would then receive the Royal Assent, but after that they became real-life laws. If you broke them you went to prison.

The State Opening and the rituals associated with the Throne and the Woolsack, on the other hand, were apparently pure theatre. Bagehot, in his great work on the English Constitution, called Victorian England 'a disguised republic'. The theatricality provided the disguise, and although Bagehot did not spell it out, it had a perfectly justifiable purpose.

In the theatre you sit in the dark with the rest of the audience, elbow to elbow like spiritualists at a séance, sharing and supporting the illusion. But the spectacle also draws you in, engages your sympathies and changes your mood. You begin to believe the actors on stage are real people. Your feelings are tugged to and fro. Pity, lust and fear are pumped out of you. Afterwards you come out into the street feeling as if you have had a satisfying emotional work-out. Political theatre has the same effect.

The stage has often been blamed for corrupting society; the debate continues on the influence of television violence. But it also has its defenders. Schiller, in his essay on *The Theatre Considered as a Moral Institution* written at the end of the eighteenth century, argues that the audience can be inspired and uplifted by a display of nobility. In political theatre, too, the display of nobility also plays an uplifting and inspiring role. Ignorant racists, or so the argument goes, encouraged to watch the television news read to them every night by a theatrical black newscaster who is manifestly middle-class, unthreatening and unchallenging, an authority figure who is himself deferential to authority, will grow in time to be less prejudiced. In the same way the public has traditionally had its gaze directed to the Masque of Order.

Dressed in Bagehot's disguise, the efficient republic stages the dignified charade of our timeless institutions: the Monarchy, the Church, the House of Lords, the Law. Watching the show, we believe we are in safe hands, we are reassured: our houses will not suddenly explode, bearded ruffians on horseback will not gallop down the street and seize our wives and daughters, money will retain its purchasing power, order will be preserved. More important, uplifted by the spectacle, we ourselves will behave in a way that will ensure the preservation of that order. Belief in the shared illusion inhibits insurrection.

During the State Opening, order was being maintained by brute force, by the sharpshooters on the roof. But it was also being maintained by the nobility and deference on display below. When the illusion worked, we were no longer aware of the stage machinery, of the vacuum behind the Throne. The Queen was a real Queen, the Lords were real lords. But, as in the theatre, it depended on our willing suspension of disbelief. If we refused to believe in fairies, Tinkerbell would die.

CHAPTER TWO

The Loaf Wards

━━━

In 1769 builders uncovered a little stone cavity in the north wall of the choir of Ely cathedral. It contained a dismembered skeleton. From the length of the thigh-bones, antiquarians estimated that its owner had been well over six feet tall. He had been, they decided, a patron of the Abbey, born before the Norman Conquest. He was probably the earliest officially recorded lord.

His identity was confirmed by a collarbone, which had been smashed either with a heavy sword or with a battle-axe, and also, surprisingly, by the absence of a skull. Both features matched the historical evidence in a poem describing his death, the original manuscript of which had been destroyed in a library fire twenty years before the discovery of the tomb. The headless man was Lord Byrhtnoth, pronounced Bright-noat, and he had been killed fighting the Danes in August 991. *The Battle of Maldon*, written a few years later, the story of his last battle, is heavily laced with propaganda, but it provides us with several clues as to how warlords were transformed into the kind of lord the English have always traditionally loved. The poem begins by describing the raid by ninety-one Danish ships on the coast of Essex. The local Saxons have called out the *fyrd* or Home Guard, and Lord Byrhtnoth is their commander.

He was sixty, a white-haired nobleman with big estates near Ely and many of those fighting with him were his tenant farmers. He had been an *ealdorman* – the nearest word in modern English is *alderman* – or Crown-appointed local governor since he was twenty-five, and was responsible for maintaining roads, bridges and fortifications. He also judged cases with the Bishop in the local courts, and was allowed to keep a third of the fines.

Historians have traced links of friendship and intermarriage between the Royal Family and those the King appointed to high office, and Byrhtnoth's estates had been held from the Crown by his father-in-law. At that stage, though, there was no question that he had any official hereditary right either to the estates or to his position as a local governor.

Despite two hundred years of Saxon occupation, life in England was dangerous and unstable and Byrhtnoth's relationship to King Ethelred was like that of an army commander to his general. His proudest boast was his loyalty to the Crown, and his status and estates depended on that. If he betrayed the King, he would be executed or disgraced and his estates called in.

He was also one of the Witan, the Wise Men, and the Witanagemot, or Assembly of Wise Men, was the embryonic House of Lords. From time to time they even met in the royal Palace at Westminster, though more often in the provinces.

Lord Byrhtnoth was on record as having spoken there more than once in defence of the monasteries, attacking the 'greed and madness' of those who wanted to turn the monks out of their rich livings. In an assembly dominated by bishops, abbots and priors, this was a conservative line.

The Church members of the Witan had the edge over most of the secular lords in being able to read and write. One of the earliest surviving records of such a council is a parchment of laws or 'dooms' drawn up at the end of the seventh century by the King of Kent and endorsed by his Witan. In some cases the bishops signed even before the King. Their convoluted signatures are followed by a column of smudgy crosses and marks, the signatures of the illiterate lords.

The Church leaders also had the distinction of being the first members of any such assembly to be elected: they were chosen by their fellow priests, their election confirmed afterwards by Rome. The Witan also included a number of prioresses, who were the last women present in any English senate until 1958.

The secular lords, whether members of the Royal Family or magnates like Byrhtnoth, were summoned haphazardly by the King to provide him with specific advice. Byrhtnoth's King Ethelred was, in fact, very bad at taking it, and had become the victim of a complicated Anglo-Saxon pun on his name: christened *Ethel-raede*, meaning literally 'noble advice', he was known as the *un-raede*, not 'unready', but 'without advice'. Nevertheless Byrhtnoth fiercely acknowledged the King as his lord, just as all the farmers and labourers drawn up on the grass above the shoreline at Maldon declared their loyalty to their Lord Byrhtnoth.

As they face the pagan Danes those loyalties are about to be severely tested. The raiders have occupied Northey Island, and begin to wade ashore across a causeway too narrow for a proper battle. Byrhtnoth, with aristocratic Saxon gallantry and love of fair play, offers to withdraw his troops so that they can fight on dry land. The battle begins; he is hit by a possibly poisoned spear of French manufacture, cut down with a battleaxe, his head is severed and carried off wrapped in a cloth as a trophy.

The Anglo-Saxons were defeated and forced for the first time to pay the Danegeld, a vast treasure of ten thousand pounds of gold and silver that drained the Church and the royal palaces of the extravagant decoration and display on which their stability and standing depended.

But from the moment of Byrhtnoth's death there is evidence in *The Battle of Maldon* of a new kind of stability and standing that is being created by the poet. He now changes gear to make his propaganda point. One of Byrhtnoth's own followers, Godric, jumps on his dead master's horse and escapes:

> *. . . leaving his Lord*
> *Who had given him many a goodly steed*
> *He leaped on the horse that belonged to his leader,*
> *Rode in the trappings that were not his right,*
> *And his brothers with him both galloped off.*
> *Godwine and Godwig recked not of war*
> *But turned from the fighting, took to the wood,*
> *Fled to the fastness, and saved their lives.*

This is the worst thing they could have done: even though they know Byrhtnoth is dead, Godric and his brother have broken their oath to their lord. The hero of the day, after Byrhtnoth, is an old soldier who weeps for his master, determined to die:

> *I am old. I will not go from here,*
> *But I mean to lie by the side of my Lord,*
> *Lie in the dust with the man I loved so dearly.*

This theme recurs again and again in Anglo-Saxon writing of the time: Wulfstan, Archbishop of York under King Ethelred, preached a sermon, known because of his name as *The Wolf's Sermon to the English*, in which he declared that '. . . it is the greatest betrayal of all in the world that a man should betray his Lord to be killed or driven into exile for life'. Wulfstan did not practise what he preached. While Byrhtnoth's widow, living in reduced circumstances near Cambridge, embroidered a Bayeux-like tapestry of the battle of Maldon and her husband's heroic death, Wulfstan remained Archbishop of York under the Danish King Canute.

But the propaganda continued: in another Anglo-Saxon lament, *The Wanderer*, there is a description of a man who no longer has a lord. Without such a focus of adoration and source of patronage, he has no role, no place in society, nobody to look to for protection. With a lord, he had a horse and comrades and was invited to the feasts and gift-giving at the great hall. He is 'deprived of the counsels of his beloved lord' and he spends miserable nights, dreaming of the good old days when he could 'embrace and kiss his Lord, and lay head and hands on his knee'.

This was clearly as unreal and fantastic as a modern commercial, and we have to ask what the writers of the time were trying to sell. Who was this idealized figure, the 'Lord', and why was he held up for universal adoration?

Clearly, part of the answer is that he was the man who provided the money, the horse, the feasts and the gifts. This is confirmed by linguistic archaeology, if we scrape away at the word 'lord'.

According to Thomas Carlyle and others, *king* was derived from *cunning*, and indicated an early meritocrat. In fact, the word comes from the same root as *kin*, and has to do with family. The king was anointed head of the family and guardian of the tribal land, ritually wedded to the earth, and crowned on a sacred rock.

Lord had nothing to do with family or tribe or the land. It came from the Anglo-Saxon *hlaf-weard*, or guardian of the loaf. The bread was made by his lady, the *hlaf-dige* or loaf kneader, and he and his wife fed it to the *hlaf-aetas*, loaf-eaters, bread-consumers or servants who worked for him. *Lord*, therefore, must originally have meant the master of a small farm, and by extension the master of a community. The lord remained someone, as is clear from *The Wanderer* and *The Battle of Maldon*, on whom you were economically dependent. But why should raw economic dependence have been glamorized and sold to the public as a political ideal?

The concept of the lord was not something that the Saxon Byrhtnoth and his ancestors had brought with them from Eastern Germany. When Tacitus had visited the area eight hundred years earlier, before the raids and migrations into England, there was no talk of loyalty to lords. There were chieftains, certainly, and strict class divisions, which amounted almost to a graduated caste system. In what sounds like an evocation of a golden age of open government, Tacitus describes a Saxon tribal assembly when every man, woman and child attended a gathering in a natural arena in the open air and listened to the debates of their chiefs and priests and tribal elders. But their first loyalty was to their blood relations. They looked up to their tribal chief, but what mattered, as in a Scottish clan, was family and kinship.

By the time of the battle of Maldon, that had changed. The old tribes, except for those in the Celtic heartlands, had been dispersed by raids and invasions. A society had evolved in which individuals were employed to fight and work with strangers and more recent immigrants. The warlord-employer, who might also be a foreigner, became the new focus of loyalty.

This could not have been achieved, though, without an intensive, sustained propaganda campaign, traces of which are evident in the *Anglo-Saxon Chronicle*. Loyalty to the family, ties of blood, its writers told their readers and listeners, always had to give way to their first allegiance, which was to their Lord.

It was a new vertical allegiance, replacing the old horizontal solidarity of shoulder-to-shoulder tribal loyalty. Byrhtnoth's men were portrayed as looking up to and adoring him as their idealized lord and leader. Byrhtnoth himself, like all the other military commanders and local governors, looked up to and adored Ethelred as his idealized and anointed lord and king. In the interests of national self-defence, the people were being conditioned, irrespective of tribe or family, into deference and obedience. A hierarchy had developed, a vertical chain of command.

The Normans confirmed and formalized this pattern. As superior administrators, they strengthened the system. The responsibility of local lords to call out the *fyrd* was precisely defined. Every lord was assessed according to the value of the land he held, and had to provide a certain number of armed and mounted soldiers. If he failed to do so he paid a tax that covered the equivalent number of mercenaries. When he attended the Witan he spoke as a tax-payer. In the same way his own tenants were assessed for the amount of produce they were bound to deliver to their lord in payment for their land. Money and services flooded up the channels originally cut for pure warlike adoration and loyalty.

The Witan, even in its most primitive forms, had always been associated with the idea of order. Under the Roman occupation Cogidubnus of Chichester, a collaborator-king, had a circle of headmen which was incorporated into the Roman provincial organisation as the *ordo*. What was new was the restoration of a vertical vision of order after centuries of post-imperial tribal chaos. It was inspired by a vision of the Shining Ladder, and it came to represent a fixed and unchangeable arrangement of society: in the words of Mrs. Alexander's Victorian hymn *All Things Bright and Beautiful*

> The rich man in his castle
> The poor man at his gate,
> God made them, high or lowly
> And order'd their estate.

It was an arrangement Shakespeare saw echoed in the frets of a guitar, the ladder of sawn grooves in the neck of the instrument marking the length at which each string produced the right note. As Ulysses says in *Troilus and Cressida*

> Take but degree away, untune that string,
> And hark what discord follows.

Degree was the guarantor above all else of social harmony, of order, and for the House of Lords it to remain of primary importance. 'Order!' is the one word no Lord Chancellor, as Speaker of the Upper House, has ever needed to use. The Lords were Order Incarnate.

Their own order has traditionally been policed by the heralds, represented at the introduction of every new peer by Garter King of Arms.

The first mention of heralds as armorial watchdogs is in connection with jousting at the end of the thirteenth century, and this is the period from which quaint Norman-French terms have survived, like gules, azure and sable – red, blue and black. Heralds began as stewards at international tournaments, paid at the end of each day's jousting in broken armour. Recognition marks on shields and flags to rally to in battle had existed throughout recorded history. With lords from all over Europe making their names in spectacular single combat, they had to establish a reputation in a largely illiterate society, stamping an exclusive logo on the public consciousness. The right to do so was enforced by the heralds. If a Bavarian nobleman with a Red Cow on his shield found himself facing an identical Red Cow from Essex, it was the heralds' fault.

Lord Rix the former Whitehall farceur, with whom I discussed the question of coats-of-arms in a hospitality suite at the BBC, told me it had started with the order of battle at Agincourt, and he was near enough right. The system had begun, in fact, a few years earlier in 1348 under Edward III, who instituted the Order of the Garter. But it was Henry V who had put the heralds on an official pay scale: in 1415 he ordered the drawing up of the first Parliamentary Roll of Arms appointing one herald specifically to superintend the Garter ceremonies, and at the same time to be the senior authority, the Principal King-at-Arms. He was now in charge of everything to do with escutcheons, banners, livery and coats-of-arms, including the list of those nobles liable to be summoned to Westminster.

The heralds still exist, though pleading poverty. I went to see the new Garter at the College of Arms, a seventeenth-century building with a decorative double staircase in grey stone standing behind elaborate wrought-iron gates set with painted shields facing the Thames just south of St Paul's. Like the cathedral, it had survived the Blitz almost unscathed. I arrived early and waited in the high panelled Court Room, used for investitures. It was distinctly Masonic, hung with portraits in oils of earlier Garters, and there was a wall plaque recording that the Court Room had received funding from the F. M. Kirby Foundation of Delaware. In the window recesses there were brightly painted models of heraldic animals. It was dominated by a high wooden throne, on top of which, near the ceiling, two painted wooden cherubs with prominent penises gestured vaguely to left and right.

Two informally dressed Indian businessmen arrived and were welcomed by one of the heralds, a nice middle-aged man in a well-cut suit, to talk about a trademark. They were led off like customers at Harrods being taken to see cigars or jewellery.

I was taken out of the front door and along a stone balcony to a separate set of rooms occupied by Garter. It reminded me of a lawyer's office in the Temple or a schoolmaster's room at Eton. Garter was talking to a timid young man in glasses, and waved me in, continuing his conversation. He was out of costume, a chunky man in a grey suit with a slightly retroussé nose. His real name was Peter Llewellyn Gwynn-Jones, and he was the son of a major from Cape Town. 'He can have a lion affronté but I don't like this spitting business. Can't he have a bucket?'

'He likes the idea of a lion spitting water.'

'Well, try and persuade him to have a bucket. And one thing I really am going to tighten up on. A lion affronté doesn't necessarily have to be shown from the front.'

The discipline was clearly military. That was what the heralds were there for, to preserve the order.

We shook hands, he offered me a cup of coffee, and we sat down away from his desk at a green-baize-covered table. I mentioned the two Indian gentlemen I'd seen downstairs. His work, I suggested, wasn't all to do with policing the aristocracy.

'No, no, a lot of trademarks. Trademarks are the worst.'

He was now scribbling heraldic patterns on the back of a brown-paper envelope. 'You've probably seen – some Rastafarian wants to use the Lion of Judah. That really won't do. That is somebody's family crest. And we get very cross indeed about these people who buy title deeds, the Manorial Society. Some of them even manage to wangle their way on to guest-lists at the House of Lords, calling themselves Lord this and Lord that when they have no right to it whatsoever.'

Scanning a list of manorial lords it was possible to sympathize with Garter's predicament. By buying the title deeds to various manors, Bupendra Arora had become Lord of Grittenham, Jacques Bichsel Lord of Hackford, Achille Chiorando Lord of Brampton, Elsie Downer Lady of Crouch, Nabil el Nagy Lord of Wicklewood, Ramesh Ghatge Lord of Harthill, Sadie Marks Lady of Shovelstrode, and the Podd family – Victor I., Victor T., Stephen, Brittany Victoria and Natasha Renée – Lords and Ladies of Newcastle, Winston, Wightfield, Halton and Little Holland-on-the-Sea. Günter Straub had become Lord of Westhall. This, Garter explained, was exactly the kind of thing that the heralds had been brought into existence to stop. The coats-of-arms in painted wood and stone and stained glass in the House of Lords were a statement of exclusivity and privilege. They, and no one else, were the lords, and the College of Arms was there to protect them.

Every new life peer was automatically approached by the College of Arms and asked if they wanted arms. The College received no government funds and was not a charity.

One former pitman, Lord Blyton, who surprised the *Sunday Telegraph*'s courtly columnist Kenneth Rose by accepting a cigarette from him at an embassy party, pinching out the one he already had concealed in the other hand and popping it into a tin with other half-smoked dog-ends, arrived at the College of Arms and enquired how much they would charge.

'Three hundred pounds, my lord.'

'Three hundred quid? Right, then, I want a couple of greyhounds, a pint of brown ale, and crossed darts.'

'I'm afraid that would not be permitted, my lord.'

'Then you'll not get your three hundred quid!'

Denis Thatcher's old golfing chum, Bill Deedes, received the standard invitation when he was made a life peer, and wrote back, smugly explaining that his family already bore arms, and had done so since the seventeenth century. He directed their attention, if they doubted it, to *Burke's Landed Gentry*.

He was irritated by their reply. The coat-of-arms granted to his Deedes ancestor in 1656, reproduced in the *Landed Gentry*, had been assigned by Garter during the Interregnum, that was to say between 1649 and 1660, and all grants made by that Garter had been declared null and void at the Restoration. The Deedes family arms were therefore invalid.

This had taken place before the present Garter's time. Shortly before my visit, there had been a turbulent period in the history of the Garter. Sir Colin Cole – 'Crest: *Issuant from flames proper a centaur forcene the human parts also proper the equine parts argent and crined and unguled or drawing a bow of the same bound and stringed gules the arrow gold barbed and flighted also argent*' – had once so irritated the Duke of Edinburgh with his less than perfect grasp of procedure when rehearsing some ritual with him and the Prince of Wales that the Duke had shouted, 'Oh, piss off, Garter!' His career, however, had run its full term.

His successor, Conrad Swan, formerly Rouge Dragon Poursuivant and York Herald, was the son of a doctor from British Columbia, originally called Swen ciski. Educated at St George's, Weybridge, he had married into the grand Roman Catholic family of the Earls of Iddesleigh. Having been admitted to the hugely snooty Catholic Order of the Knights of Malta as a humble Knight of Honour and Devotion he graduated to a slightly less humble Knight of Grace and Devotion, and then put forward the name of his own son-in-law.

Preparing details of his son-in-law's eligibility to an order that requires in some cases four armigerous grandparents or proof of noble descent on your father's side for seven hundred years, Swan committed some trivial error, misplacing a date, and had been compelled to hang up his tabard and tights 'on grounds of health'.

Naturally I made no reference to this, but asked Swan's successor what he felt about the crossed darts and greyhounds. He wasn't keen. He preferred the traditional devices. 'The thing is, if you want to suggest speed and you draw a rocket, the rocket will probably be obsolete in a few years. An arrow expresses the same idea and is timeless.'

We talked about the use of obscure heraldic language. I said I was intrigued by the use of the word 'fesse', meaning a band across a shield, because in modern French it meant a buttock. Garter said he wasn't aware of that, but he thought that jokes in general about the odder-sounding Norman-French terms were overdone. It was a shorthand understood by those involved and if he was talking to a member of the public he would probably use ordinary words.

I asked him about the coat-of-arms chosen by Lord Rix of the Falling Trousers, formerly Brian Rix, master of the Whitehall farce, which, Rix had told me, included two spotlights.

Garter again seemed uneasy. He pulled the brown envelope towards him, roughed out a shield, and showed me that traditional 'rondels rayonnant' would look very like spotlights. On Rix's coat-of-arms they are actually described as 'two suns in splendour'. Someone had talked to him the week before who wanted tennis rackets, and he again roughed out some shapes on the back of the envelope showing that 'rondels fretted' would give very much the same impression.

'Look at this.' The coat-of-arms in front of him showed three rather gloomy rams' heads against a background of what could have been dark green geometrical foliage. 'Aztec temples. Here's a man who thinks he's discovered an entirely untouched Aztec temple and he wanted it on his coat-of-arms.' He indicated the dark green geometrical foliage. The geometrical white spaces between did indeed look like the steps of an Aztec pyramid. That, after all, was his job: to contain the present in the disciplines of the past.

'Then there was something in the paper about me disapproving of Harry Secombe's motto. Not true. His motto is "Go on", which, if you read it across, spells "Goon". I happen to think that's rather nice.'

I thought it was worthwhile asking him why he thought the vertical element played such an important part in the traditions of the House of Lords: family trees growing upside down, estates and titles 'descending' from generation to generation, the Shining Ladder.

He finished his doodle. 'Do you know, I think the answer is very simple. When you're writing someone's family history in long-hand, you begin at the top of the page and work down. Simple as that.'

For a moment I felt badly deflated, like someone in an old-fashioned *Punch* joke: collapse of stout party. I walked out through the Court Room, looking again at the strange imaginary animals, gryphons and camelopards and sea dogs, unable to avoid as I thanked the receptionist seeing a letter addressed to Dragon Rouge Pursuivant.

Then I remembered the Book of Revelation. It is also full of mythical beasts, all of deep significance for the early Church: a lion, a calf, a beast with the face of a man, and a flying eagle, all with six wings and 'full of eyes', a red horse and a great red dragon with seven heads and ten horns 'and seven crowns upon his heads'.

It would probably be hard to trace a direct connection between the visual language of heraldry and the beasts of Revelation, but that was where the Shining Ladder came from.

CHAPTER THREE

The Gilded Tomb

My first visit to the Lords, to begin thinking about this book, had been three years earlier, in the days of Old Garter King Cole. All the lights were on and the Peers' Lobby was a dazzling Victorian jewel-box of carved stone and painted plaster, coats-of-arms and elaborate Gothic furniture in polished wood. The intricately worked brass doors of the Parliament Chamber dominated the space, gleaming like gold and surmounted by a leggy lion and unicorn flourishing heraldic banners. The doorkeepers, tall, authoritative men in starched wing collars and black tail coats, were standing at their high desks like waiters checking reservations in an expensive restaurant. They consulted their printed lists, wrote names on tickets of stiff white card. The crowd was a mixture of Glyndebourne and Royal Ascot.

There was still half an hour to go before the ceremony was due to begin and behind the brass doors Mrs Thatcher, about to be turned into a peer, was having a dress rehearsal. A girl from the *Sunday Times* Style section had seen her going in: 'She looked terribly funny. All in red, and that funny walk. As if she was being pulled along with a chain through her nose.'

Given Mrs Thatcher's feelings about the place it seemed to me quite possible that she was. She described it afterwards as 'a very *nervy* occasion . . . It was such a *hot* day – too hot to be wearing such heavy clothes.'

What was overwhelming about this practical demonstration of

the British Constitution at work was the extravagance of the design budget. At first sight, the Lords' end of the Palace of Westminster looked like the Disney Corporation's idea of the Age of Chivalry: a kind of historical theme-park, a cross between a Hammer House of Horror and Liberty's. What was most striking about it was how remote it was from the real world.

Earlier I had walked up from Westminster underground station, opposite the statue of Boadicea driving her chariot with the knives fitted in the wheel-hubs. Foreign tourists, international democracy slowly on the move, the workers of the world united, were dawdling on the pavements in the heat, come to see Big Ben and the Houses of Parliament. Gift shops were selling coloured postcards of Princess Diana or of snarling London punks with cockatoo combs. There were heaps of rude T-shirts and black plastic policemen's helmets. Outside the Commons' entrance a real policeman directed me in through Westminster Hall.

Inside the high vastness of the medieval building, with its long expanse of stone-flagged floor beneath the hammerbeam roof, it was cool and dark. The tourists had thinned to a trickle and it was possible to imagine all the early elements of government, the Treasury, the Exchequer, the Law Courts, evolving, as they did, from booths and back offices along its walls.

I waited to go through the security scanner at the top of the flight of steps where the silver knob had fallen off Charles I's stick at his trial and nobody had bent to pick it up for him. I followed two Japanese girls and a black American through an electronic door-frame, putting my feet as directed into two bright metal footprints and waiting for ten seconds while the scanner glowed red and then clicked to green.

I asked another policeman for directions, walked through the wide Victorian corridors with their high wall-paintings of scenes from British history, and suddenly found myself on the other side of a pair of elaborately decorated glazed doors, part of the elegant crush in the Peers' Lobby. That was the moment you left the real world of democracy behind.

I was directed to wait on the right of the brass doors, with some of the peers' wives. Standing on the other side, pink in the face and having obviously had a good lunch, was Sir Denis Thatcher Bt, spectacles gleaming, happily exhibiting the famous gap between his front teeth. Beside him was his daughter Carol, and behind them, looking bronzed and sinister, the Boy Mark.

Having pulled a plastic bald cap over my head and painted a black gap between my two front teeth every night for eighteen months in *Anyone for Denis?* at the Whitehall Theatre in the early Eighties, I felt a moment's embarrassment.

Just at that moment a kind of religious silence fell in the Lobby. Even the after-lunch Thatcher party stopped talking. A pair of glazed Pugin doors opposite banged open, and a solemn procession appeared. First, a man dressed in black knee-breeches and a black coat with a bit of black braid hanging down the back of his collar. Then another man, similarly dressed, wearing a ceremonial sword and carrying the huge gilded Mace over one shoulder. This was the Yeoman Usher. Then a man carrying what looked like an embroidered fireguard, known as the Purse, and finally the Lord Chancellor.

Lord Mackay of Clashfern, heir to St Swithin and St Thomas More, was a short, bustling man with a red face. He was wearing a full-bottomed grey wig with a little hole in the top and his long black gown with pale gold lace facings. The gown was vast at the back and would have dragged along the black and gold tiled floor if it had not been for his train-bearer, a busy little woman in black with buckled shoes, knee-breeches, an eighteenth-century coat with a bit of black braid down the back of her collar, and glasses. The great brass doors opened, and as they went through she caught up with Lord Mackay, tucked the trailing ends of his gown into two little buttoned fastenings on his sleeves, then dropped out of the procession.

The rest of the cast, various spivvy figures in shiny suits and odd aristos, cleared their throats and swung in behind. The great brass doors closed and the head doorkeeper held up his hands to address us. 'I *would* ask you to keep your voices down until prayers are read.'

Prayers were always read, as it were, on a closed set. I asked a younger hereditary why he thought this was. He gave it considerable thought. 'The thing is, we have to turn round and kneel on the bench behind us, and I don't think peers like the idea of showing their arses.'

As it turned out, prayers that day provided the *Guardian* with a joke. Their man upstairs, standing with eyes averted in the wooden vestibule to the press gallery, overheard the Bishop of Guildford reading from psalm ninety-three: 'Ever since the world began hath Thy seat been prepared. Thou art from everlasting.'

We were now let in, most of the audience taken up to the galleries. A few of us were allowed in on the ground floor, described on my ticket, suitably enough in my case as a Denis Thatcher impersonator, as 'Below the Bar'. This was that low solid rail of polished wood, a Victorian remake of the original Bar at which traitors were tried in the old Chamber, and which always separated the peers from the Commons. The clusters of lights had been hoisted up on their electric motors, the carpet was down. It may have been the Throne – fitted, in the absence of the Queen, with its loose cover and looking like a chair made for a giant – it may have been the chinks of daylight between the panels of the coffered ceiling, but it was a still very like a stage-set – though admittedly a very elaborate and expensive one.

The windows were high and cathedral-like, a glittering mosaic of blues and reds, greens and pale yellows, obscure coats-of-arms, crests and mottoes. Between the areas of stained glass carved figures stood under decorative canopies. Below them was a narrow gallery, its brass rail now hung with a red curtain, allegedly introduced during the 1960s to spare the Lords from having to look up young ladies' miniskirts. Under the gallery were more shields and escutcheons, with carved wooden busts of kings holding little orbs and sceptres, and more ornamental panelling behind the back benches.

In front of us was Barry's gilded canopy, the energy centre of our shared central power, flanked by kneeling angels in carved and gilded wood and two tall tiers of electric candles in brass candlesticks. Before it on the Woolsack sat the Lord Chancellor.

The rest of the cast, bishops and Conservatives to our left, Liberal Democrats and Labour to our right, cross-benchers sitting in front of us facing the Throne, a few younger hereditary peers crammed between the rows of old men, talking to each other out of the side of their mouths, would not immediately have appealed to a casting director attempting to re-create history. They could have been old boys attending a school reunion in the college chapel.

There was something faintly historical about the clerks in their tie-back wigs and black gowns at the table, even about the old ladies behind them poised to write things down for *Hansard*, but the Lord Chancellor on the Woolsack was what caught the eye and fired the imagination: he looked exactly like the Lord Chancellor on the Woolsack in the first woodcuts of the Lords in session five hundred years ago. Admittedly the full-bottomed wig was wrong for the period, and on top of that he was wearing a little flat eighteenth-century cocked hat.

Everyone was talking, and the acoustics spattered little bits of conversation about in the air, making it impossible to hear any single remark. I saw Denis Thatcher again. He was sitting up in a corner of the gallery above the Throne: then he stiffened and his smile froze. A man with a bald head and terrifying eyebrows, Black Rod, had appeared silently through the brass doors. He caught the eye of the Lord Chancellor, made a curt nod, turned round again and walked out. Something was about to happen.

Sure enough, he came back, nodded again, and the Chamber went quiet. Behind him came a more remarkable figure still. It was Sir Colin Cole, Garter King-at-Arms, in the kind of heraldic tabard worn by the White Rabbit with the trumpet in *Alice in Wonderland*. He had a plump face with deep bags under his eyes and looked as though he might from time to time enjoy a drink. He was known by all and sundry, as well as the Duke of Edinburgh, as 'Garter', and, I was told, bought his black tights at Fogal. He also did a nod.

There followed the former Sir Keith Joseph, tall, heavy-lidded and blue of jowl, sometimes known as the Mad Monk. He was dressed in a red robe and carried a cocked hat of the kind kept in boxes in the basement of Ede and Ravenscroft, vaguely reminiscent of something the Duke of Wellington might have worn at the battle of Waterloo.

He also nodded, and then Margaret Thatcher came in. She was dressed in a red robe trimmed with white fur and showing a double row of black ermine tails on the right shoulder to indicate that she was about to become a baroness. She looked at that distance like a Margaret Thatcher cuddly toy: her red robe had the texture of a fluffy dressing gown, her face was made up a flat matt pink, and her hair, puffed up at the back under the jaunty little black tricorn hat, looked soft and golden, like the fur on a teddy bear's bottom.

She also nodded, and her second supporter followed her in looking a bit vacant. He was short, bespectacled and red in the face. He nodded too. It was Lord Boyd-Carpenter, her first boss. All five, Eyebrows, Drinker's Bags, Mad Monk, Mrs T and the Old Buffer, then traipsed off round the clerks' table, moving as smoothly as figures on a mechanical clock, keeping an uncanny ten feet between them. Mrs Thatcher knelt before the Lord Chancellor she had appointed to present her letters patent, with their dark green cellulose acetate plastic seal, which the Lord Chancellor touched with his finger as tradition required. Then she got up and went to stand by the tallest of the three clerks – there are, in all, fifteen of them, all with first-class degrees, the Lords' intellectual nannies – a lean, randy-looking man with a fine hooked nose and a deep baritone reading voice. Mrs Thatcher looked very small beside him. He read out two rigmaroles, both purporting to come from the Queen, naming her as Margaret Hilda Thatcher and summoning her of her Especial Grace and Mere Motion to be personally present at our Parliament as Baroness Thatcher of Kesteven in Our County of Lincolnshire to treat and give her counsel. The new Baroness made a short affirmation in a smooth, soothing voice.

Then, Garter King-at-Arms, impassive with his wand of office, the Monk, the Baroness and the Old Buffer processed back towards an empty block of red-leather benches immediately in front of us. Garter stopped, but the others came on, turning sharply at the Bar and making their way to the empty back bench. Then all three performed a rather under-rehearsed synchronized turn and faced Garter. He had his back to the television cameras, which were transmitting the ceremony to millions all over the world, and was hissing conspiratorial commands, apparently confident that no one other than Mrs Thatcher and her little party could see his lips moving.

'Doff your hat!'

Mrs Thatcher's hat was clearly pinned on, but the two old boys doffed theirs, and she bowed obediently to the Throne.

'Sit!'

I was amazed. She sat. A few months before she had been the Iron Lady, not for turning, our elected Queen. Then he made her do it all over again.

'Stand! Doff your hat! Sit!'

I was reminded of a wild jungle beast snarling on a circus tub when the ringmaster cracks his whip. You could smell the sawdust. I was,

I realized, watching a mystery: a monarch – though, admittedly, in this case an ex-monarch – being restrained by the Constitution.

After that everything was an anticlimax. The new Baroness and her supporters left the empty benches with their robed backs to us, heading for the Throne, and she shook hands with the Lord Chancellor. Some of the peers shouted, 'Hear, hear!' and the little procession trailed out again at the other end of the chamber.

This time-hallowed ritual by which Mrs Thatcher had been introduced into the House of Lords – a hereditary peer, having been introduced earlier, even if it was five hundred years earlier, had only to shake the Lord Chancellor's hand – had been devised, curiously enough, by James I to cover his embarrassment at having sold as many as thirty-seven peerages in two years.

Until the death of Henry V, the King had always invested every new peer with the sword, cap and coronet in the House of Lords under the eyes of the old aristocracy, and had then conducted him to his new seat. From then until James's time the creation of peers had taken place at a private ceremony in one of the royal palaces, close in detail to that performed for Mrs Thatcher, but always with the King playing the central role.

In June 1615 James I, feeling, perhaps, as he sold peerage after peerage, that he was beginning to look like a floor-walker in a peers' fancy-dress department, started experimenting with a more discreet formula. Unseen by any member of the House of Lords, he handed Lord Hay his letters patent at nine o'clock at night in a private room in the King's House at Greenwich. Francis Bacon, writing to the Earl of Buckingham, explained that neither he nor the King were 'ceremonious in nature'. The heralds complained that they could find no precedents for this. Two years later, the King impulsively decided to make his favourite Buckingham a marquess, also 'without ceremony', and left Bacon as Lord Chancellor once again to square it with Clarencieux King-at-Arms. When Bacon himself was made Lord Verulam there was a ceremonial investiture, but almost all the other new creations after that were performed without any ritual whatsoever. It was then, under pressure from the heralds, that the King devised the present investiture ceremony in the House of Lords, sparing his own blushes and restoring the Lords' dignity.

A few minutes after the investiture was over it was, to use the new Baroness's own phrase, 'business as usual'. She slipped back into the Parliament Chamber in a dark blue suit and a diamond brooch, and old Lord Hailsham shifted his stick and shuffled up, slightly ungraciously, to let her sit beside him on the front bench. Suitably enough, the Lords had already got on to one of their favourite topics with a question about badgers. The late Earl of Arran was once asked in the Beefsteak Club why a debate on badgers had been less well attended than a recent debate on buggers, and he said he thought it must be because there were fewer badgers in the House of Lords.

Then the young hereditary peer delegated to answer questions was asked something about wetlands. He floundered for a bit, reading the answer with some difficulty, then concluded, 'This Government is committed to the environment.'

When a question came up about Maastricht, the new baroness heaved about uneasily in her seat, but seemed already lost in the sea of dark suits and bald heads.

Outside, in the Lobby afterwards, I saw Lady Wilson. She, like Denis Thatcher, had suffered eleven years of ridicule in *Mrs Wilson's Diary*, a fortnightly column in which Peter Cook, Richard Ingrams and I had chronicled her husband's career as Labour Prime Minister, which was eventually turned into a musical at the Criterion Theatre, directed by Joan Littlewood. Mary Wilson was entirely forgiving about it. She talked of the House of Lords with dismissive amusement. 'The best club in London, that's what they call it!'

I asked her what she thought about the new baroness. 'Oh, she'll settle down. They always talk big when they first come here from the Commons, but they soon simmer down.'

As I went to collect my bag from a row of hooks in a passage off the Lobby, I ran into a traffic jam at the centre of which was a bald, elderly peer with two hearing-aids who had stalled his wheelchair. It was Lord Thorneycroft, once the dynamic Tory minister. Then another glazed Pugin door swung open beyond him, and Denis Thatcher appeared, shouting, 'Where is he? Where is he?'

For a moment I panicked. For a moment I thought he meant me. Then behind him I caught a glimpse of the Thatcher family party assembling for a group photo. Perhaps she wasn't planning a return to power. Perhaps even she was taking it seriously.

Then the burly, grey-suited figure of the Cockney photographer, Terence Donovan, appeared at my side. He put an arm round my shoulders, shook my hand, jerked a thumb in the direction of the glazed door, which had now swung shut, and whispered conspiratorially in my ear, 'Guess 'oo I got in there.' He paused and looked round to see if anyone was listening. 'Ol' Fatcher!'

It seemed to me that we the people had done it. She had not been Queen after all. The real Queen had summoned her of her Especial Grace and Mere Motion to be personally present at her Parliament to treat and give her counsel, and she had come. Not for four million pounds, the figure she was rumoured to have been paid for her memoirs, but for eighty pounds a day expenses. She was safe in the Lords. She might, like a moth in a killing bottle, flutter about merrily enough for a while but, as Mary Wilson had predicted, she would soon settle down.

Outside in the sunlight on the steps, in a yellow suit and with a thick shillelagh under one arm, was the old Labour leader from the Commons, Michael Foot. I asked him if he had seen the ceremony. 'Certainly not.'

'Oh, I thought you would have enjoyed watching the enthrone-ment.'

'Enthronement?' He chuckled grimly. 'En-tomb-ment, you mean! En-tomb-ment!'

CHAPTER FOUR

The Brains of Europe

‒‒‒‒‒

Among the angels, powers, strange heraldic beasts and the opening of the seven seals he sees on the Island of Patmos, the author of Revelation records one central image, which is of God enthroned in glory.

> And behold, a throne was set in heaven, and one sat on the throne;
> . . . and there was a rainbow round the throne, in sight like unto an emerald. And round about the throne were four and twenty seats; and upon the seats I saw four and twenty elders sitting, clothed in white raiment; and they had on their heads crowns of gold.

That is the vision of monarchy, the single ruler on the throne, surrounded by his council. Whether or not St John's vision was original, a memory of an ancient Babylonian wall-painting, or came from some other Middle Eastern mystical source, it is an image that has shaped our political institutions for most of our history. Like the Shining Ladder, it was a vision of order that became enshrined at the centre of Roman Catholic belief, and government. The nature of the twenty-four 'elders' in their golden crowns became the subject of a violent disagreement, like that of the thousands of worshippers in white, seen by St John in similar visions, but the image of God enthroned above was the single most important idea of government that medieval Europe inherited from the official Christianity of the Roman Empire.

In AD 312 the Emperor Constantine, in the midst of a bitter civil war, saw a solar corona in the shape of a cross filling the sky. Knowing only that the cross was the symbol of a small and persecuted mystery religion, the Emperor ordered his soldiers to paint it on their shields, and won the next battle. He immediately declared Christianity the official religion.

From then on the Church rose in the uncanny likeness of the dying Empire, resurrecting its hierarchical structure, even preserving, in Church Latin, its language. Every diocese, the secular term for an administrative district under the old Empire, was ruled by a bishop, responsible to an archbishop, responsible to the Pope-Emperor in Rome. Once, citizens of the Roman Empire had been entitled to appeal over the heads of local courts to the Emperor. Now, members of the Roman Church could appeal over the heads of local courts to Rome, to His Holiness the Pope.

This Ghostly Roman Empire was slow to take root in England. Christian worship had existed in Army bases under the Roman occupation, but only began to establish itself in the country a hundred years after the last legions had gone. It came from Ireland, brought by Columba in the middle of the sixth century. His Celtic version of Christianity spread through Scotland, Northumberland and Wales, owing no allegiance to Canterbury, and certainly none to Rome. When Augustine arrived in the south, sent by the Pope, and preached to the Saxon King, who insisted on listening to him out of doors for fear of his magic, he laid the foundations of the Church in Kent.

In 664, at the Synod of Whitby, the Celtic Church, except for Wales which succumbed a century later, surrendered its independence. Its delegates acknowledged the Roman form of service, the official Roman date for Easter, and – the ultimate proof of loyalty – their willingness to pay tribute and taxes to Rome.

If there was a dim nostalgia for the old order of the Roman Empire, it found fulfilment in the Roman Church, in an established tradition, in discipline maintained by rank, order based on order. Every element of the hierarchy was celebrated and sung as theatre: not only in the costumes of the Pope in his sevenfold crown and the Bishops in their high golden mitres, in the shape of the flames of fire that had burned above the Apostles' heads at the sending forth of the Holy Spirit, in the plainsong and incense, in the golden glory of the brightly painted churches, but in the poetic images at the core of their belief. If God was always directly overhead, he was linked to earth by the Shining Ladder, represented by nine orders of angels: Seraphim, Cherubim, Thrones, Dominions, Principalities, Powers, Virtues, Archangels and plain Angels.

Monotheistic Christianity recognized the individual as more important than the tribe, and this presented a political problem. How was order and hierarchy to be maintained among so many divinely created individuals? Should Christians acknowledge the temporal ruler or the voice of their individual conscience? The orders of angels offered at least an ideal pattern.

Dante, in the *Paradiso*, explains how that divine order is maintained. Meeting one of the lowest-ranking angels, he asks her if she never dreams of aspiring higher, of being nearer to God. Her answer is that they all exist in love, within God's will, and it is not God's will that they should change places. They remain where they are, suspended in Divine Love like a foetus in the womb. If the angels in heaven can be happy like that, men and women should be too.

For those who felt nevertheless that they needed to move in the hierarchy, there were equally beautiful images of the system that allowed for movement, with the angels ascending and descending the Ladder that Jacob saw in his dream. There was even a theological device that permitted the King, in the image of God, to promote a lord to higher office without disturbing the harmonious stillness of the Golden Age. As a member of sinful humanity, a man or woman might think it possible to climb closer to God by good works, and these were certainly encouraged by the Church, but everything depended on Divine Grace. Touched by the Grace of God, any man or woman could rise to holiness and sainthood, to be a little lower than the Angels. Touched by the King's grace, a pageboy could rise to become an earl.

This image of a divine hierarchy became inextricably tangled in the language of secular government: even God was *Dominus*, the Lord, the great Loaf Ward and Provider. God above was the source of all authority. Beneath God came the Pope, then the King, then the bishops and the lords, then the people, class by class, from rich to poor. The power of the bishops in this hierarchy was very great. In Saxon times, when England was still divided into the warring nations of Kent, Northumbria, Mercia and Wessex, the bishops represented their own kingdom at federal level in a way that rivalled the authority of local kings. As members of the Church, they belonged to an older hierarchy, international rather than national. Rome meant full-blown Federal Europe, with priests from France, Spain or Italy long before the Norman Conquest promoted to English bishoprics, just as English bishops reigned in Cologne or Turin. They exercised, too, a supernatural authority: Christ, medieval Christians believed with a blind passion, had given St Peter and the popes who followed him the keys of heaven and hell. Those they excluded from the Mass would burn for ever in a lake of fire. Perhaps because of this their local secular authority and influence was often politically more important than their role as churchmen.

Stigand, the Anglo-Saxon Archbishop of Canterbury mentioned by the Mouse in the Pool of Tears scene in *Alice in Wonderland*, was an utterly corrupt figure, and William the Conqueror carried up the beach at Hastings a banner blessed by the Pope with the commission to sack him.

Earldred, Archbishop of York, was little better, a member of the old English Establishment who, according to a contemporary writer, 'amused the simplicity of King Edward the Confessor' by persuading him that by ancient tradition Bishops of Worcester automatically became Archbishop of York at the same time and pocketed both salaries. He was moved, according to the same writer, 'more by bribery than by reason'.

Nevertheless, when William the Conqueror was crowned in Westminster Abbey on Christmas Day 1066, it was Stigand who put the crown on his head, and Earldred who called upon the Anglo-Saxon lords, just as Roger de Mowbray called upon the Norman lords, to acclaim the new King. William was interested in preserving order and continuity and the Anglo-Saxon bishops were part of that order. He insisted on the Anglo-Saxon Coronation service that had been in use for two hundred years and he also hung on to the Witan.

By the time of his death almost all Anglo-Saxons in high office had been replaced by Normans – Stigand had escaped unpunished to retire to his country house at East Meon in Hampshire – but the embryonic House of Lords still had sufficient corporate dignity for William's heir to issue an edict restoring the laws of Edward the Confessor, 'together with such emendations to it as my father made with the counsel of his Barons'.

To complicate matters, many of the bishops were aristocrats first and churchmen second. Roger de Mowbray, who led the Norman lords in acclaiming William in the Abbey, took his name from the village of Montbrai, just south of Coutances in Normandy. As a local landowner he bought the job of Bishop of Coutances, and therefore sat in the Witan in England as one of the lords spiritual, but his cousins and uncles were there as ordinary landowning lords.

Indeed, the purchase of the bishopric of Coutances proved a good long-term investment. The title of Lord Mowbray fell into abeyance in 1476, but thanks to a cunning expert in peerage law it was revived in 1877 by the Lords' Committee for Privileges on the evidence of a letter written in 1484 by Richard III to the Duke of Norfolk. Cokayne's *Complete Peerage* called the Committee's decision 'extraordinary', since 'as a matter of historical fact' the new peer's ancestors had not held the title. Undaunted, the present Lord Mowbray was still to be seen, a charming figure in a moustache, a black eyepatch and a rose in his buttonhole, taking an active part in governing the country at the end of the twentieth century.

But indistinguishable as a bishop and a lord might be when on horseback, armed and leading his own troops as a feudal landlord, there was a difference between them that continued to split the House of Lords for centuries, dividing the lords spiritual from the lords temporal and causing much bloodshed.

The lords temporal frequently rebelled against the Crown, the more powerful among them from time to time actually laying claim to it, but their focus of loyalty was to a national hierarchy; the lords spiritual owed their first allegiance to Rome. This conflict was most famously demonstrated in the twelfth-century clash between Thomas à Becket and Henry II, but the case of Becket's predecessor as Archbishop of Canterbury, Anselm, gives us a vivid picture of the split in the Witan soon after the Conquest.

Anselm, who was born in Aosta, was the priest who heard William the Conqueror's last confession in 1087, an extraordinary genius who argued the existence of God on entirely rational grounds, and based on the image of the Shining Ladder. His argument, crudely expressed, envisaged a kind of Test Your Moral Strength machine at a fairground: if there was a scale of goodness on which a human being could hammer up a high score, there must at the top of that scale be a goodness that cannot be exceeded, a bell to be rung representing infinite good.

As a contemplative he was reluctant to become Archbishop: prayers were said in the Witan but to no effect, and he was eventually dragged physically to his enthronement. He himself said afterwards that it would have been hard to tell whether a crowd of sane men were struggling with a lunatic, or a sane man was being carried away by a crowd of madmen.

Anselm's argument, as it was between Becket and the King a century later, concerned the supremacy of English law: anyone tried in English courts still had the right to appeal to Rome; the Church, as a European institution based in Rome, retained its own courts to try members of the clergy, who had their own scale of punishments.

The confrontation occurred at an extraordinary session of the Witan. Conventionally, according to William the Conqueror's obituary in the *Anglo-Saxon Chronicle*, it usually followed a regular provincial circuit.

> Three times a year he wore his crown as often as he was in England. At Easter he wore it at Winchester, at Whitsuntide at Westminster, and at Christmas at Gloucester. There were assembled with him all the great men of England, archbishops, bishops, abbots, earls [a development of the old *ealdormen*, a translation of the Danish *jarl*], thanes [introduced in Saxon times and translated into Latin as *ministri* or royal ministers] and knights.

In February 1095 the Witan met at Rockingham Castle in Northamptonshire. It was attended, under duress, by the bishops, abbots and the 'entire nobility of the realm'. They were to remain there until they had reached a verdict on Anselm's patriotism 'by common consent', a unanimous vote.

It is one of the earliest records of how the lords sat and how they debated. Perhaps because it was to resolve a matter of potential conflict between Church and State, they began with a divided session: the lords spiritual met in the chapel at Rockingham, the lords temporal with the King in the great hall. The hall would have looked like a primitive version of the Parliament Chamber, with a throne at one end and separate benches for the bishops, abbots and senior churchmen when they came to join the debate.

Crowds of pious people climbed the hill to the castle to support the Archbishop, in a sense prefiguring the role of the House of Commons. In any case, the presence of a mob outside had a marked effect on the debate.

Archbishop Anselm found himself in a difficult situation: acknowledging as he did the European supremacy of Rome, he would have preferred to limit participation in any debate to his fellow churchmen in the chapel. As it was, most of the bishops disagreed with him, and he could count on the support of only two, both Anglo-Saxons: Gundulf, the Bishop of Rochester, and Ralph Luffa, the Bishop of Chichester.

On the other hand the King was demanding Anselm's submission to a secular authority, and to join the lords in the hall would have looked like surrender. He chose, therefore, to wait outside, watched, if not surrounded, by his lay supporters. Even in this vulnerable position he still had the power, as Papal Viceroy, to summon individual lords or bishops to ask their advice.

The debate began early on a Sunday morning, and raged for four days. Anselm first addressed the bishops, who agreed to present his arguments to William Rufus. The next day he agreed to talk before the whole House. He spoke to an empty Throne, as the King refused to listen, but argued from Christ's words about rendering unto Caesar the things that are Caesar's and unto God the things that are God's. The mood was against him, and he insisted on a private audience with the King. William Rufus heard him, was furious, and returned alone to the Throne to ask the House how he should reply.

Eadmer, the Archbishop's chaplain and biographer, describes the primitive exchange of speeches that followed. Bishops and lords broke up into angry groups of two or three, shouting at each other. Anselm, he said, stood outside, his back against a stone wall, eyes closed and apparently dozing, watched by an adoring crowd. A group of lords found him and told him he must accept the sovereignty of English law. Anselm said it was getting late, and suggested they talk about it again next morning.

On Tuesday, the third day of the debate, William de St Calais, the Norman Bishop of Durham, recommended that Anselm should be sent into exile. Surprisingly, this swung the secular lords in

Anselm's favour: St Calais, they thought, was being disloyal to his own Archbishop. William Rufus then lost his temper. 'What does please you if these words do not? While I am alive I shall never endure an equal in my own Kingdom. If you know that his case is so strong, why did you allow me to begin these proceedings against him? Go and consult, because, by God's face, if you do not condemn him, I shall condemn you!'

Whatever he felt about the Pope, and however determined he was not to surrender any sovereignty to Europe, William Rufus was perfectly clear about the role of the lords. It was their right to advise him, and he would take no final decision without them. They, too, were already behaving in a way in which the House of Lords would continue to behave for the next nine hundred years: they were slowing things down, giving the central power time to consider its decisions, letting it feel the response of ordinary people. But at Rockingham, William Rufus did not like it. What, he wondered, had they been talking about all this time? Lord de Beaumont, another Norman to whom the King had given a large estate in Warwickshire and who was one of his closest friends, agreed that it had been a very long debate, and admitted that they had come to no useful conclusion.

The King turned to the churchmen, who had been cowed by the lords' support for Anselm. What would they advise? The bishops wriggled. They explained that they were not in a position to pass judgment on their own Archbishop, but that, if the King wished, they would ignore any future orders from Anselm: send him, as it were, to Coventry.

This set off another storm of protest from the lords, which embarrassed the bishops, 'who knew that the eyes of all were turned on them'.

In the end, on the fourth day, with many members of the Council having slipped away during the night pleading urgent business elsewhere, they agreed a longer postponement, and Anselm arranged a compromise. The lords should send representatives to attend all Church courts and councils. In other words, all European decisions would be ratified by the sovereign power. But the Church would keep its own courts, European institutions, on English soil, and English people sentenced by English courts would retain the right to appeal to Rome. William Rufus accepted this, but grumpily.

A hundred years later, Henry II did not. He wanted one law and one scale of punishments dispensed under the royal cipher, the symbol of the shared central strength of England. That meant taking charge of both the barons' courts, the old local assizes of the kind attended by Lord Byrhtnoth, and those of the Church, which were still answerable to Rome. As a former Chancellor, his old friend Thomas à Becket seemed the ideal man to help him do it. He was not.

A priest in Worcester killed a man and raped his daughter. Becket, as Archbishop, put him in a Church prison and refused to release him to stand trial in a civil court. Aware that the King thought Church courts too lenient, Becket began to impose heavier sentences. A priest who stole a silver chalice from St Mary-le-Bow in Cheapside, London, one of the Archbishop's own churches, was unfrocked and branded. A canon of Lincoln who murdered a knight and insulted the judge of a civil court was fined, flogged and exiled. This made matters worse. To send a man into exile was a punishment reserved for the Crown and the civil courts. The Church courts were getting out of hand.

In the autumn of 1163 the King summoned the Witan, this time to Westminster, and almost identical scenes were played out as they had been at Rockingham. This time the full House met in one room, probably near the present Parliament Chamber, in the King's Palace of Westminster.

Becket was there, and so was the King. Henry proposed that in future all 'criminous clerks' – ordained members of the Church guilty of serious offences – were to be handed over to a civil court for sentence and punishment. Becket, the bishops and abbots had a permanent majority in the House, and voted against the idea.

Henry II had an even worse temper than William Rufus: one commentator described him as a ruddy-faced, horny-handed horseman, more at home giving orders from the saddle than debating on his feet. His eyes became bloodshot when he was angry. He shouted at the bishops, his voice cracking: he was not asking them to break Church law, he was asking them to swear obedience 'to the customs of the kingdom', as had their predecessors.

There was a second vote. At that time there was no discreet shuffling through lobbies. It was a system that survived, oddly enough, in the trial of a peer by the House of Lords until 1934, when each peer was required individually to pronounce his judgment of 'Guilty' or 'Not Guilty'. With the eyes of the whole company on him, every member, beginning with the most recently elected bishop or the youngest landowner summoned by the King, gave his answer. It was a severe test. In this case it involved only the churchmen, the youngest priest voting first and Becket, as Archbishop, last.

They all gave in. Criminous clerks would be handed over to the secular courts; they swore that they would obey the customs of the kingdom. But they added what amounted to a let-out clause, a wrecking amendment, with the phrase 'saving their order'.

Seven years later there was what amounted to a full session of the Witan at the King's hunting lodge at Clarendon, near Salisbury. Becket and the bishops again played for time in a closed session, but after a three-day debate the secular lords lost their tempers and burst in on them. According to Gilbert Foliot, the Bishop of London, 'they threw back their cloaks and shook their fists at us'. The speech he wrote down was good rousing stuff.

> Listen, you people who despise the law of this country and disobey His Majesty! These hands, these arms, these bodies of ours are not ours, they belong to our Lord the King, and they are ready, if he as much as nods, to take revenge for every insult he has to suffer and to do whatever he wants us to! Any decision he takes entirely on his own is right by us! Think again, think about what he is asking for, or there will be trouble!

This was the kind of oratory that Becket and the bishops understood, and the King drew up what were called the Constitutions of Clarendon for them to sign. Clause Three confirmed the compromise reached by William Rufus and Anselm, requiring the presence of civil magistrates at all Church courts, but it went further: once 'criminous clerks' had been sentenced, they would be tried in the civil court and sentenced like any layman who had committed the same offence. They would have no right of appeal to Rome.

Facing the angry lords opposite, each churchman, beginning with the most junior prior, pressed his signet ring into the warm wax. When the parchment was finally laid before the Archbishop, he refused, but even without his seal, the Bill became law.

Becket then began a campaign of public penances, which could only be interpreted as highly ironic, punishing himself for having given way to the King, and refusing to co-operate with the King's officers. When the Witan met again, this time at Northampton Castle, Henry outmanoeuvred him. Asking for the accounts from the time when Becket had been Chancellor, he raised the threat of embezzlement charges. Becket appealed to Rome, and the King had trapped him: in taking this step, Becket had broken the law of England.

The debate – nobody called it a trial – took place in a full session of the Witan. The bishops were 'excused' from passing judgment, which was left to the earls, barons and senior judges, 'certain sherrifs and barons of the second rank, men full of years'.

Becket dramatized his position by carrying his own cross, like a European flag. Gilbert Foliot, the Bishop of London, who did not like him, made a satirical speech at his expense: if the Archbishop carried his cross, perhaps he would like the King to carry his sword? That would certainly make 'a brave show'.

The Throne, however, as it had been for Anselm's speech, was empty. The King did not want a confrontation and was waiting in an upstairs room. Becket denied the right of any civil power to challenge him and walked out of the Chamber to jeers from some of the lords, spoiling his exit by tripping over a bundle of firewood near the door.

The Archbishop went to France, excommunicating those bishops he saw as collaborating with the King. It was the arrival of these bishops to complain to the King that prompted Henry's famous outburst, with its snobbish reference to Becket's father having been a butcher. 'What wretched drones and traitors I have nourished and promoted in my household! They allow their Lord to be treated with such utter contempt by a middle-class clergyman!'

The four knights cornered Becket at just after four in the afternoon of 29 December 1170, near the Chapel of the Virgin Mary on the left of the nave in Canterbury Cathedral. They found him, tall and gaunt in a black skullcap and cloak, surrounded by terrified monks.

The knights were drunk, in full armour, with only their eyes showing through slits in their helmets. Each carried a sword in one hand and an axe in the other. Fitzurse, their leader, flicked off the Archbishop's skullcap with his swordpoint. Becket gripped a stone pillar, surrounded by his monks and chaplains, and refused to be moved. In what must have been a familiar gesture for a man who had himself scourged three times a day, he bowed his head, challenging them to strike. Fitzurse swayed back and brought down his sword, shouting to the others to kill. One monk, Brother Edward, raised his arm to protect the Archbishop's head, the rest screamed and scattered.

None of the survivors was sure whose sword it had been, but the first stroke cut Brother Edward's arm to the bone, slashed the top of the Archbishop's head and brought a trickle of blood down over the bridge of his nose. Within seconds he was hit again, staggered forward, a swordblade cut into the left side of his head, he fell, and two of the knights struck at him as he lay on his right side; another sliced into the top of his tonsured skull, laying bare the brains, while the fourth knight's sword shattered on the stone floor of the cathedral.

Then Hugh of Horsea twisted his swordpoint inside the skull, spilling Becket's brains over the stone paving, and shouted, 'He won't get up again!' The knights ran out of the cathedral, chanting, 'King's men, King's men, King's men!'

They were Normans. They had conquered England as part of a Norman Empire that, at its height, extended southwards to the Mediterranean. But they were Eurosceptics, and they had the support of a majority of the divided Witan.

The European response to Becket's murder was surprisingly mild. The Pope found Henry innocent of any direct involvement in the murder of the Archbishop: the knights had acted impulsively and on their own initiative. Nevertheless, the King must revoke the Constitutions of Clarendon. The clergy, who were European officials, would appear before the civil courts only for hunting offences, and the clergy, as everyone knew, were forbidden to hunt. Once again, as under the first Roman Empire, those accused in English courts could appeal to Rome.

There was a final, humiliating punishment. The King of England, representing the united strength and shared power of the nation, was required to do penance at Canterbury.

Henry II walked into the cathedral in his bare feet and knelt at the newly erected stone tomb that marked the grave of the martyred Archbishop. There, he was forced to put his head into an opening in the stone through which it was possible to see Becket's elaborately decorated coffin. In this position he was given one stroke of the lash by every member of the cathedral staff, beginning with the youngest monk.

CHAPTER FIVE

The Lord Chancellor's Dance

———

I was brooding on the Lord Chancellor's wig, on a new wooden wig-block at Ede and Ravenscroft's. On a shelf above were other wig-blocks. Some of them were a hundred years old, pitted by pins, and looked like ancient mummified heads.

Five ladies, ranging in age from eighteen to fifty-eight, were working with horsehair. It arrived, bleached, in ten-inch-long paper-wrapped bundles like spaghetti, and was woven into a silk cap so that it stuck up initially like sugar-stiffened punk cockatoo plumes. It was treated with chemicals to prevent the wearer contracting anthrax and what one lady called 'other nasty diseases'.

'The skill is to blend it by judicial' – this seemed a good word in the context – 'mixing of the hairs. Otherwise it would look a shocking white, you see, like nylon.'

There were no patterns. Ede and Ravenscroft had been making wigs since 1721, copying them from generation to generation since they set up at their first premises in Searle Street. 'There were times when wig fashions got a bit silly, but not the judges'.'

The Lord Chancellor's wig had three lines of stitching across the back and a few stray strands of horsehair were still being 'frizzed' into an imitation of a spinsterly perm, a froth of pan-scourer grey curls. I recognized the little hole in the top. I asked whether that was to let out the heat.

'That is called the coif. Before they wore wigs, lawyers in the old days used to wear a little white cap called a coif, and that is where they wore it.'

The lady working on the wig was backcombing the stray horsehair with a metal instrument she told me was called a picker, and explained that a bald Lord Chancellor had the option of a silk lining to stop the horsehair irritating his scalp.

Lawyers, like their costumed fellow performers in the Lords and the Church, were innately conservative, and the Lord Chancellor's wig was usually bequeathed with the job. 'Lord Mackay of Clashfern would normally have inherited his predecessor's wig, but Lord Hailsham had pulled it about so badly we've had to make him a new one. He used to drag the front down. He could never keep anything tidy on him, you see, because of his leg. He was irritated by the pain.'

The idea of the inherited wig, itself an irrational inheritance from a high fashion long since dead, was typical of the law. The Lord Chancellor's wig and gown, like the Woolsack, where Lord Hailsham would also ease his pain by muttering, 'Bloody fools!' at the Bench of Bishops six feet away, safe in the knowledge that on the mad *Alice in Wonderland* constitutional stage-set he was outside the Chamber, were part of a theatrical display of mystical authority.

If the Church traced the origins of its power to God incarnate in the person of Christ laying His hands on the head of St Peter, English law traced its authority back to the Creation itself. The Saxon King Alfred, credited with writing down our first laws since the Romans, prefaced the book with his own family tree, a pedigree that went back generation by generation to Adam. It included in the upper bifurcations of its roots both Noah and the god Wotan. This, again, was the vertical hierarchy, all things beginning in God. God was above, so our roots searched deep into the sky. The law, too, came from God, and was 'handed down' from one age to the next. As Tennyson wrote of England:

> *A land of settled government,*
> *A land of just and old renown,*
> *Where Freedom slowly broadens down*
> *From precedent to precedent.*

From the earliest days lawyers harked back to some imagined

age of good law, the unpolluted source: like King Alfred, they looked back to the past for their authority, reluctantly modifying that original truth precedent by precedent, but maintaining order as they maintained the law.

A chancellor, or *cancellarius*, was originally an usher in a Roman court. The word came to mean a lawyer, then a lawyer in a royal household. As he had to be able to read and write, he was always a priest. Later, chancellors appeared who were plain working lawyers, not bishops. Since the beginning of the eighteenth century, every Lord Chancellor has been made a peer on his appointment.

But when he took his seat in the Witan under Edward the Confessor on the eve of the Conquest, he had the rank of bishop, and was subject to the political tug-of-war between Westminster and Rome. He was always, therefore, in some sense a party politician. But he was also the Law Incarnate.

At the State Opening of Parliament, the Queen represents our shared power, the Lord Chancellor our shared law. When the Queen is not there, the Lord Chancellor acts as her stand-in, representing our shared law and our shared strength, both seen as outside the control of party politics.

Every time there is a change of government there is a new Lord Chancellor, and he always finds himself in the same dual role, enforcing and bending precedent. The Earl of Mansfield, at the end of the eighteenth century, looked at Sir Joshua Reynolds's newly finished painting of his great friend David Garrick dallying between two beautiful women, Tragedy and Comedy, and said that he was often in a similar position. 'Inclination draws me one way, and a long string of precedents in the other.'

The Lord Chancellor's close theatrical association with the Crown, with the magic force-field outside the political debate, goes back to the beginning. The *cancellarius*, as a priest, was the King's chaplain. The Lord Chancellor is Keeper of the Queen's Conscience. When Lord Hailsham had the job, he dismissed the question of keeping the Queen's conscience as 'ridiculous', but since the Reformation the Lord Chancellor has been required for that reason to be a Protestant.

This finally changed under Mrs Thatcher, but under rather bizarre circumstances. The Tory Attorney-General, Lord Rawlinson of Ewell, who was expected to be the next Lord Chancellor, was a Roman Catholic. An Act of Parliament was passed, the Lord Chancellor's job as Keeper of the Queen's Conscience was thrown open to anyone, then Lord Rawlinson fell out of favour and the Protestant ascendancy remained unbroken.

Perhaps the most comic and revealing theatrical image from the Woolsack dates from the turn of the century, when the Lord Chancellor was the reactionary first Earl of Halsbury. The third Marquess of Salisbury, the Tory Prime Minister, liked to sit next to him on the red silk cushion, and they made a very odd couple: Salisbury a vast bearded giant, Halsbury with his large bald head, no eyebrows and legs so short his feet didn't touch the floor. What made the image so rich was its constitutional blasphemy: it was like an actress joining a bishop at the altar to celebrate Holy Communion. The Lord Chancellor was Speaker of the House, and in allowing a party politician to trespass on a sofa sacred to the Law he was committing a scandalous breach of decorum. But the image reflected the political reality: a Tory Lord Chancellor was always a Tory.

In appointing generals and archbishops, Salisbury wrote to his Lord Chancellor, he could ignore party politics: in choosing judges never. 'There is no clearer statute in that unwritten law [of our party system] than the rule that party claims should always weigh very heavily.'

As the *Solicitors' Journal* wrote at the time, 'Lord Halsbury has never shown his contempt for the opinion of the profession – and, we will add, of the Bench – so markedly as in the appointment of Lord Justice Henn Collins. The way to the High Court Bench is once more shown to be through contested elections and general service as a political hack.'

But unlike hereditary peers, Lord Chancellors competed for their place there – Lord Mackay of Clashfern was said to owe his position to a general desire to keep out his rival Lord Donaldson of Lymington – and unlike other peers who had been Members of the Commons, they did not win their place exclusively through political service. The Lord Chancellor was always a battle-scarred old legal mercenary. He had fought his way up the legal profession, arguing cases not for love or political commitment but for money.

As meritocrats, Lord Chancellors often came from humble beginnings. The reactionary Earl of Eldon, who opposed the Reform Bill of 1832 and was accused, like many Lord Chancellors before him, including Becket and Bacon, of having made a fortune out of the Woolsack, was born plain John Scott, the son of a provincial coal-merchant. Lord St Leonard's father was a barber, Lord Sankey's a draper and undertaker. Writing in 1824, Canning was amazed at how open the job was to talent, wherever it came from:

> It is one of the noblest and most valuable prerogatives of the Crown of England that it can take from the walls of Westminster Hall [the Hall was an early permanent home of the Law Courts] the meanest individual – and when I use the term meanest, I use it not with reference to talents and intellectual endowments, but to birth and original station in society – and place him, at once, in the head and front of the peerage of England; and I never wish to see the day when the Crown is deprived of that beautiful prerogative.

Even in Canning's time the 'beautiful prerogative' was exercised by the Prime Minister, and sometimes the offer of high office over-rode party loyalties, as in the early career of Earl Jowitt – a name he insisted was pronounced Joe-itt – Clement Attlee's Lord Chancellor. He had originally been a rather sudden convert to socialism.

On 30 May 1929, he stood for Parliament as a Liberal and was elected. On 4 June, five days later, he was offered the job of Attorney General in the new Labour government and took it, resigning his seat as a Liberal MP. Lord Birkenhead at the time described him as 'hurling himself upon the socialist omnibus as it was turning at full speed into Downing Street'. Churchill, more bluntly, said that he had 'disgraced the name of rat'. When Jowitt's childhood friend Clement Attlee, who described him as 'a nice, bright, clever little chap, never gave me any trouble', asked him to become Lord Chancellor in the Labour government of 1945 he did not hesitate. He collected the Great Seal from Buckingham Palace, and then had to ask his colleagues whether or not it gave him a seat in the cabinet. It did.

Not everyone had accepted the job. When Attlee's government fell in 1951, Churchill tried to cast a cabinet whose names at least would convey a sense of the good old days, combining unity with continuity. He wanted a Lloyd George and an Asquith. Lloyd George's son Gwillym accepted the Ministry of Food, but Cyril Asquith, the former Prime Minister's nephew, refused the Lord

Chancellorship. He wasn't well, and felt that Churchill 'mustn't be saddled with a lame duck on the Woolsack'. The name of Gavin Simonds had also been suggested, but Churchill had never heard of him. Simonds was a High Court judge, and had once distinguished himself as a barrister by speaking for twenty-four hours in defence of the crooks in a case involving forged Portuguese bank-notes.

When Simonds was offered the job of Lord Chancellor, he hesitated. He was nearly seventy and felt he would be 'embarking on an unknown sea'. He said he would like time to think it over. Churchill scowled. 'How long do you want?'

'Well, I want to talk it over with my wife.'

'Where is she?'

'In the country.'

'When will she be back?'

'About six o'clock.'

'That's too late. I have to tell the King by six o'clock. You must take this fence by yourself.'

Simonds had accordingly jumped. What he described in his memoirs as 'his political adventure' lasted three years, until Churchill sacked him in the next reshuffle, but he became a passionate Tory spokesman in the Lords. His performance in persuading the peers to allow commercial television, during which he repeatedly insulted the BBC, left Lord Reith 'shocked and disgusted'.

His slogan was 'Trust the people!' The people loved classical music: 'The crowds waiting outside the Albert Hall at Easter were not waiting to hear some melancholy crooner mouthing an erotic melody: they can hear that on the BBC.'

Those who heard Viscount Simonds pleading the Government's case in the second debate must have begun to understand the 'open hostility' of the judge during the Portuguese bank-note case. Competition, he argued, did not lower standards: 'Does Shakespeare live? Has that immortal voice been stilled? Is that hand of glory withered? Shakespeare reigns. And why? Because Shakespeare is chosen by the people, and not by the BBC!'

Some Tory peers were so appalled that they voted with Labour. Lord Reith accused him in the *Observer* of 'surrendering television to the brute force of money'. Simonds was furious. 'Lord Reith questioned my sincerity and in effect charged me with prostituting my high office for party advantage. I will confess I saw red.'

The Lord Chancellor's role had traditionally made him vulnerable to this kind of attack. What Simonds called his 'high office' was inevitably associated with the bewigged judge, the Speaker, the figurehead of the House of Lords as the ultimate Court of Appeal, the Keeper of the Great Seal. To find a party politician under this disguise, whether he was motivated by personal greed or mere 'party advantage', was always a shock.

His role as Speaker was largely ornamental. It was the shrine of order, when the word was never shouted to restore it, and certainly not by him. He was there to ask them if they were 'Content' or 'Not Content', and to announce the result of the vote if they divided, but he still represented Authority.

If the architects, carpenters and central-heating engineers are responsible for the scenery at the House of Lords, the prompters and stage managers are always the lawyers. They check the production against the script. All stage business is sacrosanct, and though in practice he might have to consult with the more experienced clerks, the ultimate authority on such traditions remains the Lord Chancellor. Marcia Williams, Harold Wilson's secretary, used to say that the one advantage of having Lord Gardiner to dinner when he was Lord Chancellor was that he knew when to sit down: he might be a failed actor with a fourth-class degree from Oxford, but he knew about protocol.

Lord Halsbury needed guidance about the official reception when he became Chancellor, guests at which included the Lord Mayor of London and 'Tum-Tum', the future Edward VII. 'You will have to provide a feed of some sort,' his predecessor wrote, 'for the various retainers, clerks, train-bearers, tipstaves – strange creatures who gather themselves together out of all the forgotten crannies of obsolete jurisdiction for that occasion. This consists I think chiefly of cold beef, not without beer. It would be quite convenient to receive the Prince in the private room at the House of Lords and not admit him into the general reception. He is a very dangerous guest: he once got into your predecessor Lord Cairns's dining room and ate up all the judges' luncheon.'

He might need advice from the experts, but the Lord Chancellor's office gives him a mysterious authority. He is, after the Archbishop of Canterbury, the first subject of the realm, before the Prime Minister and before the Speaker of the House of Commons. It was this, more than any clear constitutional role, that made his mystical dance so bewildering. Shuffling those few steps to the left, he preserved in his wig and costume the image of the Law, the appearance of the objective judge, but his advice to the House was entirely partisan: he was arguing the Government's case as craftily as any defence lawyer trying to save a criminal from prison.

He was a judge, too, when he presided over appeals to the House of Lords. In recent years the work has been left more and more to the law lords, the Lord Chancellor having more than enough to do in appointing other judges and supervising the working of the nation's courts, but on the increasingly rare occasions that he hears an appeal he is above politics.

Curiously enough, when Lord Mackay was playing that role he rarely wore his wig. When he was hearing an appeal he and the committee of law lords wore suits and sat at a horseshoe-shaped table in a committee room upstairs, listening to the arguments of barristers in wigs and gowns. Later, when the judgment of the House of Lords was finally given, usually on a Thursday afternoon when the Parliament Chamber was otherwise empty, he resumed his wig and gown and sat on the Woolsack, for the law lords' formal vote.

The history of the Lords as a Court of Appeal goes back to its first sharing of royal power. As early as the twelfth century, appeals were heard by a commission of five judges, with a few cases referred to the King and his Council. However, the role of each House was clarified when the Commons insisted that they were principally concerned with taxes and money, and wanted nothing to do with legal decisions or appeals. The Commons would give their advice and consent in the making of new laws, in grants of subsidies, and in matters concerning 'the common profit of the realm', but the right to sit in judgment had always belonged, and always would belong, to the King and the Lords. While the right to appeal to a higher European Court was suspended, between the time of Henry VIII and the reign of Mrs Thatcher, the House of Lords remained the highest court in England. Appeals were heard in the Parliament Chamber before the Chancellor and the few qualified judges in the Lords, who were often outnumbered by lay peers keen to join in the questioning and vote on the outcome.

From the transcripts of Lords' proceedings, it is clear that untrained peers wasted a lot of time. As with the hereditary peers in political debates, there was the argument that lay peers provided instinctive common sense, but they also produced reactionary judgments, reflecting the political balance of the House.

Nevertheless, Lords' appeals often succeeded. Between 1712 and 1714, for instance, the Lords reversed the judgment of the lower courts in nearly a third of the cases they heard.

By the middle of the nineteenth century, lawyers were exasperated, and in 1844 the Lord Chancellor virtually put an end to interference in appeals by lay peers. When Daniel O'Connell, the Irish leader, was convicted in Dublin of conspiracy, he appealed to the Lords. The case was heard by the Lord Chancellor, supported only by former Lord Chancellors and hereditary peers who had been judges. They overturned the conviction, and lay peers, keen to vote against what seemed to them too dangerously liberal a judgment, were warned off by Lord Wharncliffe, a government minister.

> I cannot help suggesting your lordships should not divide the House upon a question of this kind, when the opinion of the Law Lords has been given upon it, and the majority is in favour of reversing the judgment. In point of fact, my Lords, they constitute the Court of Appeal, and if noble Lords unlearned in the law should interfere to decide such questions by their votes instead of leaving them to the Law Lords, I very much fear that the authority of this House as a court of justice would be greatly impaired.

In 1883, when Lord Denman attempted to vote, for purely political reasons, in a case involving the radical Charles Bradlaugh, his vote was ignored by the Lord Chancellor and also in the official law report.

Meanwhile, with an increasing amount of work falling on the Lord Chancellor and the few lawyers in the Upper House, Queen Victoria recommended the introduction of so-called law lords, life peers who would share the burden of hearing appeals. They would need the authority conferred by membership of the Upper House but need not be given hereditary titles.

In 1856 Sir James Parke was invited, with the Queen's encouragement, to become the first law lord. Parke was an alarming figure. When, on a hot day in court, he asked for the windows to be opened and was told they had not been made to open, he sent for twelve carpenters, one to each window, to take them out of their frames. 'Every word he uttered,' his biographer wrote, 'was like a die stamped by a mighty engine.' But not even Sir James carried sufficient weight to survive as a life peer, as the Queen had wished, 'for and during the term of his natural life'. Lawyers refused to accept that others should be sent to the Lords with titles loaded in their loins and lawyers not. After six months as a life peer his title was made hereditary.

The first actual life peer, one of four Lords of Appeal in Ordinary, did not take his seat in the House until the passing of the Appellate Jurisdiction Act of 1876. This came in the wake of a revolutionary Bill, passed in 1873 by a Liberal government, that ended the Lords' right to hear appeals altogether. After three years of debate, under a Tory government, it was restored, but in future the Lords were to have professional assistance. There are now twelve law lords, and since 1876 appeals have been considered in the Lords only if they raise an important question of law.

Until 1948 cases were still heard in the Parliament Chamber, sitting at what Lord Newton described in 1938 as 'a sort of miniature tea table, the sort of thing you would see outside a second-rate café in Paris'. During rebuilding after the House of Commons was bombed in the Second World War, the lords found a committee room where they have met ever since.

The other part of the Lord Chancellor's role is as Keeper of the Great Seal. The use of seals became formalized under the Normans: following their custom, orders were signed by the King, and countersigned with the Seal. Henry II wanted the law to be the same for everyone, a shared law with no exceptions for criminous clerks or members of European organizations like the Roman Catholic Church, and that demanded a rival source of authority, higher than the King himself. The King, as the lawyers defined it, was under no man. He was under God and the Law.

Even before him, kings had come to acknowledge the extent to which order depended on law, law on order, and that even they ranked second to that concept. Part of the rigmarole used in the writ of summons to a modern life peer, the reference to the Monarch's 'Especial Grace and Mere Motion', was a distinction between what a king or queen did as a human being and what they did, by Grace and Motion, in their role as a ruler under the law. Thus they acknowledged the independent power of the Great Seal of England and therefore of its Keeper.

The Seal consisted of two moulds, originally made of silver but now of alloy. Since the Norman Conquest the front has carried the image of the monarch on the Throne and the back that of the monarch on horseback. Generally, the seal has been treated with respect, but James II famously dropped one set in the Thames when escaping on the horse ferry, and when Henry Brougham was Lord Chancellor, he was said to have used his to play Hunt the Slipper at country-house parties.

Until 1874, a salaried clerk known as the Chaff Wax softened the lump of red wax in hot water, clamping it round a ribbon or tag on the parchment document, and then squeezing it flat. More recently, the wax was replaced by granules of cellulose acetate plastic, green for a peerage patent, red for a judge or a bishop.

When a government falls the Lord Chancellor goes, and his Great Seal is ceremonially smashed by the Sovereign. Lord Hailsham's father surrendered the Seal in 1938, and described it getting 'two gentle taps from the King, carefully calculated to do no possible damage', so that he could keep it as a souvenir. Lord Simonds, sacked in 1954 by Winston Churchill to make way for his friend Sir David Maxwell Fyfe, the first Earl of Kilmuir wrote that 'The Queen hit the old Seal some hefty blows.'

The Throne, the Woolsack and the Parliament Chamber were all created in the light of the Shining Ladder. They had, in the practice of ritual theatre, slowly transformed warring hooligans into some kind of civilization. Others would argue that they were historic lumber that had obstructed and retarded the development of a just society.

But some comprehensible process was at work. The Mace had once been an iron club for smashing another man's skull on the battlefield. By some mysterious alchemy, the repetition of these rituals had transformed its iron into gold.

CHAPTER SIX

The Barons' Beef

Despite the brooding presence in full armour, carved in gilded wood on the canopy above the Throne, professional historians would be cautious about admitting any shared political identity between King John's barons and the present House of Lords. To carry the connection back any further would infuriate them.

I mentioned the use of the word *ordo* to describe the Royal Council of Cogidubnus at Chichester in Roman times to the most distinguished historian of the House of Lords, Enoch Powell, and the famous cat's eyes narrowed in a wince. 'I think you would find it extremely difficult to establish any direct connection between the *ordo* and the House of Lords.'

The same is true of many of the liberties I have already taken. Byrhtnoth did not receive a writ of summons to an official Parliament, was not technically called Lord Byrhtnoth and does not figure in Cokayne's *Complete Peerage*. The gatherings at Rockingham and Clarendon could be described as Great Councils or Royal Councils, and a great deal of printer's ink and paper has been expended by academics in quarrelling about which was which. Constitutional historians usually date the emergence of an upper House as a distinct institution from the 1340s, and, as we have seen, they were not called 'the Lords' for another two hundred years.

But King John's barons were adopted as official ancestors by the Parliamentary Committee supervising Pugin, and their presence at Runnymede unquestionably marks an important moment, both for the Lords as governors and for the rule of law their future assembly would come to represent.

The oddest eye-witness account of what happened in June 1215 is from a man who would have had a seat in any early House of Lords as Abbot of Bury St Edmunds, and the summons in Norman-French his bishop would have received to a meeting of the Witan was already phrased as it would be for the next seven hundred years. Laying aside all excuse and delay, as he loved and honoured the King, he was requested to go to London on a particular day in the Church's calendar 'to treat with us of our great and arduous affairs and the common benefit of the realm, since it is expedient to have your advice and that of the other Magnates of our realm, whom we have caused to be summoned there on that day'. Abbot Hugh, like all the Bishop's senior clergy, would have been included in that summons.

From the few fragmentary reports of what was said in the Witan, the tone of their oratory sounds oddly familiar to a modern fan of the Lords' more colourful style. King John had lost Normandy in 1204, most of the Norman nobility in England were beginning to think of themselves as English, but a few had been caught fighting with the enemy, one of them pleading rather fatuously that 'his body might have been fighting for the King of France, but his heart was with King John'. This prompted Lord d'Aumale, described as 'a very valiant gentleman and a good knight, but so crippled with gout that he had to be carried in a litter', to say that 'if King John ever had the good fortune to get his hands on the hearts of those whose bodies were fighting against him, he hoped His Majesty would throw them down the privy'.

Runnymede, however, was not a meeting of the Witan, and Father Hugh was not invited to it. He had recently been elected Abbot, and he travelled to Windsor simply to have his appointment confirmed by the Crown.

When he arrived, he was told that the King was in conference with the Archbishop of Canterbury, Stephen Langton, and would receive him the following day, 10 June 1215, 'in the meadow at Staines'. Abbot Hugh seems to have been unaware that anything of importance was going on. According to his own account, he arrived, found a great crowd at Runnymede and waited for hours at the back. After 'much discussion and exchange of views', a courtier identified him, took him through to the King, who gave him the formal kiss of peace confirming his appointment and invited him to dinner at Windsor Castle.

The 'discussion and exchange of opinions' was King John's great confrontation with his barons. Literate priests were there, making notes, but historians now believe that most of the business of the day was, as Abbot Hugh described it, a public debate. Demands were shouted by the barons and either agreed or rejected by the King and his ministers. Those agreed were written down as the Great Charter.

Despite the impression of normality given by Abbot Hugh's ceremonial confirmation in office and the invitation to dinner, the King and the barons – what amounted to a rogue opposition party who had taken the law into their own hands – were on the brink of civil war. The signing of Magna Carta provided little more than a breathing space, but it represented a strengthening of the position of the members of what would become the House of Lords, an acceptance on their part of a wider political responsibility, and the tightening up of procedures by law.

The crisis at Runnymede was to do with money. First there had been the war with France, then King John's elder brother Richard I had emptied the English treasury to take a crusading army to Palestine and had been arrested on the way home by the Austrians. The ransom for his release was raised from individual lords in the form of a heavy personal wealth tax.

Financing foreign wars put a great strain on the lords and the whole feudal system. The word *feudal* came from *feodum* or *feudum*, Latin meaning fee: the lords and bishops held their lands from the King in return for the fee. Henry II and his sons extended this from what had been the loyal provision of troops or their equivalent in money to the grudging payment of taxes in cash, often collected by corrupt tax officials. Lords who were unable to pay forfeited their castles, their wives and children were taken hostage, and in one case starved to death.

What strained the system to breaking point was the loss of their honour and dignity. Centuries before the lords had been mere *hlaf-weards*, men with money, but had been transformed first into charismatic war-heroes by the Anglo-Saxons, and later, in the age of chivalry, into superior beings, worthy not only of loyalty but of adoration bordering on worship – barons and earls in shining armour. With the exception of one Anglo-Saxon, Lord Waltheof, executed soon after the Conquest, no lord, whatever his crime, had suffered the death penalty or the various disgusting mutilations practised on lesser criminals. Even on the battlefield he was sacrosanct: bowmen and foot-soldiers might be slaughtered in heaps, but providing the lord wore his coat-of-arms and displayed the necessary heraldic emblems, he was treated as a member of a strictly protected species, emerging from battle at worst bruised. This was partly because of ransom value, but also for fear of powerful reprisals, and because armour had been developed that would have protected Lord Byrhtnoth even against a Danish battleaxe, but most of all because the lords were seen as a sacred caste.

To ask these heroes of chivalry to raise armoured knights, attendants and foot-soldiers was one thing. To force them to pay a crippling tax was to unmask them as ordinary mortals. It caused the old upward-looking romantic loyalties, which bonded each layer of society to the one above, to come seriously unstuck.

What is remarkable about Runnymede is the visible emergence of a militant committee of lords challenging not only the King but direct government from Rome, and defining English liberties on behalf of the entire people by law. Both sides had appealed to the Pope to arbitrate, and King John had even knelt before the high altar of old St Paul's, officially surrendering his sovereignty to the Church. In practice, despite the terror felt by most Christian citizens of excommunication, handing authority over to Rome made very little difference to the outcome of the crisis.

A month before Runnymede the Pope sent three directives: first, to John, telling him to listen to the lords' complaints and treat them fairly; second, to the dissident lords, demanding respect for the King and threatening them with excommunication if they resorted to force; and third, to the Archbishop of Canterbury, telling him that the crisis was all his fault. It was his job, as Rome's man in England, to maintain peace and order. In the event of trouble he was to support the King, who had agreed in the meantime to raise another army for the Middle East.

At this point a delegation from the dissident lords arrived in Rome. The Pope received them, listened to their case, and wrote a fourth directive ordering them to provide whatever troops the King needed for his Crusade. If there was any further trouble, he was sure it could be settled by 'the judgment of the lords in the King's court according to the laws and custom of the realm'.

None of the directives arrived until weeks after the dissident lords, leading what they called 'the Army of God', had seized the City of London, the confrontation had happened and Magna Carta had been agreed, stage-managed by the Archbishop, Stephen Langton.

Magna Carta was therefore an English initiative, devised by the Archbishop and the lords temporal, and the first great piece of parliamentary business, a primitive series of Bills argued through clause by clause and set in permanent form by the lawyers.

Great Charters – or legal agreements defining the powers of government – were already being drawn up to establish the rights and liberties of the nobility in Italy, Spain and Hungary. What made Magna Carta different from the others was that it included safeguards not simply for the nobility but for everyone else. It also involved the third force in the triple alliance who believed so passionately in order: the lawyers.

The early lawyers, clerks in holy orders, literate and well-educated churchmen, brought with them from the Church courts to the civil courts the inherited authority of the old Roman Empire: Church Latin. Clerks had been present at Rockingham, Clarendon and Westminster. Agreements had been made and ratified by bishops and lords pressing their signet rings into the hot wax, amendments had been debated and carried, and the law clerks had written them down. But it was in Magna Carta, in clause after clause, that the law emerged as the third partner in the mystical part of government, separate from the Church and separate from the King, the guardian of something sacred that had 'come down' from a more virtuous past.

Magna Carta, like all the other Great Charters of the time, recalled a Golden Age. Guided by the rising class of church law-clerks, the people of Sicily in their charter asked the Pope to remember the days of King William the Good. In England they called on King John to remember the laws of St Edward the Confessor, the good old English king before the Normans came.

Bad King John has recently been reassessed as not having been so bad after all. Historians have praised his diligence in scuttling round the country from local court to local court, continuing the work of his father Henry II in standardizing the administration of justice. His own respect for and encouragement of the law, and his taste for clearly defined arrangements, played into the hands of those demanding a legal constitution, and he had to sign some disagreeable clauses. Among other things, he had to agree to a Committee of Public Safety, made up of twenty-four lords elected from among their own number, making decisions on a free vote and commanding an army of twelve thousand knights. This sounds like a crude prototype of a Lords' committee, but it had more teeth than some of the more sophisticated assemblies that followed it. If four or more lords protested at the way in which he was behaving, the King himself, in signing the Charter, authorized them to 'distrain and distress us [*distringent et gravabunt nos*] in every way they can, namely by seizing castles, lands and possessions, and in such other ways as they can, saving our person and those of the Queen and of our children, until in their judgment amends have been made'.

A sub-clause authorized the general public – members of the future House of Commons – to join in: 'Anyone in the land who wishes may take an oath to obey the orders of the said twenty-four Barons in the execution of all the aforesaid matters, and to join with them in distressing us to the best of his ability.'

As soon as the 'discussion and exchange of opinions' was over, the law-clerks drew up several copies of a parchment scroll. Under the eye of the Archbishop, King John and his Chancellor fixed the Great Seal to each. They were dated June 15, five days after the start of the negotiations witnessed by Abbot Hugh.

Magna Carta not only protected the lords from the King, it protected the people from the lords. Clauses thirty-nine and forty showed the lords' concern for those who would eventually be represented in the Lower House. No 'free man' – and that meant not only bishops and lords but 'merchants' and 'villeins', who had been dismissed until then as 'worthless' before the law – was to be deprived of his property, outlawed, exiled or imprisoned except by 'the lawful judgment of his peers [his equals] or by the law of the land'.

Most important of all for the future of government, the summoning of Parliament was established legally and accepted by the King: in Clause fourteen, he agreed that 'to obtain the common counsel of the realm about the assessing of an aid [the equivalent of a money bill] we will cause to be summoned the archbishops, bishops, abbots, earls and greater Barons individually by our letters'. The King's sheriffs and bailiffs would summon anyone who held an estate from the King when a new tax was to be imposed and it has been estimated that this would have produced a House of eight hundred members. The assemblies were to happen at a fixed place and on a fixed date, with at least a month's notice to be given of every session. Writs of summons would also specify what business was to be discussed.

Magna Carta was followed by chaos. Copies of it were distributed throughout England, but for the next forty years no stable power was concerned to enforce it. The Pope, resenting an English 'Army of God', annulled it as soon as he discovered its existence, ostensibly finding it offensive to his honour and dignity as Pope. Louis IX of France, who was called in later to arbitrate, found it offensive to the honour and dignity of a king.

But the lords persisted. Twenty years later, Stephen Langton, who was still Archbishop Canterbury, insisted on a milder version being signed when Henry III began to rule in his own right in 1232.

What the Pope and Louis disliked in Magna Carta was the germ of a rival creed. If the Church, the King, the lords and even the lawyers believed in a vertical hierarchy, a Shining Ladder that had its origin in a dream of a Golden Age, Original Truth, Paradise, God in the Highest, another equally ancient belief was rising to challenge it.

In establishing, or as its framers insisted, re-establishing the rights of 'freemen', Magna Carta was evoking another Golden Age. In the reign of St Edward, before the Norman Conquest, man might not, as Rousseau would claim of his own imaginary Golden Age, have been born entirely free, but he had been born with a measure of freedom and certain inalienable rights. Those rights were not graciously initiated from above by the King or the Pope, but were bargained for on the level meadow at Runnymede under the threat of violence.

Heaven, ultimately, might have existed, and might exist again in a Golden Age to come but here, below, on earth. Nor was it a realm where angelic happiness sprang from an acceptance of God's will. Heaven could be bargained for, clause by clause, and as free merchants and villeins won more freedom, so the lords would lose it. It was the beginning of what Richard Trench called the Industrial Principle, as lethal to the hierarchy and to the lords as carbon monoxide. It was the Dream of the Bright Horizon.

CHAPTER SEVEN

The King's Needs

As the lords and the bishops continued to battle for control with the King and the Pope, two unexpected things happened. One was the emergence as leader of the dissident lords of Simon de Montfort; the other was a spontaneous movement inside the Roman Catholic Church.

Simon de Montfort was an unlikely founder of English parliamentary freedom. His father was a brute, who had crushed and massacred the Cathars on the French border with Spain, and de Montfort himself had upset the lords by marrying the King's widowed sister Eleanor, who had taken a vow of chastity. The wedding had been celebrated quietly in the recently completed Palace of Westminster, but royal marriages were subject even then to the approval of the lords, and the lords had not been consulted. As a Frenchman born in France, he also belonged to a race that, since the loss of Normandy, the Anglo-Norman lords now hated. John's successor Henry III had surrounded himself with men they saw as foreigners. The Duke of Savoy, a brother of Henry's new French wife, was building a palace for himself just south of what is now the Strand. Another brother, Boniface, famous for his good looks and still in his twenties, had been made Archbishop of Canterbury.

Simon de Montfort, having been made Earl of Leicester, moved into opposition, taking over the leadership of the twenty-four lords appointed to enforce Magna Carta. Sometimes the number had been reduced to fifteen, sometimes even to twelve, and it had continued ineffectually to challenge the King for control of the shared power. In 1258 they had met him at Oxford, to try to restore the authority and rule of law that had been agreed at Runnymede, and the Provisions of Oxford were the first agreement since the Conquest made in English.

The King was involved in increasingly unpopular, expensive wars and in opposing him de Montfort found himself a hero, particularly in the towns. He had also become a close friend of a leading member of the new movement in the Church. Its adherents saw the idea of hierarchy, of the Shining Ladder, as a once-useful chain of command that had become petrified. The obvious drawback to the Ladder as the central pattern of Church government, and therefore of secular government, was that it seemed to contradict the historical doctrine that Christ had been born in a stable, to the wife of a Jewish carpenter.

Under the feudal system, the bishops had become landlords and warlords, wealthy, powerful men living in castles and attended by foot-soldiers and servants. How could Christians be called upon to respect such a hierarchy, in which God the Creator in his human form would have come somewhere below the lowest acknowledged social rung?

One answer came from St Francis of Assisi who died in 1226, having founded his order of friars, who would live, like the Apostles, in poverty.

Even the secular lords shared this concern, and one of the first objectives of the original standing committee of twenty-four was the reform of the Church. But the Church was beginning to reform itself. In England one of the leading early reformers was the Bishop of Lincoln, Robert Grosseteste, 'Robert Bighead' in Norman-French. He was an intellectual, a scholar who had read the pre-Christian authors of Greece and Rome. When Grosseteste became the close friend and confessor to de Montfort, they discussed not only Aristotle on tyranny and the ideas of poor friars in Oxford on what they called the Body Politic. They also talked about Christ's humble beginnings on earth. The man who was soon to shape the government of England was exposed to the first seminal ideas of both the Renaissance and the Reformation. In his will, made in 1259, de Montfort specifically mentioned 'the poor people of his land', his ploughmen and farmers.

As Henry III pursued his expensive war in Sicily, flouting the agreements on regular Parliaments and using foreign mercenaries to defend him in England, de Montfort rallied a minority of lords, but a majority of prosperous townspeople. When it came to the great battle of Lewes in May 1265, he brought with him 15,000 Londoners. From Fletching below the Downs, he led his men in a dawn attack on the King's encampment, finding paths to the east near what is now Lewes prison. At first, the Londoners were badly cut up by troops under the command of Henry's son, Prince Edward. Then de Montfort's forces drove the King's army down the steep hill below the High Street to St Pancras Priory where, cut off by the river Ouse behind them, they surrendered.

Both Henry and Prince Edward were captured, and de Montfort made history by summoning the first Parliament not made up exclusively of lords and bishops. He called knights from the shires and burgesses, or town councillors, from the cities. It was the beginnings of a House of Commons, representing not commoners but 'communes' or communities.

Almost at the same moment, the old ideals of chivalry, associated with the Shining Ladder, began rapidly to crumble. Later in the same year, at the battle of Evesham, all the lords who had supported de Montfort, whether they were wounded or captured unharmed, were slaughtered on the battlefield. Although he was the Earl of Leicester, de Montfort himself was stabbed to death, his body stripped, chopped up and put on obscene display.

But perhaps Prince Edward had learned his lesson: he came to the throne in 1272, and during the course of his thirty-year reign he called sixteen parliaments, all of which included representatives of the shires and cities as well as the lords. They now met, with increasing regularity, in the old Palace by the river at Westminster.

In April 1341 this joint assembly finally separated to form the two Houses of Parliament. The old Witan had often divided to discuss particular issues but this was the first time that the parliamentary rolls recorded a summons to two different institutions: the House of Lords, known in Norman-French as *les grantz*, the great ones or magnates, who were called individually as the owners of great estates and raisers of troops, and the House of Commons, known then as 'those of the commonality'. Those invited were told that they were 'to debate and consider among themselves, the magnates separately, and the knights of the shires, the citizens and the burgesses separately, how to meet the King's needs'. The separation was really to do with tax. Until then the sum to be raised from the communes for the King's needs had been calculated on a percentage of 'movables'. Now the annual total for the King's needs was set at a fixed sum.

The lords and the bishops would be assessed individually on their estates, but the rest of the community, the successful tradesmen and craftsmen in the towns and the independent landowners who farmed small estates in the counties, would negotiate with the commissioners through their representatives in the Commons.

This strengthening of the power of the secular element in government was accompanied, apparently quite fortuitously, by a weakening of the influence of the Church. Agreeing to pay the same kind of fixed annual levy, a large proportion of what were known as the 'minor clergy', though they included the heads of abbeys and monasteries founded before the Conquest with long-established seats in the Witan, simply withdrew from Parliament. Attendance was a duty, like jury service, and they took advantage of a period of administrative incompetence to get out of it. No writs of summons had been issued for some years, and when they finally arrived, the minor clergy said they were 'not sanctioned by custom', and that they were 'amazed to receive them'.

This produced an odd freak in constitutional history: a purely clerical assembly, the Convocation, which negotiated its taxes with the Crown without any right to advise on how the money was spent. It also meant fewer churchmen in the Lords.

What the new system meant for the Lower House of Parliament was an important modification of the old hierarchical machine. Raising the money for the King's needs had successfully transformed the old Shining Ladder into a sort of vertical money-pump, but with new controls.

Under the Normans and their passion for discipline, leaks had been sealed, joints and junctions tightened. The Domesday Book specified exactly how many 'hides' of farm produce each estate could provide and the lords siphoned it up. When they were allowed to commute their quota of armed and mounted troops into a cash tax, the wealth was sucked up again, providing the King's power, the money to pay the Army. Only the House of Lords had, in theory at least, any control over the taps. Now the Commons had effectively installed taps and stop-cocks lower down.

It was not a period of great parliamentary distinction: when Edward III consulted the two new Houses about the wisdom of pursuing wars in Scotland and later in France, both were non-committal and the King therefore acted on his own initiative.

Constitutionally, however, things were falling into place. During Edward's absence in France the lords and the bishops, who had traditionally withdrawn to their own separate chambers for any detailed discussions, formed their first joint committee of six lords and six bishops. If this sealed the unity of the Upper House, it did not make their report any more decisive. 'They had debated with great diligence and deliberation as they had been asked, for which the Lord King thanked them very much, but it was not fully agreed what the King should do concerning the business.'

Almost more important, Parliament began to meet regularly, at least once a year, summoned by law rather than at the request of the King.

There continued to be times, in emergencies, when Parliament met in provincial cities like York, but in principle it had now come to rest at Westminster. It was no longer a touring show, and the stone, having stopped rolling, began to gather moss.

For the law-clerks, who dipped their goose-quills in the ink and drew up each new parchment roll of those summoned to the Lower House, the names of the knights of the shires and the burgesses were often new, and required investigation.

The sees of the bishops, Chichester, Rochester or Durham, never changed, and neither did the names of those abbeys and monasteries still included in the post-1340 parliaments. But when they came to the secular lords the same lethargy served to strengthen the aristocracy in their hereditary claims. They had usually to do no more than copy the list from the previous year. The roll of those summoned became fixed. The earldoms and baronies began to appear immortal. As the lazy law-clerks copied them from one roll to the next, new faces appeared in Parliament bearing the same old names. The principle of the lords' hereditary right to a seat in Parliament became established.

To understand how these two Houses of Parliament worked, it is necessary to imagine the riverside at Westminster before Big Ben and the Victoria Tower, when there was no road between the Palace and the Abbey. The construction of the complex of buildings had been begun in early Saxon times from a little fishermen's chapel on Thorney Island, a mudbank in the Thames under what is now the river-front of the new Palace of Westminster. According to legend, it was miraculously visited by St Peter; as he appeared all the candles lit of their own accord.

Since then, the halls and residences of a royal palace had been built, including the Minster, now the Abbey – that gave the place its name – with an abbot and a full complement of monks. All that survived into the twentieth century is Westminster Hall and, now on the other side of the main road close under the walls of the Abbey, the Jewel Tower. Beneath it in wet weather it is still possible to see the water of the Tyburn, the stream that winds through London from the old place of execution at what is now Marble Arch to the Thames where it emerges at the southern end of the old Thorney Island, now buried under the Victorian foundations. For centuries the Jewel Tower was the home of the Lords' archives, which are stored today in the Victoria Tower. It is now a little museum, containing among a few other things a rusty sword buried in the mud of Thorney Island before it all began.

Like Westminster Hall, originally built by William Rufus, the old Palace echoed the Abbey in buttresses and pale stone.

With the Thames at Westminster running due north, the huge roof of Westminster Hall lay roughly parallel to it, but veered off to the north-west. At the southern end of Westminster Hall, there was a C-shaped range of buildings facing the river.

Its northern wing was St Stephen's Chapel, a dazzling challenge to the Sainte-Chapelle, which Henry III had seen in 1248 on a visit to Paris. It had been begun by his son, Edward I, and completed by his grandson, Edward III, a few years after the two Houses separated. It was brilliant with stained glass and glittering floor-tiles, wall-paintings in deep blue, spangled with golden stars, vividly coloured saints and angels painted under enamelled arches, gilded martyrs high up under delicate stone canopies, while more stars glittered from the deep blue of the vaulted roof.

From the west doors of this royal chapel, close to the southern end of Westminster Hall, there was a flight of steps up to what was called the White Chamber. It was eighty feet long and forty feet wide

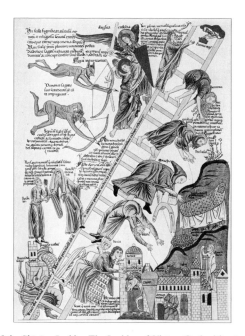

The Dream of the Shining Ladder. The Ladder of Virtue. God, ultimate authority, the source of all life and protection, is thought of as vertically overhead. The steps of the Ladder gave their names to the ideas of class, rank, grade and order "under God" With the Ladder generally accepted as the natural pattern of things, those seen as being born to the upper rungs became less vulnerable to gravity than the laity and clergy shown here "falling into temptation".

Jacob's vision of the angels ascending and descending from heaven.

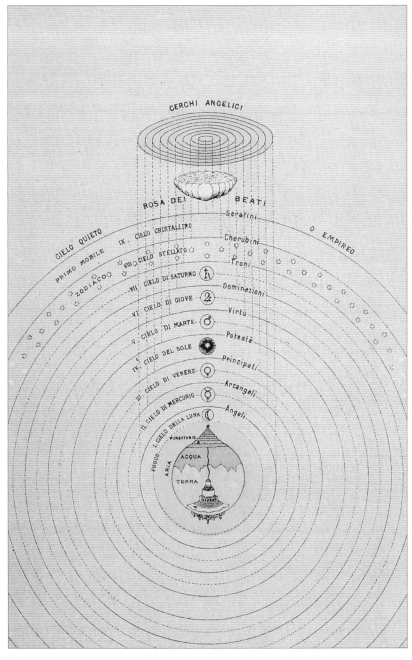

The Orders of Angels. An illustration from Dante's *Paradiso*. The celestial class structure, eternal and unchanging.

The Three Estates. The equivalent structure on earth. A French scheme, drawn in 1450, of the Pope above the King and his Nobles above the People. The tree image here seems to hint that power originates from below: later family trees, with their roots in heaven, give hereditary power divine authority. Nobility and People were further classified in Tables of Precedence, still sometimes used at municipal dinners, where the younger son of a baronet ranked higher than a senior academic.

The Mediaeval House of Lords. The design of the peers' robes and the shape of the woolsacks already appears to have been established. Edward I, (1272–1307) joined here by the King of Scotland and the Prince of Wales, presides over a House – the Commons did not yet exist as an assembly – dominated by Lords Spiritual whose first allegiance is the the Pope in Rome.

A victory for the Eurosceptics. The King challenges a Papal "Bull", commanding the loyalty of all his subjects except those still in thrall to the Catholic Church.

The birth of the Church of England. Henry VIII as Head of Church and State tramples the Pope.

A Seraph. A panel from the ceiling of the old Painted Chamber where the Lords and Commons first met, in a workshop for restoration when the Palace burned down.

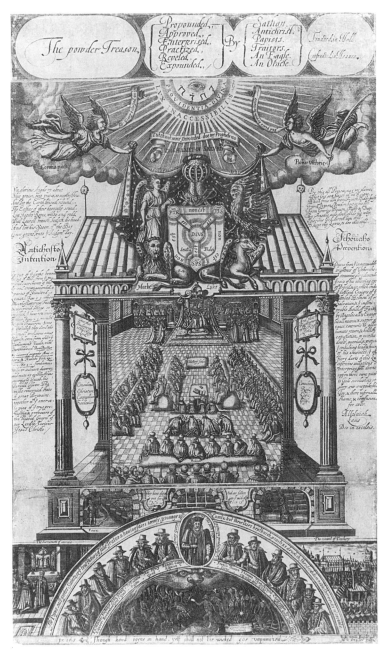

The Powder Treason: James I, enjoying the direct authority of God above; the Catholic Church, once the guarantor of order, as Antichrist or the hellish European threat: Lords and Commons are undermined by Guy Fawkes and "the Pope's saltpetre saints", bent on terrorist outrage.

Queen Anne at the State Opening. With the creation of twelve new peers to ensure the government had its way on the Treaty of Utrecht in 1712 the hereditary authority of the House of Lords became vulnerable to the political party in power.

Their Lordships' House. The State Opening of 1769 in the Queen's Chamber hung with the famous Armada Tapestries. Even with a Cabinet consisting almost entirely of peers, they exercised their real power through the control of seats in the Commons.

Revolution! With no place on the old Ladder, now set in stone, Queen Caroline and her attendant Bright Horizonists mount a challenge.

and ran north–south, parallel to the river and following the line of the present Palace, with clear windows high up under the roof.

At its southern end, parallel to St Stephen's Chapel, was the Painted Chamber. This was the King's State Bedroom, the meeting place of Parliament. Like Liebknecht and the German socialists who scrambled into the Kaiser's bedroom to celebrate the revolution in Berlin in 1917, the members' presence in that part of the Palace had real political significance: they were all tax-payers, they shared the King's housekeeping and the King's house.

There was a platform at the east end nearest the river, reached by a short flight of steps, with a view over the Thames through two elegant tracery windows. From there it was possible to see the Queen's Chamber, another separate hall built in stone running parallel to the river at the water's edge.

The Painted Chamber had been completed in about 1250 and took its name from the birds, lions and other animals painted on its walls. Fifteen years after it was finished there was a fire, and it was repainted with more uplifting subjects. From the coffered ceiling angels and saints looked down, hands raised in blessing. On the upper levels of the walls there were long horizontal painted panels, showing the victories of the Jews as the Chosen People. There was an attempt at primitive perspective, with realistic green shrubs and trees. In the window recesses there were symbolic figures of the Virtues, with arching angels above in golden crowns. On either side of the King's State Bed, paintings showed the Coronation of Edward the Confessor. Gold and silver glittered from every painting, and there were raised decorations of painted plaster. Up to shoulder height there was a dado, painted green and with folds to look like a curtain.

There is an early eye-witness account of the building in use when the Archbishop arrived there in January 1341. As was often the case, there was a crisis over payment of Church taxes.

He appeared at the north door of Westminster Hall, near what is now the Commons' underground car park. He was accompanied by the Bishop of London and the Bishop of Chichester, walking in formal procession, with the Archbishop's jewelled cross carried in front of him by a chaplain, attended by priests and acolytes. At the door they were stopped by two armed guards. One of them explained to him, as politely as possible, that he was not allowed in. 'Father, do not take this ill, but we are forbidden to let you enter the King's Painted Chamber where he is holding his Parliament.'

The three lords spiritual were diverted into what was called Little Westminster Hall, a room off to the left of the north door housing the Exchequer. There, the Steward of Edward III's Household demanded the payment of the outstanding Church taxes, and when that was settled the procession reassembled and swayed off through Westminster Hall. They went out through the southern doors, past the end of St Stephen's Chapel and up the steps into the White Chamber. At the end they turned left, and were admitted to the Painted Chamber where the full Parliament was in session. The doors were opened, the Archbishop took his seat, the Bishops took theirs, and their train of attendants withdrew.

Now that Parliament had a permanent home, the webs and tendrils of tradition and dignity began to form.

Some rules were purely practical, and have since been superseded. No weapons, swords, daggers, long knives, armour or even padded jerkins were to be worn in the area bounded by Westminster and the City of London. This was a come-down for the great landowning lords, who were in the habit of travelling with a small army as much for prestige as self-defence, so, as an exception they were allowed to have a single sword carried in front of them, though not in the Palace of Westminster or in the presence of the King.

When two servants fought in Westminster Hall, one killing the other, the survivor was immediately hanged without trial. Presumably to prevent other forms of hooliganism, all street games in Westminster, the City and the suburbs between were banned at the same time.

Other rules had more to do with the mystical power of ritual and repetition, inspired by the Shining Ladder, and strict order was observed in the seating of Parliament. Edward III's Throne was at the east end of the Chamber, and when the Archbishop had dismissed his cross-bearer and chaplains, he took his official seat on the King's right, where the Bench of Bishops still stands today. The Bishops of Chichester and London would have taken their seats on a bench on the same side, in the order of the dates of their consecration. Then, on their right, came the remaining bishops, abbots and priors.

Facing them across the Painted Chamber sat the lords temporal. On the King's left sat his son, the Black Prince, who was the first

Englishman to be created a duke when he became Duke of Cornwall, and establishing the place of honour to be occupied in future by all dukes. Then there were the earls, the barons, and the judges. At the west end of the room, separated from them, were the Commons: the knights of the shires and the burgesses of the cities.

Every Parliament began, as today, with a joint session and a formal speech from the Throne, promising first a debate on the King's needs, then another on points of policy and lastly an opportunity to consider appeals. Then the King and the Lords withdrew, and the Lord Chief Justice called on the Commons to elect a committee of twenty-four. It was almost always formed of knights of the shires, many of whom were closely related to members of the Upper House. Their role, in Norman-French, was to *entrecommuner* or 'inter-commune' with the Lords. The Commons were then dismissed and ordered to return to the Painted Chamber the following morning 'at sunrise'.

At dawn the King's needs and the points of policy to be decided were read out in more detail, then the Commons, like the Lords, withdrew to their own chamber to debate. Once they had voted and come to a decision, their committee returned to report to the Lords and to argue the Commons' case.

The Lords were also there to settle disputes between members of the Upper House. One of these cases involved the long-running quarrel between Lord Zouche of Ashby, who had allegedly abducted an heiress, and Lord Grey of Rotherfield, who claimed that she was engaged to him. The case was settled in Zouche's favour with the Crown demanding the traditional marriage tax. Grey appealed to the Pope, without success, and the argument rumbled on. Five years on he and Zouche fought, and Grey was bound over to keep the peace. A year later, the pair began to argue in the Painted Chamber in front of the King. There were 'hot words', and Grey went for his dagger. This time both men were arrested and imprisoned. Zouche was given bail and reappeared in Parliament, and the King asked the Lords' advice on what should be done with Grey. They found Zouche innocent and sentenced Grey to go to prison.

The Commons debating chamber was either the monks' refectory in Westminster Abbey or the Abbey Chapter House. The Lords, when they withdrew, climbed the steps to the low platform at the eastern end of the Painted Chamber and found their way through a series of narrow lobbies to the Queen's Chamber. It was the stone building overlooking the river, also painted with allegorical figures of spring and winter, and was provided with a long cellar running the length of the building, with doors opening on to the riverbank, originally intended for the Queen's wardrobe.

This was the cellar chosen by Guy Fawkes to stack with gun-powder before a State Opening three hundred and fifty years later. Fawkes having failed to blow it up, the Queen's Chamber was to remain the home of the House of Lords until 1801.

CHAPTER EIGHT

In the Kremlin

The survival of these ancient ideas of hierarchy to the end of the twentieth century owes much to the Church, to the Law, to the innate laziness and love of habit of the British people, but it is no coincidence that the House of Lords, as the last shrine of the old order, should be staffed by administrators, doorkeepers and messengers who are all former members of the armed services.

One of Burke's indictments of the French Revolution is that it broke 'the great essential link between the officer and the soldier'. That link, he says, was subordination, and on that link the whole system of pre-revolutionary Europe depended.

Black Rod, when I went to see him in 1994 in his busy office off one of the red-carpeted corridors, was a retired sailor, Admiral Sir Richard Thomas, former commander of HMS *Fearless*. In Edward III's time, Black Rod was a courtier, a member of the Royal Household, the Usher of the newly founded Order of the Garter. He took his name from the black stick he used to clear a passage through the crowd on ceremonial occasions. Since then, the Order of the Thistle has appointed a Green Rod, the Order of St Michael and St George a Blue Rod, and the Order of the British Empire a Purple Rod. Black Rod seemed more sinister, and his appearance was suitably menacing. He was the man with the terrifying eyebrows, the gleaming dome of a head and he had cavernous and unblinking eyes.

I began by quoting Lord Grimond's joke about the House of Lords not being thought a worthy target by serious terrorists.

The black eyebrows bunched together in a severe frown and he dismissed the suggestion with the kind of irritation you would expect from a former admiral who had once commanded HMS *Fearless*.

'No, no, we are a target here, and I recognize that. Now, if people are after you they will observe you, they will see there is a pattern. You meet the same people every day on the way in to work. Lord Nonesuch always comes every day, say, at eight thirty. So you vary the pattern, you vary the way you police, you vary the emphasis. Sometimes we search cars, sometimes we don't. If you were to stand on the other side of the road and watch us you wouldn't find a pattern. Let me give you a glass of gin.'

His hospitality was characteristic of the place, though Sir Richard seemed less at ease than most of the staff who run the Lords. Watching him glide along the red-carpeted corridors when Peter Horsfall persuaded him, in his own phrase, 'to go walkabout', the large observant eyes under the eyebrows looking balefully ahead, I sensed a studied remoteness. He was the CO on his tour of inspection, not on easy terms with the peers he was employed to protect.

In his office he settled down behind his desk, fixed the unblinking eyes on the middle distance, and prepared to answer my questions.

Peter Horsfall had told me that the Duke of Edinburgh had had a hand in Sir Richard's appointment. I asked him if this was true. 'Absolute nonsense. We barely know each other.' The post of Black Rod was traditionally filled by senior officers of each of the three services in turn, and he remained, first and foremost, an old salt in dry dock, still very military in a way that Peter Horsfall was not.

I asked him how long it had taken him to learn the job from the Air Chief Marshal he had succeeded. He sniffed and thought. 'A day and a half. But I had a fair amount of experience.' It had really been a move from one part of the Establishment to another. He had spent eight years at the Ministry of Defence, so he knew how Whitehall worked. He had been happiest when he had commanded HMS *Fearless*.

'It's every sailor's dream to have your own ship. I had that. Being an admiral's not so much fun – you command the Fleet but you're always on someone else's ship.' Being Deputy Supreme Commander of the North Atlantic hadn't been much fun either. 'You have an American on top of you and an American underneath you. It's different. You have to rather tiptoe through the tulips. But living in

America taught me, oddly enough, more about England. You begin to understand that even the Italians do things quite well. But what we English do best is ceremonial. We pride ourselves on being ace at ceremonial and we get a lot of encouragement. I mean you may think the Queen's Speech is rather a potty little exercise but it does show' – he seemed momentarily flummoxed as to what it showed – 'the Queen in Parliament.'

How did he feel, after working in Washington and Brussels, about coming back to all the dressing-up and wearing wigs?

He looked at me sharply, the eyes under the great eyebrows and the huge dome distinctly hostile. 'I don't *wear* a wig!'

I remembered that he didn't. It was an embarrassing moment, as if I had accused him of sporting a hairpiece in the evenings, but I persevered, pressing on to the core of my thesis. The House of Lords and the armed services were the last bastion of rank and order. They understood the difference between commissioned officers and other ranks. Surely his military background must be a help. 'I'm not so sure about that. Things have changed a lot in the services over the last few years. A lot of the old barriers have been broken down. There are greater technical demands being made on fighting men, you're working with trained brains who have to think outside discipline. For example, we had a farewell party last night for' – he made a very slight pause to add weight to the Christian name – '*George* Martin, one of the doorkeepers.' His train of thought had continued without a break apparently unaware that he had moved from ship to shore. 'Ten or twelve people from the Establishment Office, old doorkeepers, Hailsham, Jenkins. No, the division between officers and other ranks is now markedly less than it was. I think that's true across the board.

'I'll tell you a story. A doorkeeper finds a peer smoking in one of the non-smoking areas and says, "You shouldn't be smoking in this part of the building, my lord." So the old boy says, "What's that got to do with you?" The doorkeeper says, "Well, it is my duty to help you keep the rules, my lord." Then the peer spots an ashtray. "What's that ashtray there for, then?" And the doorkeeper pushes it across to him and says, "So you can put your cigarette out when I tell you to, my lord." '

That story seemed exactly to capture the atmosphere of the House of Lords. Whatever he said, the notion of rank and old-fashioned social deference was still there, but it depended on both sides observing the rules of the game. It was like a virus that seemed to infect everyone who worked there, a kind of Wodehousian country-house germ that leaked from the old peerage, producing a desire to perform a continuing charade of Life at Blandings Castle: the doorkeepers and attendants muttering, 'my lord', their half bows as they delivered their lordships' messages and opened doors for them. It might have been incubated by the thick carpets, the Gothic panelling, the endless shelves of leather-bound books, the portraits of former members, even by the ritual politeness in the Chamber. But everyone in the end seemed to catch it, the doorkeepers more acutely than the peers themselves.

Peter Horsfall had caught it too. In his flat under the eaves at Christmas-time the walls were covered with more than a thousand cards suspended on ribbons. 'Working for the peers is the best side of working here. I can count on one hand' – a thought crossed his honest brow – 'or perhaps two hands, the number of nasty things that have happened here. One of them will be rude perhaps, and I'll think, "Hang on, how old is he?" '

Where he evidently felt happiest was with the liveried man-servants: twelve attendants and twenty-three doorkeepers. There, too, order survived, with the same kind of stepped hierarchy that existed among the peers, from generals down through the ranks to the private soldiers: there were ex-infantry men in the Commons; in the Lords they were ex-Household Cavalry or Foot Guards.

I tried to press Peter Horsfall on this. Was there anything in writing? No, there was no set rule, that was how it happened. The best job, he reckoned, was the Redcoat, who hailed taxis at the Peers' Entrance and pocketed the tips. One old boy had hung on to it for nineteen years. A less popular chore for a retired guardsman was being 'the Bishops' Boy'. He had to help the bishops on and off with their robes and to keep the roster of who was on duty to say prayers. They are a distinguished body of men, and essential to the running of the operation. They have even been accused of voting. When the Lord Chancellor asked the peers if they were 'Content' with a Bill, a good strong bellow of agreement would pass it without the peers having to be counted through the lobbies in a division. Late at night when the doorkeepers were tired of standing by the doors, rumour had it that they would strengthen the bellow of assent so that everyone could go to bed.

They learn their job minding visitors in the Strangers' Gallery. The trickle of tourists, students and Boy Scouts who took the traditional cure for admiring the House of Lords of coming in and watching them, were on the whole well behaved. Notices in quaint red and black Gothic characters, like church hymn boards, warned them against causing any disturbance, and they seemed quickly lulled into obedience by the slow rhythm below: door-keepers and attendants coming and going among the red benches delivering messages, a peer shuffling in, a peer shuffling out, one peer on his feet, apparently ignored by the rest, droning on about wildlife.

There was the dramatic moment when militant lesbians had suddenly produced lengths of climbing rope and abseiled down into the Chamber, allegedly with the connivance of the bearded socialist peer Lord Monkswell, but in the normal course of things the worst disturbance was someone shouting a protest, when they would be taken downstairs and locked in a room until the end of the day and they were peacefully released.

Such a leisurely working day gave new doorkeepers time to study their copy of *Dod's Parliamentary Companion*, a kind of *Who's Who in the Lords* with a little black-and-white photograph of every peer. *Dod's* was their bible. It told them where a peer had gone to school and to which clubs he or she belonged. Some of the keener trainees kept their own little notebooks with drawings and their personal observations, which was a help when they graduated to standing downstairs in the Chamber.

Often, Peter Horsfall said, when peers were 'popping up and down' in a debate, even the *Hansard* writers were confused and turned to the doorkeepers for help. Fortunately they worked in teams of three, so one would usually know. It was the doorkeepers, too – often old sergeants who had barely used a typewriter – who had to service the word processor feeding the blue television screens throughout the building that announced who was speaking and what was being debated. That was generally considered to be their worst job.

What they really enjoyed was looking after their lordships. I asked one senior doorkeeper how they were told to treat the peers. He thought about it, then said with absolute seriousness: 'With exaggerated courtesy.'

I understood the seductive power of the place for so many old Labour men, trade-union bosses and revolutionaries who had sworn to abolish it. After a few weeks of being called 'my lord' and bowed through doors by former non-commissioned officers of the Brigade of Guards, anyone would accept their upper rung on the Ladder. It was what Thackeray, writing soon after the Reform Bill of 1832, called Peerage-Worship, or Toadyism Organized. 'How,' he asked, 'can we help cringing to Lords?'

Even the police volunteered to work there. Peter Horsfall called them by their Christian names, and they took a share of the peers' traditional whip-round at Christmas, like a Christmas box for the old retainers at a country house. Some years it raised as much as £10,000.

The cleaning in the Commons is done by a firm of outside contractors but the Lords still have a permanent staff of forty-two housemaids. Having tea after one of the State Openings, they were all friendly, desperately discreet and slightly giggly, like old-fashioned maids at some vast Victorian house. They chattered away about how well the ceremony had gone, about Denis Thatcher worrying that no one would sit next to Margaret, and then Jim Callaghan had come along, and Denis had slapped the person next to him on the back and thanked him for making it such an entertaining morning, and what a wag Denis was. They said he frequently shook hands with the Queen with a cigarette cupped in the other hand, and that as far as the Queen was concerned Denis could do no wrong. They all wanted to go on an outing together to see round Buckingham Palace.

Underpinning the country-house charade, Peter Horsfall himself still saw the organization in military terms.

'If you think of me as the regimental sergeant major here, the Yeoman Usher – that's the man who carries the mace – is the adjutant.'

The adjutant, I remembered from Army days, was a major, the one who did most of the commanding officer's dirty work in terms of daily administration and discipline.

'Black Rod is commanding officer. Look at it this way: I can't be away when Black Rod's away.' That, too, tallied with what happened in the Army. The two people of whom everyone was afraid were the regimental sergeant major and the colonel.

Even so, the military hierarchy had become blurred by other administrative patterns. The Clerk of the Parliaments looked after the offices that managed relations with the House of Commons, the printing, secretarial work, legal affairs and accounts. Peter Horsfall, working under Black Rod, looked after the fabric of the building, although following a review by Mrs Thatcher's government, some of his responsibilities had been handed over to a Director of the Works, who managed the upkeep of the entire Palace of Westminster with a budget of £20 million a year. 'They have specialists in furniture restoration and people repairing the stoves and so on.'

He was also officially responsible for the heating and lighting engineers, the general maintenance and catering personnel. That meant going beyond loyal permanent staff, and all new or part-time staff had to be checked as potential security risks. 'It doesn't matter if they've got something on their record, as long as they declare it. You can't take anyone at face value. A terrorist of any calibre, I'd have thought, could work for some firm for a year to build up a bit of a reputation and get references.'

So far, he said, there had been only minor breaches of security, and they had been the work of outsiders: a German photographer had slipped past the policeman on duty at the Chancellor's Gate, while he had been out directing traffic, and Greenpeace had taken advantage of the scaffolding on the Victoria Tower to climb the outside from a lorry in the middle of the night and unfurl a protest banner. His own civilian staff, whom he invited me to meet at one of his monthly co-ordinating meetings when, as he put it, he 'got everything sorted out', seemed loyal and entirely reliable.

Some of the staff, it must be admitted, had moved on from the world of P. G. Wodehouse as I discovered at the Co-ordinating Meeting which Peter Horsfall had invited me to join. I arrived with time to spare, and called in to renew my own security pass.

The security headquarters at the Lords, the Pass Office, was a double-decker Portakabin, newly clad in black glass, in a gloomy courtyard, with the conventional airport equipment for examining luggage, steel frames to step through, metal detectors and black-uniformed staff. On the noticeboard there was a stern letter. It warned peers not to bring strangers to the House of Lords 'in disregard of the regulations'. Any attempt to circumvent the rules, it said, would be reported to the Speaker, the Lord Chancellor, but the mood in the Pass Office was affable in the extreme. A big West Indian security officer was exchanging banter with a Cockney in a hard hat carrying a parcel.

'Man, you leave dat tin' dere, I'll be round the corner, an' *runnin'* !' Then he collapsed into helpless giggles.

Upstairs, where my photograph was taken and my pass fixed in a plastic holder on the end of a chain, there was a more intriguing conversation going on in an inner office. 'You can knock me out a couple of one-liners anyway, bearing in mind who it is we're gonna meet. Like "What's the odds on Cardinal Hume?" or "How do you get the white smoke up the chimney?"'

I wondered, briefly, which peer was visiting the Vatican and why his security guard thought he would be meeting the Pope, let alone why he would need jokes to entertain His Holiness. Then I collected my new pass and set off to find Major Horsfall.

His office, on the ground floor just off the Chancellor's Gate, was severe. It had Pugin wallpaper and a Gothic door, but there was a word processor, printer and photocopier occupying most of the room and a desk for his secretary. His own desk, by the shuttered window, was a plain table covered with a sheet of glass under which there were various lists and telephone numbers. 'This is a trick I picked up in the Army. People are amazed when they ring me up. I've got all the answers. I just read them off from under the glass.'

We walked through outdoor passages, narrow courtyards and finally through Westminster Hall to have a cup of coffee in Plod's Café, so named because it was favoured by the police, down some steps through a doorway on the west side of Westminster Hall, under a vaulted stone ceiling. Baked beans, mushrooms, rashers of bacon and scrambled eggs steamed in stainless steel containers, dished up by plump ladies in white hats and overalls. A democratic queue of MPs, peers, workmen and security guards lined up with trays to collect their breakfast on big white plates, to have their tea poured out from big sloshing stainless steel teapots, and to pay at the till.

Upstairs again, he led me through another Pugin door, this one marked Television Interview Room, a long room with a narrow wooden table and more Gothic chairs, and handed me a one-page agenda. Each of the thirty-eight items had a number between 12 and 94, and a column to say who had raised it. One item had been raised by the Yeoman Usher, one by 'Nine Peers'.

They could have been the staff of any big hotel or conference centre: men in grey suits, some carrying briefcases, two younger women in raincoats, then two tearaways who arrived late. It was summertime, and one had a gelled brushcut and a brown shirt, the other an orange short-sleeved sports shirt. Both carried plastic carrier bags, one bright blue, one bright green. Major Horsfall whistled between his teeth.

'You can tell the workers. Got their jackets off.'

The brushcut remained perky and unrepentant. 'Sorry about that! Recess time!'

They began with some general talk about trouble with the chimes of Big Ben. Peter Horsfall expressed his surprise that a spokesman quoted in the *Daily Telegraph* had said, 'Brian O'Boyle will soon sort it out' rather than 'Mr O'Boyle, our resident engineer, will soon sort it out', and then began to crack through the agenda at a brisk trot.

A new room had been created out of an attic, and he wanted to congratulate them on keeping down the cost. 'Thirty thousand pounds, the estimate was for that room, we got it done for two thousand five hundred. So well done all concerned.'

A new handrail was being installed in one of the public corridors, but it was a firm they hadn't used before and they were taking their time. 'OK. Keep chasing. Right, shall we crack on, Barry, and leapfrog Chris?'

Two more men arrived, one with a cheery smile and a bald head. 'Morning, sorry we're a bit tardy!'

Major Horsfall persevered.

A section of the roof of the Parliament Chamber had been reassembled in a laboratory in Cambridge and squirted with water from various angles in an attempt to find some more efficient way of waterproofing the tiles.

'Now we come to the continuing work on cleaning the stone.'

This was the business of pigeon droppings. The building had been treated with pigeon deterrent, which, it turned out, was doing more damage than the droppings. The man in charge of the work was apologetic. 'Some of that pigeon repellent gel is thirty years old, and it's very hard to get off.'

Peter Horsfall sounded more critical. 'There's very bad staining, particularly round the Peers' Entrance.'

'Well, we haven't used that pigeon repellent for eight years.'

The Throne was being restored, as well as the spare throne at Cholmondeley Castle. Lady Trumpington had had problems about the air-conditioning.

Lord Ampthill still hadn't got the brass lights he asked for six months ago. It was the only time in the meeting when Major Horsfall became slightly beady. Lord Ampthill had been promised his lights in January, they must get a move on. Lord Ampthill sounded a man to be reckoned with.

There was resentment about the expense of the new sound systems recommended by the BBC. 'Thirty thousand pounds this year, forty thousand next year, and another thirty thousand for the Moses Room.'

A bleeper went off, and the bald-headed man with the grin bustled out of the meeting.

Black Rod had come on very strong about the new security lights being installed in Palace Yard. Westminster Abbey wouldn't allow them to be fixed to the outside of the Abbey. Then, with a perceptible brightening of their mood, they came to the problem of smoking.

A small persecuted band of smoking peers, it seemed, had found a basement room where they were allowed to smoke, but the extractor fan had driven their stale smoke up through the stained-glass window above into the room of one of the clerks, who was a ferocious anti-smoker. An experimental bit of double glazing had been tried but the clerk was still complaining. A humane discussion ensued about the poor smoking peers having nowhere to smoke, and how the problem was complicated by the air-conditioning. 'Recycling makes it worse, you see.'

Then, again, the mood changed. This time there was real anxiety. Works offices in the basement round what Horsfall called the Bandstand, a convergence of corridors beneath the Chamber of the House of Lords, were to be moved. 'By having them all central, you see, it should make their work easier. I could see that when I walked round with Black Rod. Of course, it'll mean losing the Kremlin.'

A real shudder ran through the room.

Nervous looks were still being exchanged when they moved on to the lavatories. Then, almost at once, there was a happier atmosphere.

Lavatories at the House of Lords, like the Throne and the Woolsack and the old-fashioned deference of the doorkeepers, were somehow sacred. Anywhere else on earth except the House of Lords they are a great leveller. For generations in England dustmen have stood shoulder to shoulder with dukes as 'Gentlemen'. At the Peers' End of the Palace of Westminster, hierarchy survives, and it is enforced.

Baroness Mallalieu, one of the glamorous intellectuals brought in by Labour, was surprised to be stopped at a door marked 'Peeresses' by Barbara Castle. The old Labour star explained that it was for the wives of peers – 'You are not a peeress, you are a Woman Peer' – and led her some considerable distance to somewhere more suitable.

The peers' lavatories are marked 'Peers', a word that some-times takes on added significance when a door stays open to reveal a row of lords standing at the trough as if by way of demonstration.

Stuart Braham recalls an amusing encounter when, scorning the sign on the door, he was using the peers' urinal. Believing himself to be alone he released a loud fart, which was greeted to his consternation from inside one of the cubicles by a cry of 'Dirty bugger!' Humiliated, he tiptoed out, passing in the doorway the then Archbishop of Canterbury, Lord Runcie, who innocently took his place at the stalls, leaving the clerk to imagine the expression on the face of the emerging peer.

Now the staff were glowing with satisfaction. Peers had demanded heating in some remote thunderbox, and there had been fears it would involve damage to a Victorian glass-mosaic floor. The head of the electrical department won universal praise with a proposal for overhead coils.

There had also been something near to panic when a bench used by the peers when they were polishing their shoes had disappeared from another lavatory. It had been found in a workshop, and the meeting sighed with relief. Finally, peers had complained about lavatory mats getting 'tatty'. This was considered with deep seriousness. Peter Horsfall had been in to have a close look at them. 'They're coir with red edges. The coir's easy enough, but I'm not sure about the red edges.'

Someone said the tiles looked nicer bare.

'Do they really need mats?'

Peter Horsfall nodded gravely. That was what the peers were used to, they had to have them. 'But they've got to look right. They'll look right when they're good.'

The meeting came to an end, and I confessed to being puzzled by one thing. What was the Kremlin, and why were the staff so attached to it?

'Come with me, I'll show you!'

He led me off on a whirlwind tour of the building. The first door he opened revealed an unfamiliar view of the Parliament Chamber. I realized we were inside the canopy over the throne.

'There was a clerk, Sir Peter Henderson, and when he retired and the peers made speeches of appreciation, he sat hidden up here listening to them.'

We passed through smoking rooms with low Pugin armchairs, reading rooms with Pugin paper-racks, whips' offices where only the telephones belonged to the twentieth century, and even looked into the tiny room allotted to Baroness Thatcher. She had apparently already complained about it being too small, and was cross at having to share a coat-hook downstairs in the hall.

Everything was decorated in the same heavy Victorian Gothic, polished leather and dark carved wood, with austerely framed pictures of former parliamentarians on lattice-patterned wallpapers of dark olive green.

The new office discussed at the meeting was being made at the end of one corridor. The walls were bare plywood and electric cable was being stapled into channels sawn in the wood. Afterwards, Peter Horsfall said, it would all be papered in Gothic lattice-pattern and mocked up to look like Pugin. He seemed pleased. Tradition had been maintained, money had been saved.

Walking through with Major Horsfall was indeed very like being back in the Army. During my National Service, a lot of time was spent flushing out 'skivers', those idling when they were meant to be on duty. Officers and sergeant majors would make a stately progress through the camp, suddenly throwing open doors. If anyone was caught there would be a roar of rage from the sergeant major, a few sharp words from the officer and, in extreme cases, the man who had been lying on his bed having a smoke would be marched off in double-quick time to the guardroom.

Now, in this post-Wodehousean, post-hierarchical age, the effect was not quite the same. Wanting to show me a typical Lords' committee room, he threw open a door.

The room was in darkness and, at the front of several rows of modern stack chairs, a lone figure was silhouetted against a large television screen, watching football. Peter Horsfall turned on the lights. An elderly security man rose in an unhurried manner to see who it was. There was no roar of rage. Peter Horsfall nodded to him. 'All right, Ken?'

'Yes, thanks.'

He did admittedly leave the lights on.

We walked along concrete-floored, neon-lit underground passages and carpeted administration offices in the cellars below the Chamber where computer screens flickered among a controlled chaos of wall-charts, files and papers.

We walked outside through grubby grey courtyards, and Peter Horsfall stopped to point up at the roof. 'Look at that up there! Infilling! I think that looks terrible!' He indicated a row of steel-framed windows, new offices fitted into space in the roof, square and ugly behind the blackened stone of Barry's Gothic battlements. 'Portakabins!'

We went, finally, down a steep flight of wet steps directly under the Victoria Tower. At the bottom was a basement room with lagged pipes all over the ceiling. The walls were damp and hung with coloured pin-ups: a wide white smile, a long glistening back and a provocative bottom in lacy white pants; a very pink girl with a pair of huge breasts sporting only a tiny pink G-string. Sitting alone reading the *Sun*, his feet up on a plastic-topped table, was a man in jeans and a leather jacket.

'Morning, Bob!'

Bob recognized Major Horsfall with a slight wrinkling of the forehead. 'Oh, hello.'

Peter Horsfall betrayed no sign of irritation. He introduced me, explaining to Bob that I was interested in the House of Lords and that he'd like to show me the Kremlin. Bob got to his feet and patted the top of one of the lagged pipes above his head for a key. Peter Horsfall filled in while we waited. 'This isn't the Kremlin itself. The Kremlin's in there. It's the bar where a lot of the staff go drinking.'

He said all the best parties were held in the Kremlin. It was stocked with drinks, which was why it was locked. Bob still couldn't find the key. He found some other keys but they didn't fit. He had a slightly mournful South London accent and told Peter Horsfall while he was trying them that a lot of the maintenance staff were worried about the rumours. 'There's talk of losing it, making it into offices. We're very big on tradition here. This bar goes back a long time and we like it, right? It's a tradition, like the blocks of wood for the State Opening.'

On the way up the wet cellar steps, Peter Horsfall remained silent on the plans for new offices but explained about the blocks of wood. 'We used to have these huge blocks of wood, you see, like Victorian railway sleepers, for people to stand on at the State Opening. Blokes were carrying them in. I told them two men to each but, of course, they had to try lifting them on their own. One chap had a heart attack, dropped down dead, so we had to introduce these new light stands on frames.' He shook his head and blew through his teeth. We crossed the courtyard and went back into the Palace. He was obviously still thinking about the railway sleepers. 'I agree with him, though. It's not the same.'

CHAPTER NINE

The Saint with Two Heads

In the summer of 1520 two remarkable men went together to Canterbury Cathedral to visit the shrine of St Thomas à Becket, murdered over three hundred years before. One was Erasmus, the Dutch philosopher and satirist, then working as a parish priest in Kent, and the other was the founder of St Paul's School, John Colet.

In the crypt below the nave of the cathedral, in the holiest part of the shrine, a monk showed them the fractured skull of the martyr set in silver. 'The top of the cranium,' Erasmus wrote, 'is bare for people to kiss. There in the dark hang the undergarments, waistbands and breeches of haircloth with which the Bishop subdued his flesh. The very sight of them is horrifying and makes one ashamed of our softness and our comforts.'

Relics were big business. The cathedral records still contain annual accounts of the income from pilgrims who visited each altar, not counting the tips collected by monks who acted as guides. Water from a sacred well under the chancel 'mixed with the saint's blood' was bottled and sold as a cure for various diseases. At Walsingham, Colet and Erasmus had even been offered milk said to have been produced by the Virgin Mary. Relics made money because they represented a link with Original Truth. To kiss the skull of St Thomas à Becket was to make contact with the authentic past, like kneeling before a hereditary earl or accepting the judgment of the hereditary Chamber.

Colet was invited to kiss the skull, and Erasmus recorded how amused he was at Colet's expression of nausea as he did so. Then the monk on duty opened a trunk and produced jaws, fingers and a decomposing arm. Finally he showed them some bits of ancient linen rag, which, he said, 'the saint employed to wipe the sweat from his face or neck, the running of his nose, and things of that sort incidental to the human frame'. Colet found them 'disgusting', but, to Erasmus's delight, pretended to brush them with his lips.

The description of the visit is of particular interest because it was written by Erasmus himself, a man with a highly developed sense of humour. Jokes had always been made about the authenticity of relics: Chaucer's pilgrims to Canterbury two hundred years before talk about them as 'pigges' bones'. But the gently satirical tone of Erasmus, as one of the Church's leading intellectuals, is indicative of a new mood, and spelt trouble for the traditional veneration of relics and shrines as symbols of authority – rungs in the Shining Ladder that linked the present to the holier past.

The two men climbed the steps to the nave of the cathedral, passing through the South Porch where they saw portraits of the three knights who had killed the Archbishop. They were like Wanted notices, the men's names recorded underneath 'in order that no one hereafter might assume them as titles of honour'.

Canterbury was the provincial headquarters of the European Superstate. Through Canterbury the Roman Catholic Church was regularly pumping vast amounts of money out of England as it had for a thousand years. There were fees for every compulsory church service from baptism to burial, taxes, rents and tithes, and Becket's tomb was the suitably imposing centrepiece of a vast financial organization triumphantly commemorating the King's act of submission. One visitor described it as being 'composed of pure gold, adorned with jewels, and enriched with magnificent gifts'. Erasmus was dazzled:

> Everything shone and sparkled and flashed with rare jewels of extraordinary size. Some were bigger than a goose's egg. The prior showed the jewels one after another, touching them with a white wand and adding the French name, and what it was

worth, and who gave it, for the principal ones were presents from royal visitors.

Eighteen years later, in the winter of 1538, with Henry VIII confirmed by both Houses of Parliament as Supreme Head of the Church of England, the tomb was demolished. Two huge chests of gold and precious stones were dragged out of the cathedral, every stained-glass window that made any reference to Becket's martyrdom was smashed, 'so that there should be no more mention made of him never'. The image of his martyrdom that had formed the centre panel of the Archbishop's Seal for centuries was replaced with an image of the Crucifixion, and Becket's official saint's day was struck from the calendar.

Becket possessed, it turned out, not one but two skulls, and this was widely publicized. Both had holes in the top of the head to match the description of his murder. The one set in silver that Colet had hesitated to kiss was shown to be a recent fake, but all the bones that could be found, some almost certainly those of the Archbishop, were ordered to be taken out without ceremony and burnt.

To underline his break from Rome, Henry VIII ordered a play to be performed in Canterbury, *On the Treasons of Becket*. Henry II was now the hero, a noble English king sorely tried by an emissary of Rome who had 'lifted himself up with intolerable arrogance above the authority of the King and the common laws'. Even the three knights were reinstated. According to the official proclamation, Becket had 'given opprobrious words to the gentlemen', wrestled with one of them, 'violently shook and plucked him in such manner as he had almost overthrown him to the pavement of the church'. The knights had acted only in self-defence.

It may have been a triumphant blow for English sovereignty, but it was a damaging one to the Shining Ladder, and it was to have long-lasting consequences both for the future of Parliament and for the status of hereditary peers in the House of Lords.

Canterbury was not the only place to hear the sound of breaking glass. During the previous century the House of Lords had been split in the struggle between Lancaster and York, and with aristocratic leaders on both sides hanged, drawn and quartered, its membership was seriously reduced.

Recognizing the potentially sacred nature of heredity, Henry VIII saw the aristocracy as a vital part of the new order that would replace the Church. Eight years earlier, in the middle of his divorce from Catherine of Aragon, he sent a directive to Clarenceux King of Arms, signed and dated at Windsor in April 1530. Clarenceux, who originally took his name from the Duke of Clarence, was one of the official heralds appointed at the time of Agincourt, responsible for all of England south of the Trent. 'Henry by the Grace of God King of England and of France, Defender of the Faith and Lord of Ireland' ordered all 'mayors, sherriffs, bailies, constables and other our officers, ministers and subjects' to assist 'our trusty and well-beloved Thomas Benoit, otherwise called Clarenceux King-at-Arms' in his enquiries on a tour of inspection, officially known as a Visitation, during which he was to check all crests and armorial designs. Wherever he found 'false armoury and arms devised without authority, marks unlawfully set or made in scutcheons, squares or lozenges', whether they were 'in stone, windows, plate, set upon churches or other places, banners, standards, pennons or coats-of-arms', he had orders from the King to smash or destroy them. Given the already ancient tradition of setting coats-of-arms in stained glass, carving escutcheons in stone or painting heraldic devices on wood, this was tough stuff. If it sounded like an act of religious fanaticism, a forewarning of the smashing of Becket's windows at Canterbury or the breaking of sacred images that came with the full Reformation, that is exactly what it was. Smashing Becket's tomb was a largely political gesture. Purifying the aristocracy was political reform when the lords were about to meet more frequently than they ever had before.

Only four annual Parliaments were called in the 1490s, none between 1505 and 1509, none between 1516 and 1522, none between 1524 and 1529. Then in 1530 Henry VIII made his first demands on the Church, asking for the repayment of the then immense sum of £100,000, which he claimed he had already spent on his divorce from Catherine. As he pressed on, severing one by one the sources of papal income and creating an Anglican Church independent of Rome, both Houses were forced to sit for months on end and this pressure continued for the best part of seven years. What became known as the Reformation Parliament reformed Parliament itself, and an erratic series of stormy annual general meetings became a hard-working if pliant core of national administration. There was also an intensification of parliamentary ritual, which Henry himself encouraged on the evidence of his reading.

In *The Education of a Christian Prince*, written in 1516, Erasmus had described a 'limited monarchy, checked and lessened by aristocracy and democracy'. The term 'limited monarchy' had already been used in the previous century by Henry VI's Lord Chief Justice, Sir John Fortescue. France was an absolute monarchy, England was a mixed monarchy, a *dominum politicum et regale*, the power shared between Parliament and the King. Erasmus explained what a limited monarchy meant. According to Aristotle, there were three pure forms of government: monarchy, the rule of a single man, which could degenerate into tyranny; aristocracy, the rule of the few, which could become oligarchy, the rule of a gang or *junta*; democracy, the rule of the people, which could always slide into mob rule. The perfect balance, he concluded, quoting the Latin author Polybius, once existed in Rome, with a first consul, a senate and the assembly of the people. It had been the foundation of Roman greatness.

Henry VIII recognized this as his own existing system. King, Lords and Commons were the three elements of government: the Commons subordinate to the Lords, the Lords subordinate to the King, but each modifying the others and neutralizing the dangers inherent in their purest forms. 'We at no time stand so highly in our estate royal, as in the time of Parliament,' Henry told both Houses, 'wherein we as head, and you as members, are conjoined and knit together into one body politic.' The King was mystically present in Parliament, and Parliament shared his nature. 'Whatsoever offence or injury is offered to the meanest member of the House, is to be judged as done against our person, and the whole court in Parliament.'

If this was true it represented a big shift from pure Shining Ladderism, in which King, Lords and Commons had been three discrete orders vertically organized under God and the Pope. It echoed the new image of God, as preached by the Protestants: an omnipresent power that was as accessible to the people as it was to the priests. If the King's dignity was present in the humblest member of the House of Commons, then the humblest member of the House of Commons shared some of the King's power. At the same time, Henry was insistent on the maintenance of a show of order.

As early as 1516, a new distinction had been drawn between the lords temporal and spiritual, to the advantage of the peers. They were entitled to be tried only by their equals, by the House of Lords itself. The bishops were merely 'Lords of Parliament'. They did not possess noble blood, their seat in Parliament went with the job: out of office they would stand trial like any other citizen. But the presence in Parliament of the lords temporal had been ordained by birth, and they were to take their places according to an unchanging order. Like the King, they acknowledged the supremacy of the law: the Lord Chancellor, the Law Incarnate, took precedence over all but royal dukes. Otherwise the lords sat rank by rank, dukes with dukes 'according to the antiquity of their creations', earls with earls, and so on down to the barons. Even membership of Lords' committees was restricted to peers of the same rank, earls debating with earls, barons debating with barons.

When it came to a spoken vote the tellers took it bench by bench, beginning as they had for centuries with the most junior creation and working up to the most senior. Discipline was strict, but on rare occasions peers were reprimanded for 'disorder' or 'sitting confusedly'.

To enhance the Lords' theatrical dignity Henry himself ordered yards of scarlet silk and bags of copper nails to decorate the Painted Chamber in which both Houses met for the State Opening. Long canvas cushions, stuffed with wool and covered with scarlet silk, like the Woolsack, were tied to the nails to cover the benches and the Bar. The Throne was the centrepiece, with the royal arms embroidered in gold, scarlet and blue behind it, and the peers had to bow to it as the symbol of the Royal Presence on entering and leaving the Parliament Chamber. To the left and right of the Woolsack, and facing it, were three more scarlet-covered sacks to accommodate the King's Counsels, the Masters of Chancery and the Lords' Clerks. On state occasions, when peers wore their red robes, the Painted Chamber blazed with scarlet.

But if the House of Lords grew in ritual authority it was to prove itself pathetically weak as the senate Erasmus had told the King was there to check him. The House was now almost exactly balanced between the lords spiritual and the lords temporal, with fifty abbots and bishops, including the Bishop of Llandaff, Jorge de Athequa, Catherine of Aragon's confessor who spoke hardly a word of English, and fifty-three lords temporal. Both sides contained strongly conservative elements, led by the old Archbishop Warham, but when the King moved against Rome and against the hierarchy they themselves represented, they offered very little resistance.

Henry made use of a wave of popular resentment against the priesthood, with their exorbitant fees and charges, and left it to the Church's own Convocation to raise the £100,000 he had chosen to claim for his divorce expenses. When they offered £40,000 he roared at them, and they agreed the full sum, sending him a loyal letter of thanks for defending the Catholic faith and for protecting them against the Lutherans 'whose books and works were everywhere dispersed to the intent to blemish and hurt the estimation of the prelates and clergy and to bring them into common hatred and contempt'.

The King fully intended to bring them into a lot more hatred and contempt. He already had inspectors at work digging out instances of buggery, lesbianism and other moral turpitude in the rich monasteries and convents that would justify his closing them down.

For the moment, though, in 1530, he turned to the Commons and the Lords to cut off the Church's sources of income. The first Bill, limiting the 'mortuary fees' charged by parish priests, went straight through the Commons and received little opposition in the Lords. According to the diarist Richard Hall, the bishops recognized that it would not affect their own income, and took it on the chin, 'making a fair face'.

The second Bill in the same session, which limited the legal fees charged by priests, made them 'frown and grunt', and brought the Bishop of Rochester, John Fisher, to his feet in protest. The Bills, he said, were outrageous. They would bring the clergy into 'servile thraldom, like to a bond maid, or rather little by little to be clean banished and driven out of our confines and dwelling places'.

A member of the House of Commons, he told them, had recently accused the priesthood of being 'vicious, ravenous and insatiable'.

'What, are we all of this sort? These men seek to reprove the life and doings of the clergy, and so finding fault with other men's manners whom they have no authority to correct, omit and forget their own, which are much more out of order.' He urged their lordships to 'resist manfully this violent heap of mischief offered by the Commons'.

It was an odd reversal for a member of the Church whose traditional occupation was pointing out the faults of others, but roles were changing, and Fisher was right to warn the Lords that in destroying the priests' authority and privilege they were threatening their own. 'You will see all obedience withdrawn, first from the clergy, and after that from yourselves.'

He was answered by the Duke of Norfolk, 'half angrily and half merrily', who told him that clever priests were not always the wisest of men.

Fisher was increasingly isolated. If the Lords' constitutional power had been as great as defenders of the old House of Lords in future centuries liked to imagine, the Bills would have died. Instead, the King ordered joint committees of both Houses to push them through, and the Commons showed themselves a great deal more vigorous in committee. When one of the lords spiritual appealed to precedent, a member of the Commons reminded him that thieves had traditionally robbed people on Shooter's Hill. Did that make it lawful?

Supported by the King, the Commons pressed on with a third Bill to stop the clergy from farming, brewing and selling corn. The Lords rejected it. The King ordered another joint committee, and, finding all the lords temporal against them, even the bishops gave in.

The King also terrorized individual members. If governments in later times controlled the House of Lords with the threat that they would flood the Chamber with new peers, Henry VIII won by draining it of old ones. While he filled every bishop's seat that became vacant with one of his own chaplains and appointed Cranmer Archbishop of Canterbury to steer the legislation through, he also made sure that those who opposed him stayed away. One sixty-year-old conservative bishop came to the conclusion that he was too old to travel to Westminster. Bishop Lee decided he was too busy with his duties in Wales. Lord De La Warr, another conservative, wrote to say that regular attendance at Westminster over the past three years had proved too painful and expensive. Lord Darcy, who had already spent time in the Tower for suspected treason, pleaded 'age and debilities', and Lord Conyers, who would lose his head on the block three years later, gout.

Most of them offered their proxy vote to the new Lord Chancellor, Audley, formerly Speaker of the House of Commons, suggesting he used it as he thought fit. Lord De La Warr actually left a square on the page as 'a window for to put in whom it shall please the King's Highness to appoint'.

Their terror was understandable. Fisher, like the former Lord Chancellor Sir Thomas More, went to the block for refusing to acknowledge Henry as head of the English Church, having been tried as a private citizen. Henry had been stalled briefly when Fisher narrowly escaped death from a pailful of poison mixed by a man called Richard Roose, which killed several members of his household. The King, living in dread of being poisoned himself and wishing to make it clear that Roose had not been working on his instructions, devised a new and horrible punishment for all poisoners: Roose was boiled alive. The King, whatever his lip-service to Erasmus's ideas of limited monarchy, got his way, and the House of Lords did little to restrain him.

When the House of Lords did make a mild protest it was usually on non-religious matters, reflecting its members' perennial concerns as landowners. When a Bill came in to stabilize rents on agricultural land by limiting to 2,000 the number of sheep that could be kept by any tenant farmer, the Lords passed an amendment allowing farmers to count sheep in 'long hundreds', 120 instead of 100.

De La Warr, with other absentee opponents of the Reformation like the Earl of Essex and Lord Lisle, was among the first to ask for Church land after the dissolution of the monasteries. But the reputation of the Lords as an institution was above reproach. 'There is no unquietness, no tumultuous fashion,' one eye-witness wrote, 'there is no cheeking or tauntyng of any man for showing his mind.' They never spoke more than one at a time, they could say anything they chose and be sure of being answered gently and courteously. Sleaze was unheard of. 'There is no man speaketh for any carnal affections or lucre of the promotions of this world, but everything is done for zeal of the commonwealth.'

Ironically, the zeal of the Commonwealth was the one force that the House of Lords was unable to survive. If politics until now had been largely ecclesiastical, theology became inextricably political, and the single most symbolic move came not in the Lords but in the Commons. In 1548, twelve years after the dissolution of the monasteries, as the Lords continued to meet in the Queen's Chamber down by the river, the Commons moved into St Stephen's

Chapel. Candles and crucifixes were carried out, and where the high altar had stood, they installed the Speaker's Chair.

The Shining Ladder, too, was now deconsecrated, out of the dim religious light and exposed to critical public gaze. Like much other Roman Catholic lumber, it would soon be pulled down and smashed.

CHAPTER TEN

The House of Lords Abolished

Burke's assertion that nothing in the French Revolution, 'not to the fashion of a hat or shoe', was left to accident, was also true of the English Revolution that swept away the House of Lords in 1649. The same militant belief was at work that Burke condemned in France, Trench's 'industrial principle', severing links with the past. It was religious rather than secular Bright Horizonism, but in the course of it theological ideas emerged into the light as political aspirations, and the Revolution expressed itself at every stage in vivid public theatre.

What seemed to be the final assault on the Shining Ladder had begun in the Reformation, in the century before, in the celebration of the Mass. For the old Catholics, the power to turn bread and wine into the Body and Blood of Christ resided entirely with the priest, as a member of a sanctified hierarchy, originally ordained by Christ himself. He might be corrupt or drunk or unshaven or smell of onions but when he intoned the words *Hoc est enim Corpus meum* the transubstantiation happened.

Protestants argued that the recipient also had a role to play. Unless he or she believed, it remained bread and wine, even if the Pope himself had consecrated it. If they received it in faith then it became the Body of Christ. Power passed from the hierarchy to the individual.

The same principle was at work in the provision of English translations of the Bible to every church in the country, as ordered by Henry VIII. Instead of accepting dogma in Church Latin they did not understand, individuals could argue about the meaning of the Christian faith from the original sources.

If this seems irrelevant to the existence of the House of Lords, the conclusions that followed from it were not. When Church authority was challenged, as Bishop Fisher had warned them, all authority was challenged. The Church hierarchy now came under close historical scrutiny, and the same hostile interest would soon be taken in the origins of the secular hierarchy, the nobility. The Shining Ladder depended on respect for unbroken continuity, on a belief in a divinely inspired process at work in civil institutions, as slow and natural as the growth of a tree. Bright Horizonists looked for a Golden Age, either in the past or the future, into the likeness of which the present could be hammered by human effort, and they had turned first to the early Church, when Christ as God Incarnate had instructed the first disciples.

When John Calvin of Geneva re-examined history, he came to the conclusion that Jesus Christ had never ordained any bishops. St Peter had been commissioned to take charge of Christ's flock, and authority had passed into the hands of locally elected 'presbyters' or elders. They might have appeared to the author of Revelation high in the sky in white robes and with golden crowns on their heads, but on earth they were democrats.

This had political consequences a long way from Geneva. In Scotland the new 'Presbyterians' turned the bishops out of their palaces. Bishops no longer existed. Politically the Presbyterians' ideal constitution would have replaced King, Lords and Commons with God, the Presbyters and the Faithful, effectively putting government in the hands of the elected elders.

More moderate scholars pored over the letters of St Ignatius, condemned for his Christian faith to be eaten alive by wild beasts in Rome in AD 115. Ignatius had not only been Bishop of Antioch, he had written about the importance of Christians 'submitting themselves' to the elders, who should in turn be 'tuned to their Bishop as strings to a lyre'.

Whether or not the elders had originally been elected, there had been a hierarchy, and in England that doctrine for the moment prevailed. But the Bright Horizonists were on the move there too, and the Church of England, cautiously balanced under Queen

Elizabeth so that it respected both the old Catholic tradition and the new ideas of the Reformation, became increasingly keen on following the Scottish pattern. When James I, already King of Scotland, came south in 1603, the battle over the bishops began in deadly earnest. He had been appalled by the Scottish Presbyterians, who kept their hats on when they met him and called him by his Christian name. Men who refused to genuflect before the Sacrament or bow to the altar were hardly likely to bend the knee to their fellow men.

Alarmed by the bishopless Christians he had seen in Scotland, James I arrived with the determination to preserve the hierarchy of the Church in the interests of social stability. He found even the English bishops in the grip of the fundamentalist fever. Nine of them met him at Hampton Court soon after his Coronation, all in favour of a more primitive form of worship in the Church of England with bare churches, simple vestments, less ritual and no bowing to the altar or kneeling.

This was the kind of dictatorship of style, politics expressed as theatre, that fascinated Burke. Rearranging the order of the Ten Commandments, the Puritans had promoted to number two the ancient Semitic ban on making 'any graven image, or the likeness of anything that is in the heaven above, or in the earth beneath, or in the water under the earth', on bowing down to them or worshipping them. In trying to scrape off the accumulated traditions of centuries and re-create primitive Christianity, the Puritans raged against every kind of holy picture, decoration and display. To begin with they identified it with Catholic idolatry. Zeal-of-the-Land Busy, the hypocritical Puritan preacher caricatured in Ben Jonson's *Bartholomew Fair* of 1614, condemns even the dolls and rattles for sale on the stalls as 'Popery'. But the condemnation would soon be extended to everything associated with the 'dignified' side of government.

In 1614, during the procession to the State Opening of Parliament, 'with trumpets sounding', the crowd watched the old theatrical display of the House of Lords as the embodiment of order. First came the lawyers on horseback, 'riding two by two', the Masters in Chancery, the King's legal advisers, the Masters of Requests, the Barons of the Exchequer, the Justices of the Courts of Common Pleas and King's Bench, and the two Lord Chief Justices. After them came Poursuivants-at-Arms, privy councillors, and two more heralds. Then the lords, the barons of Parliament, the bishops in order of their consecration, two more heralds, the viscounts, the earls, the great officers of state and two archbishops, two gentlemen ushers, one of them Black Rod, and behind them the Prince, soon to be Charles I. Finally, riding at the back, there was the Earl of Shrewsbury with the Cap of Maintenance, the Duke of Lennox with the Sceptre, the Earl of Derby with the Sword of State, the Lord High Admiral, then the Earl of Suffolk, as Lord Chamberlain, and last of all King James.

Suddenly the horse ridden by one of the bishops whinnied and reared out of control, the Bishop lost his hold on the reins and fell heavily on the cobbles. There was little sympathy from the crowd, and it was one of the lords temporal who got the cheer when he shouted, 'One bishopric pulled down!'

He may have regretted the joke. His own horse immediately reared and threw him. But both accidents were prophetic.

Following his meeting with the nine bishops at Hampton Court, James appointed the Bishop of London, Bancroft, the most conservative he could find, as Archbishop of Canterbury. This had the effect, in the House of Lords at least, of blackening the bishops still further in the eyes of the Puritans: not only were they associated with the King, who was married to a Catholic and suspected of Catholic sympathies, but as a conservative block under Bancroft's leadership they found themselves voting with the few remaining Catholic peers.

The lords temporal were in trouble for different reasons. At a time of religious instability, the House of Lords under Queen Elizabeth had remained entirely stable, with a membership of sixty throughout her reign. James I not only filled the House with his boyfriends, like George Villiers for whom he revived the dukedom of Buckingham which had died out a hundred years earlier, but shamelessly raised money by selling peerages.

References in correspondence of the time always mention the same charge: 'Candish' – Cavendish – 'or Chandos (I remember not which) are to be made Earls, and to pay £10,000,' Thomas Lorby wrote in 1618. 'Buckingham, knowing Roberts to be rich, forced him to take the title of honour; and that, in consideration therefor, he paid £10,000.' 'Roper and Hollis were lorded at £10,000 a piece.' Christopher Roper, who had been offering inducements including 'fruit, falcons and a great standing bowl' for several years, even risked making a joke of his eventual ennoblement, taking the title of '10M', and his descendant Lord Teynham was still in the House three hundred and fifty years later.

Individually, the peers were providing the Puritans with plenty of material, becoming involved in a series of scandals. Some were accused of embezzlement, others of murder, still others of homosexuality, adultery or rape. The Castlehaven case combined all three: Mervyn Gay, Lord Castlehaven, was accused of having an affair with Lawrence Fitz Patrick, and of assisting Giles Browning to rape Lady Castlehaven, said to be 'the wickedest woman in the world'. Castlehaven was executed. But it was the sale of honours that appalled the then Garter King-at-Arms Sir Edward Walker. 'The frequent Promotions to Titles of Honour and Dignity since King James I came to the Crown of England took off from the respect due to nobility. The curtain being drawn they were discovered to be men that heretofore were reverenced as angels.'

At a time when the monarchy was showing itself increasingly contemptuous of Parliament as a whole, the Lords did their best to restore their angelic order. In 1621 they appointed the first Committee for Privileges 'to investigate the ancient rights of Barony'. When Charles I created the new earldom of Banbury in 1626 'with precedence before other Earls of ancienter Creation', the Committee for Privileges threw it out. The King argued that the new earl was old and childless, and after two years of lobbying individual peers he finally got his way. But the committee insisted this was to be the last time, and when Charles tried again a few months later, asking that the new Lord Lovejoy should take precedence over the recently ennobled Lords Fauconbridge and Lovelace, they refused point blank.

It was in 1626, too, that Mr Justice Dodderidge, settling a disputed claim to a title, ruled that a peerage was 'fixed in the blood'. No one could take it away; no one could renounce it; it was an immortal essence. This went far beyond anything dreamed up by the Anglo-Saxon image-makers or the Norman lawyers. Lord Saye and Sele was so elated that he even wrote to the Governor of Massachusetts to float the idea of an hereditary American aristocracy. The people needed the peerage to aspire to.

The Lords' ancient right to hear appeals had fallen into disuse, but under Charles I they eagerly re-established it. Details of precedence and procedure became all-important, formally incorporated in the 107 Standing Orders. Peers were forbidden to make 'personal, sharp or taxing speeches'. They were to refer to a speaker in the third person, as 'the peer who spoke last', and never by name. They were allowed to wear their hats in the Queen's Chamber but were to take them off when they rose to speak. The Standing Orders also defined the Lords' superiority to the Commons. If they needed to communicate with the Lower House they could send a note to St Stephen's Chapel by a messenger. If the Commons wanted to communicate with them, the message must be delivered by a Member of Parliament standing bare-headed at the Bar of the House who would bow three times to the Lord Chancellor before and after he delivered the message. In any joint committee with the Commons in the Painted Chamber, peers were to sit with their hats on while the Commons stood bare-headed.

At the same time they also attempted to lay down the practical choreography dictated by Henry VIII's mystical idea of the King in Parliament.

When the future Charles I originally took his seat in the Lords on the left of the Throne as Prince of Wales he was treated with respect, used as an unofficial intermediary with the King, and thought to exercise a restraining influence in the Chamber. In 1621 when the Earl of Berkshire threatened another peer in the heat of a debate he apologized particularly to Prince Charles. If the Prince had not been there, he said, they would certainly have come to blows. But when the Prince left his seat and talked to the Lords with his back to the fireplace on the right of the Throne there was outrage. Bishop Burnet accused him of 'breaking all decency of that House'. He was literally out of order.

But the real constitutional problem came up when Charles was King.

Constitutionally, as part of both Houses' squaring up to the monarchy, the House of Lords took a tough line. When Charles I allowed eleven years to go by without summoning Parliament, the Lords revived an idea from the time of Magna Carta. Parliament, they agreed, need not wait to be summoned by the King: it could in future be summoned by the Lord Chancellor, or by a committee of twelve peers.

Physically it was more difficult. When he appeared, the King walked into the Queen's Chamber, stood with his back to the fire out of habit, and talked to the lords man to man about the crisis which was shortly to lead to the outbreak of civil war; the clerks wrote down what he said, and then, as soon as he had gone, struck it from the record. He might, as monarch, as Henry VIII had put it, be 'ever representatively sitting in Parliament', but as far as the House of Lords and its privileges were concerned, he had not been there because he was not sitting on the Throne.

While the Lords as guardians of the shrine of the Shining Ladder were quibbling over points of procedure, the Bright Horizonists' assault on the King, and since he was ever representatively sitting there, on the royalist elements in Parliament, was reaching its climax. It had been continuous since the reign of James I, and one of the Puritans' fiercest pamphleteers was the West Country lawyer William Prynne. More than any of his co-religionists, he fixed on style. It was William Prynne who condemned men for wearing long hair.

> Our masculine and more noble race [he wrote in one of his broad-sheets] are wholly degenerated and metamorphosed into women. In crisping, curling, frouncing, powdering and nourishing their locks and hairy excrements they bestow more cost, more thoughts, more time and more pains upon their hairy locks and bushes from day to day than on their peerless and immortal souls.

Women's hair should not be worn short. Long hair was 'their feminine glory, and the very badge of their subjection both to God and man'.

He had come to prominence for daring, in his *Histriomatrix, The Player's Scourge or Actor's Tragedy* of 1632, to attack the theatre, and by implication the Queen who had recently appeared in a court entertainment. Since James I's time, elaborate masques had combined sublime subjects with ridiculously bad behaviour on the part of the actors. On one famous occasion the actresses representing the allegorical figures of Hope and Faith were too drunk to deliver their lines and were heard being sick in the wings, while Peace 'most rudely made war with her olive branch, and laid on the pates of those who did oppose her'. The Queen had taken part in one such masque, and Prynne was accused of sedition.

He was fined £5,000, imprisoned for life, expelled from Lincoln's Inn, deprived of his university degree and condemned to have his ears cropped. The physical punishment was carried out in public but with some sensitivity. This was officially because he was a scholar and a gentleman, but according to gossip at the time because he had promised the executioner ten shillings to go easy. Only a thin layer of skin was shaved from the upper edges of his ears. When both healed leaving no scar, his Puritan friends celebrated it as a miracle, and Prynne in prison wrote another pamphlet attacking his accusers, including Bancroft's successor Archbishop Laud. This time the sentence was the same, the fine now equal to the cost of a peerage, and the public punishment barbaric. The executioner paced round the gallows platform like a masked wrestler, branded the letters SL – Seditious Libeller – on Prynne's cheeks with his branding irons, considered that he had burned the L crooked and did it again. When he sliced off his ears he left one dangling. Prynne was sent to Mount Orgueil prison in Jersey, a Puritan martyr.

On the eve of the Civil War, in 1641, William Prynne's sentence was reversed by the Commons and he returned in triumph to London to prosecute his old enemy Laud, who was executed. Prynne was elected Member of Parliament for Newport in Cornwall, and the Commons finally drafted a Bill to exclude the bishops from the Upper House. The House of Lords rejected it. A second Bill was drafted by the Commons, and the Lords rejected that. A third Bill they simply ignored. When, as a result, a Puritan mob armed with swords and clubs broke into the old Palace shouting, 'Down with the popish lords and the bishops!' the House of Lords officially requested protection from the Commons, who refused it. When the King sent guards under the command of the Earl of Dorset, the Commons sent them away, telling their lordships that they needed protection against the King, not against the people.

When the King burst into the Commons to arrest five of its members the Lords saw their point. Early in 1642 they debated the Bishops' Exclusion Bill. The Bishop of Lincoln, one of the few bishops who attended the debate, reminded them that there had been bishops in the House of Lords 'these thousand years and upwards', but the vote went against him. The Bishops' Exclusion Bill was the last piece of legislation to receive the royal assent before the Civil War began. The empty Bench of Bishops was pushed back against the wall of the Queen's Chamber. The first rank had fallen, and with the secular peers split – roughly with ninety backing the King and thirty backing Parliament – the House of Lords as an institution was highly vulnerable.

With the bishops gone, both Houses of Parliament had made a series of demands to the King: they wanted the right to approve his choice of ministers, the final word in the appointment of judges, and the ultimate decision on the future of the Church. The King rejected all of them, and his answer came close to a written English Constitution. In *His Majesty's Answer to the Nineteen Propositions of both Houses of Parliament* of 1642, he reminded them of the Ladder. The order under God was King, Lords and Commons: monarchy, aristocracy and democracy. Each had its advantages: monarchy united a nation, aristocracy tapped the talents of the ablest people in the state, democracy engendered courage, liberty and the hard work produced by liberty. But all three, as they knew, could slide into excess. The experience and wisdom of their ancestors had moulded the present form of government out of a mixture of all three, held in place by the ancient laws of England.

To upset the balance of order of these three 'estates' would mean 'a total subversion of the fundamental laws', and would 'destroy all rights and proprieties, all distinctions of families and merit'. The country would lose credit abroad; people not born to power would be intoxicated by it. The long line of the King's noble ancestors would end with the seizure of power by a popular demagogue, a Jack Cade or a Wat Tyler. What he called the 'excellent constitution of the Kingdom' would end in 'a dark equal chaos of confusion'. Charles reminded both Houses of Parliament that under this 'splendid and excellently distinguished form of government', each had their own role. His own as King was to declare and end wars, to create peers, to appoint ministers, judges, governors and generals. He had the power of pardon but he was responsible for maintaining peace and order, without which there would be no rule of law. He commanded the respect of lords and landowners, maintaining national unity, and the respect of the people, preventing 'tumults, violence and licentiousness'.

The Commons existed to manage the household: it controlled the power of the King to impose taxes, which provided 'the sinews of peace as well as war'. As a regulated monarch, he could not squander public money on favourites or followers because the House of Commons was there to stop him. The Commons, too, had the right to accuse incompetent or dishonest ministers before the Bar of the House of Lords, who would judge them. But the House of Commons was never intended for a share in government or the choosing of those who should govern.

The House of Lords, apart from its role as the ultimate court of appeal, was 'an excellent screen and bank between the Prince and people, to assist each against any encroachments of the other, and by just judgments to preserve the law'.

Then came the clause that was to cause a great deal of trouble: 'In this Kingdom the Laws are jointly made by a King, by a House of Peers, and by a House of Commons chosen by the People, all having free Votes and particular Privileges.' Colepeper, the King's adviser, considered adding the words 'the King being the head and sovereign of the whole', but sent it off to the printers as it was.

According to the Venetian ambassador, unprejudiced persons and many members of the Upper House, including some of the leading malcontents, were impressed, and considered that the King had made a good case. Others saw their chance: if the laws were made *jointly* by King, Lords and Commons as an equal partnership, that was the end of the old idea of subordination, of Commons under the Lords under the King under God. King, Lords and Commons were 'co-ordinate'.

Members of the Commons coming to the Bar of the House of Lords began to keep their hats on. Shortly afterwards the fighting started. In the course of the Civil War the Bright Horizonists, until now concerned chiefly with popery and the rights of Parliament, began to focus their attention on rank.

The Lords were condemned by the extreme Puritan sect known as the Levellers. When their leader John Lilburne appeared at the Bar in 1646, accused of insulting the Presbyterian Earl of Manchester, he told them that the people of England had given the House of Lords no authority to judge him. That was the core of the Horizonist attack on the creed of the Shining Ladder: authority did not come from above, it came from below. The existing system of King, Lords and Commons, Lilburne told the House of Lords, was no more than a disgraceful relic of the Norman occupation. William the Conqueror had been a thief and a tyrant who had distributed peerages to his fellow gangsters for their help in enslaving England.

The Just Man in Bonds, a Puritan tract selling on street corners, made the same point. The peers were the sons of conquest and usurpation. Most important of all, they were 'not made by the people'. It was from the people that all just power, place and office in the kingdom should arise. Richard Overton's *Remonstrance of Many Thousand Citizens*, which appeared in 1646, called for the abolition of both the House of Lords and the monarchy. The House of Commons was supreme, and should be re-elected annually with constitutional guarantees to limit its powers. 'Ye only are chosen by us the people; and therefore in you only is the power of binding the whole nation, altering, or abolishing the laws. The cause of our choosing you to be parliamentarians was to deliver us from all kind of bondage.'

Lilburne and the Levellers, condemned as extremists by Presbyterians, were still a long way from demanding modern democracy: women and the entire working class were excluded from any role in electing Parliament, but as far as they were concerned the King and the House of Lords were *subordinate* to the Commons, and might as well had to go. Lilburne had done some thinking about a problem that has exercised modern reformers. According to Lilburne, any Second Chamber that was 'equally supreme' was 'an absurd nullity'. If an Upper House disagreed with the Commons, how could government go on?

The Lords found some odd defenders, none more unexpected than William Prynne, who published another of his pamphlets, *A Plea for the Lords* in 1648. Peers of noble birth and education, 'more generous heroic spirits than the vulgar sort of men', were not so apt to be overawed by the King, and they were harder to bully or seduce from the common good with honours, preferments or wealth, because they already had them. Always verbose, he revelled in Ladderist imagery: to abolish the Lords was to 'level the head, neck, shoulders, to the feet; the tallest cedars to the lowest shrubs; the roof of every building to the foundation stones; the sun, moon, stars, heavens to the very earth and centre, and even' – here he was citing the pre-Darwinian equivalent of the Ladder, the Great Chain of Being – 'men themselves to the meanest beasts.' The Lords, 'by their very nobility, peerage and great offices' had 'a just right and title to sit, consult, vote, enact laws and give judgment in all their general assemblies of state, parliaments, senates, diets and councils'. Possessing more property and having more at stake, they had, in practice, 'always been generally reputed the wisest and most experienced Commonwealth men'.

Prynne did not defend bishops or individual Roman Catholic peers, he defended the parliamentary machine, now dominated for the most part by his co-religionists. 'Parliament', he wrote, 'is the absolute sovereign power within the realm.' It was not subject to the law because it made the law. It had been making the law since Magna Carta, and whenever it wanted it could change the law to suit its own purposes. But Parliament must include the Lords as well as the Commons.

The Lords themselves attempted a counter-attack, inspired by a speech from the Earl of Manchester. A free Parliament could not survive if both Houses were brow-beaten by such 'high and visible insolences'. The Lords, they claimed, were doing everything in their power 'to vindicate and right the Parliament'.

Parliamentarians in the Commons were unrelenting. A month later, Sir John Evelyn, MP for Wiltshire, was ordered to 'go up to the Lords, and impeach the Earl of Lincoln, the Earl of Suffolk, the Earl of Middlesex, Lord Hunsdone, Lord Willoughby of Parham, Lord Bartlett and Lord Maynard of High Treason, in the name of all the Commons of England for levying war against the King, Parliament and Kingdom, and to desire their Lordships to sequester them from their House, and to commit them; and they would make good the charge of High Treason against them'.

When Evelyn accordingly walked through the old Palace, stood at the Bar in the Queen's Chamber with his hat on and read the impeachment, it was clear that the ancient dignity of the Lords was beginning to crumble.

Compromises were put forward: a single amalgamated House, with peers allowed to sit in the Commons, or a special dispensation for single-chamber government by the Commons at times of public emergency. Henry Ireton, Cromwell's son-in-law, published the more conservative *Heads of the Proposals of the Army*, recommending the retention of both the monarchy and the House of Lords. All the new peers created by Charles I since the Civil War had begun were to lose their titles, and the Commons should have a veto on any future elevations to the Upper House.

In April 1648, defeated after the brief second Civil War, the King agreed under the treaty of Newport to both these conditions.

He was too late. Ireton and the Army were now angry and talking about an elected monarchy, with a single supreme representative assembly. When Colonel Pride purged Parliament to the seventy members acceptable to the Army, excluding, among others, the ever-troublesome William Prynne, the House of Lords became of little importance. They rejected the Bill to bring Charles I to trial, they rejected the Bill condemning the King for treason against Parliament. No peer spoke in favour of either, and the Presbyterian Earl of Manchester even defended the old order. 'By the fundamental laws of England,' he told the thirty-odd peers who remained in the Queen's Chamber, 'the Parliament consists of three estates, of which the King is the first. Without him there can be no Parliament, and therefore it is absurd to say the King can be a traitor against Parliament.'

As proof of how far political power had shifted from the old vertical hierarchy to the horizontal clamour of a million individuals, there was the episode of the Prophetess of Abingdon.

While the King's fate was being decided in Whitehall by a small Army Council, a woman was let in because she claimed, like almost every politician of the period, to be inspired by God. She had had a dream in which there was a reference to binding kings in chains. She was heard with as much respect as Cromwell or Ireton, and with a great deal more respect than any peer in the House of Lords.

Condemned to death without the Lords' approval, the King took communion first thing in the morning of 30 January 1649 assuming that he would be dead by breakfast time. Then it turned out that the Army-dominated Commons had forgotten to pass the necessary legislation to deny his heir the right to succeed, and he was forced to satisfy his hunger with a piece of ordinary bread and a glass of unconsecrated claret while they assembled to debate it. His head was not cut off until long after midday.

Between the Lords' vote on 4 January against trying the King and their own abolition on 19 March, some attempts were made to save them. Cromwell himself was in favour of preserving the Upper House, telling the Commons that they were mad to alienate the peers when they needed them as allies. There was a proposal that they should be incorporated into the Commons, but Bulstrode Whitelocke, one of Cromwell's advisers and a constitutional lawyer who had left London to avoid the King's trial, warned against allowing peers to sit in a single chamber as they would exercise too much influence. The Commons set aside the motion.

One speaker in the Commons suggested retaining them as a kind of High Court, but this was stalled, and the last amendment put down by conservatives on the morning of 6 February was that the Lords should be retained without any right to vote: 'That this House *take the advice* of the House of Lords in the exercise of its legislative power.' Cromwell voted for it, but it was defeated forty-four to twenty-nine. The motion carried was that the House of Lords was 'useless and dangerous, and should be abolished'. From that afternoon the House of Lords no longer existed. No one had asked them whether they were 'Content' or 'Not Content'. They were not consulted.

According to Viscount de Lisle, a member of Cromwell's House of Lords, who recorded the event in his diary at Penshurst, none of the half-dozen peers sitting in the Queen's Chamber at the time was aware that anything had happened. There was even more noise than usual from the sound of the Army outside and the empty Throne, now bare of the royal arms, still dominated the Chamber. It was only when the Lords sent a messenger through the smoking fires outside in the courtyard where Cromwell's troops were 'guarding' Parliament and across to St Stephen's Chapel that they discovered the truth.

For the first time since the Roman withdrawal, England was released from the spell of the Shining Ladder. The Bright Horizonists had won and they set about constructing a new horizontal world. There was no king, there were no lords and no bishops. Power did not come from above, it grew out of the people.

The big chair in their lordships' House was simply a big chair.

CHAPTER ELEVEN

The Second Coming

From 1649, England managed for eleven years without the monarchy. It survived for only eight without a House of Lords, and it could be argued that the Upper House defined its role more clearly by its absence than it ever had by its presence.

In the English Revolution, as in the French Revolution a century and a half later, there were believers in the industrial principle, Bright Horizonists, who were convinced that a clean break could be made with the past: 1649 would be a new Year One, and a new heaven would be made on earth. In France the Horizonists would be hostile to all religion; in England they were Protestants, some of whom believed that this new age would be ushered in by the Second Coming of Christ. These were the so-called Fifth Monarchy Men. According to prophecy, the death of the King would herald the Second Coming. Christ's reappearance in glory would bring in a dazzling new British Empire, a successor to the Assyrian, Persian, Greek and Roman empires before it.

In practice the shock of the King's death produced a reversion to earlier and more primitive forms of government, but much of the theoretical debate about what should replace the three-tier constitution of King, Lords and Commons was extremely cautious. Those who had seized power were, after all, not ragged revolutionaries: most were pious, respectable merchants, men of property or country landowners, concerned above all to re-establish national and international confidence after years of civil war and the public execution of the King.

The Lords now found themselves without privileges or any official collective status, and the pamphlet that an anonymous group of peers published in defence of the old House had to compete with a stack of street-corner broadsheets. In it the 'peers, lords, and barons of the Realm' accused those who had excluded them from Parliament of being 'traitors and usurpers' bent on subverting the law and the old structure of government to destroy freedom and enslave the people to a 'boundless tyranny'. To set bounds to tyrants was their constitutional role. Abolishing the Upper House, they wrote, had been 'an insolent and frantic act by some members of the Commons' House,' designed to create anarchy and confusion, enabling them to seize power.

The lords, as usual, stressed the importance of order, of law, the rights and privileges of Parliament, 'and more particularly of the House of Peers'. With the King and the Commons, the ablest part of which had been forcibly excluded from the Chamber by Colonel Pride, they represented the guarantors of law and liberty against a few 'insolent and misadvised' members of the Lower House. 'In the presence of Almighty God, angels, and men' they condemned all resolutions made by the present government, denied its right to set up courts of law, to try or to condemn anyone, least of all the King, whose execution had been a barbarous act of murder. The Commons had never constituted a court of law. All the House of Commons had the right to do, the unseated lords snootily concluded, was to denounce criminals before the Bar of the Upper House, having first respectfully removed their hats. They had no right to stand there with their hats on, let alone to sit, vote or give judgment.

Perhaps the most interesting blueprint for an alternative constitution among the flood of rival broadsheets was James Harrington's *Commonwealth of Oceania*, published in 1656. Loosely fictionalizing his ideal country, Harrington's analysis of what had happened is remarkably modern in its assumptions, and offers little comfort to the lords. As a young man in Rome, he had offended the Pope by refusing to kiss his toe, and he makes it quite clear that power has nothing to do with rank or titles. 'Empire', he writes, 'follows the balance of property.' Those who own the country naturally govern it. The distribution of property and land determines the way in which the country is ruled. If one man owns the whole country it is a monarchy and he is 'King'. If the country is owned by a small group of individuals, then they constitute an aristocracy. He even develops ideas for the nationalization of land to prevent this happening. At the time he is writing, he says, the country appears to be owned by everybody, and that represents a moment of pure democracy. He is not happy with it, because it lacks stability. He goes on to discuss how this has come about, and traces the causes of the revolution to the Reformation. By breaking up the old estates and the monasteries, Henry VIII effectively signalled the end of the monarchy and the aristocracy. The old order and the old stable constitution had been undermined.

Government by a single chamber was dangerous: 'A council without a balance is not a commonwealth but an oligarchy.' The Commons had grown more powerful under Elizabeth I, and when they came into conflict with Charles I and the bishops, 'the House of Peers which alone had stood in this gap, now sank down between King and Commons'.

Oligarchy, the rule of a dominant gang, had traditionally been associated with the aristocracy, and this is the first time, long before cabinet government or the rise of prime ministers, that the term is applied to the Commons. His ideal system would limit its powers.

Cromwell, to whom he dedicated the book, should, he suggested, retire. There would be no head of state. The King would be replaced by a kind of joint Presidency, a Bench of Magistrates, chosen by ballot and serving a limited term. The Upper House would be an elected senate, and the Commons would be replaced by a popular assembly, known as the Prerogative Tribe. The Upper House or Senate would be the central element of government, and would initiate legislation and draft new laws. It would have three hundred members, of which a third would resign every year. To qualify for election, they would have to be over thirty, have served in the Army, be married, and possess goods, land or money worth a hundred pounds a year. The Prerogative Tribe would have 1050 members, who would also be compelled to resign on a regular basis. They would debate and approve the laws, and take over the role of the House of Lords as the final court of appeal. Elections would be indirect.

The vote would be limited to property-owners, who would elect deputies, who would in turn elect both chambers: 'That which is proposed by the Authority of the Senate and resolved by the command of the people is the law of Oceania.'

In real life the shape of government evolved through a series of painful compromises between Horizonists and Ladderists, between the industrial principle and the spiritual relation, between new ideas and continuity, as a series of immediate responses to a continuing crisis. There was unrest at home, war in Scotland, war in Ireland, and war with the Continent.

Initially, within days of the King's death, England was declared a Commonwealth and Free State, and every man in the country over the age of eighteen was required to swear allegiance to it. All the functions of the monarchy were provisionally taken over for a year by a forty-strong Council of State, thirty-one of them members of the Commons. It contained many of the most vocal fundamentalists, and was under pressure from a powerful Army. In 1650, adultery was made a capital offence as a concession to the Army's 'saints' or radicals.

Many practical politicians favoured a republic, governed by a single assembly, and as the House of Commons still existed it became attractive as the working model. The fact that its numbers had been reduced to a rump by the Army contributed to its romantic appeal. If the Army would only restore its freedom and stop interfering in its business, the Commons would emerge as the perfect means of expressing the nation's will.

When Cromwell dissolved the Rump Parliament in 1653, the Army argued in favour of full military government by an Army Council. Instead he appointed a Council of his own of 139 members, drawn mostly from conservative-minded members of the gentry. In constitutional terms, this was near enough primitive monarchy, or what Cromwell called 'the rule of a single person', and it was only a short time before that became reality. His nominated Council spent six months trying to control Protestant extremists, splintering into more and more warring factions, then resigned. They restored all power to Cromwell as Lord Protector of the Commonwealth of England, Scotland and Ireland.

Cromwell retained an Advisory Council, and began to move towards a more limited monarchy. He promised regular Parliaments, with a fully elected Lower House, and this met in February 1654. In preparation for it some 'decayed boroughs' were suppressed, and some new constituencies were created. The proportion of country members increased from about a fifth to two-thirds, making the House, if anything, more conservative. It consisted of four hundred members for England and the Channel Islands, thirty for Scotland and thirty for Ireland, elected by constituencies. Electors had to prove that they had at least two hundred pounds, or the equivalent in land or property. Cromwell took the role of both the King and the House of Lords, with the right of veto. He defined his system officially as 'government by one person and a Parliament'.

In January 1655, weary of listening to debates about how his power could further be limited and convinced of such a Parliament's inability to govern, he dissolved it and revived a system that had existed before Byrhtnoth's day. He divided the country into eleven districts, each under the command of a major general. Two years later, with order to some extent restored, he summoned a new Parliament, which was both strongly supportive of Cromwell and in favour of a monarchy. One of their first acts, in 1657, was to vote for the restoration of a Second Chamber and to offer Cromwell the Crown. In conversation with Cromwell, Lord Fiennes expressed what a lot of people felt: there had been enough experiments in new forms of government. The 'bond of peace' was the knot that bound the ruler to two Houses of Parliament: 'This tying and untying of the bond and continuous seeking after new fashioned knots has put these nations to much trouble, and into more danger.'

The idea of restoring the monarchy had floated in and out of focus whenever there was talk of 'the rule of the single person'. The Lord Chief Justice, Oliver St John, had even suggested crowning Charles I's youngest son, the Duke of Gloucester. Cromwell did not want the Stuarts back, but he agreed tentatively to 'a settlement with somewhat of Monarchical power in it' and, as the crisis continued to deepen, asked the much-quoted rhetorical question, 'What if a man should take upon him to be a king?'

The answer was that if a man, even Cromwell, had taken upon him at that moment to be a king the Army would probably have prevented him. Nevertheless, in the negotiations that followed the possibility always existed that Cromwell might try to found a new royal family, and that the old order of King, Lords and Commons might be restored in full.

In the face of the opposition of the Army, a compromise was reached. John Maidstone, Cromwell's steward, wrote to a friend at the time to say that he was now talking of 'another House of Parliament, instead of the old Lords, that this might be a screen or balance betwixt the Protector and Commons, as the former Lords had been betwixt the King and them'. It was a compromise that infuriated conservatives and monarchists. In offering a modified 'Other House' instead of a House of Lords, Cromwell, they claimed, was worshipping with the heathen oppressor, the enemies of the Shining Ladder. Like Aaron, he was sacrificing his principles, 'making a Golden Calf like the Egyptian Ox'.

When he announced his intentions to the Army, most of whom were fundamentally opposed to any Second Chamber, he stirred up equal fury, but he stuck to his guns. 'You are offended at a House of Lords. I tell you that unless you have some such thing as a balance you cannot be safe.' He even quoted Charles I to them. His 'Other House' was to be a safety barrier, 'an excellent screen and bank', in this case between the Army and the Commons. The Army had overstepped its authority by putting armed guards on the doors of St Stephen's Chapel and deciding which Members of Parliament were to take their seats. Now what remained of the Commons had shown signs of religious intolerance, and that could soon threaten the religious independence of soldiers in the Army. The Commons had sentenced a Quaker, James Naylor, to severe punishment for 'religious extravagance', and were openly boasting that they now possessed all the power that had previously belonged to the Lords. Without an Upper House, Cromwell told the Army, the danger was plain: either the Army would 'grow upon the civil liberties by secluding' (excluding) 'such as are elected to sit in Parliament', or the Commons would 'grow upon your liberty in religion'.

Whether or not he was immediately aware of it, the compromise had crippled his new Upper House before its birth. If he had become King, Lords and Commons would have slipped back into their accustomed places in the old Constitution. By refusing the Crown and remaining Lord Protector, he was retaining powers, like the veto on Bills from the Commons, that should have belonged to the Lords, and the old peerage did not like it. Nevertheless, he pressed ahead.

His new House would provide 'a great security and bulwark to the honest interest', not being so 'uncertain' as the House of Commons which depended upon election by the people. Cromwell's nominated Other House was an experiment that any modern prime minister, enjoying comparable power of patronage, would be wise to study. It was not a success.

Cromwell made the appointments officially with the approval of the Commons. The intention was to recall a core of dependable hereditary peers and to surround them with a larger number of life peers. In December 1657 he issued sixty-three traditional writs of summons. Of these seven were to hereditary peers; of the rest a third were to Army colonels who shared his political views, a third to country gentlemen and members of the minor aristocracy, and a third to his own relations. Only forty-two of the sixty-three accepted, and of these only thirty-seven appeared at Westminster.

Of the seven hereditary peers, only two came. One was Cromwell's son-in-law, Lord Fauconberg, and a poor peer of no importance, Lord Eure. The other five stayed away: the Earl of Mulgrave, old and ill, who died six months later, the Earl of Manchester, who had shunned Westminster since the execution of the King, the Earl of Warwick, whose grandson had just married Cromwell's daughter, Lord Wharton, and the old Puritan hero Lord Saye and Sele.

The reason that Lord Wharton failed to appear has, fortunately, been preserved, in a letter from Lord Saye and Sele. The old English Constitution, he wrote, was the best in the world, and the mainstay of this mixed and balanced government used to be the House of Lords. It was 'the beam keeping both scales, King and people, in an even posture, without encroachments one upon another to the hurt and damage of both'. The old House of Lords preserved the rights and liberties of the people against the tyranny of kings, and also by offering the image of order, the Ladder that supported the King: '. . . as steps and stairs upheld the Crown from falling and being cast down upon the floor by the insolence of the multitude'. In the circumstances, Lord Saye and Sele concluded, it would be most unjust, dishonourable and unworthy for Lord Wharton or the other hereditary peers to allow themselves to be used in Cromwell's experimental Chamber.

Snubbed by the hereditary peers and packed with his own supporters, Cromwell's Other House was not taken seriously. Snobs objected to two of Cromwell's colonels, one of whom had been a drayman and another a baker. Few people 'scrupled to own them as lords'.

John Maidstone noted that the new House was 'too thin for a screen, too light for a balance'.

At the first joint session of the two Houses in the Painted Chamber the Lord Commissioner, Lord Fiennes, explained to them why they were there. This re-establishment of three-tier government or, as he put it, 'of a chief magistrate and two Houses of Parliament', was 'not a pageantry'. It was, he said, 'a real and well-measured advantage to itself and to the Commonwealth'. There was nothing irrational, theatrical or mystical about it. Reason demanded the middle path between extremes, and this was the reasonable answer. 'It is so consonant to reason that it is the very emblem and idea of reason itself.'

It might not be a pageant, but it did not stop the antiquarian Henry Scobele from trying to compile a new book of rules on how the old theatre worked, approaching veterans who remembered the House of Lords before it had been abolished. He questioned the Archbishop of Canterbury, Lord North and Lord Buckhurst, and expressed his particular gratitude to the Lord Treasurer, 'the eldest Parliament man affirming this to be the ancient course', the first Earl of Marlborough. He did everything in his power to re-create the magic. In chapter after chapter he listed every detail of procedure, with the Standing Orders amplified: if the Lord Chancellor was ill, the Lord Chief Justice must take his place; the Lord Chancellor must always take off his hat before addressing the House, as must all the other members; the judges who sat on the Woolsacks were to keep their hats off until the lords officially indicated to the Lord Chancellor that they could put them on; no commoners were to keep their hats on in the 'room called the Lords-House' or Queen's Chamber, and attendants were allowed to stay in the Chamber only for the time it took to 'bring in their lord'. Members were to bow to the Cloth of Estate if they found it necessary to cross the floor of the House, and must 'keep their dignity and order in sitting': if they moved somewhere else it 'hindered others who sat near them' and produced 'disorder'.

Small committees were to meet next door in the Painted Chamber or the little room adjoining it. Speeches in committee could be made sitting down, but they were to remove their hats before speaking.

If a Bill originating in the Commons was passed, the Clerk was to write the words *A ceste Bille les Seigneurs sont assentis*. If it emanated from the Lords he was to write *Soit Baille aux Communs*. If amendments were added later on a separate piece of parchment, the main Bill was marked *Soit Baille aux Communs, avecque un Provision annex*: and the amendment or 'proviso' *Soit Baille aux Communs*.

If the King was to give the Royal Assent in person, the Lords would wear their full scarlet robes. The Clerk of the Crown was to read the Bill aloud. If it was a Public Bill the answer was *Le Roy le Veult*, a Private Bill *Soit fait come il est desiré*, and if the Bill had not been passed *Le Roy se avisera*. If it was a Money Bill, the King's answer was *Le Roy remercie ses Loyaulx Subjects, accept leur bénévolence, & auxy le veult*. If the King had granted a General Pardon, the answer from the Lords was *Les Prelates, Seigneurs, Communs en cest Parliament assembles au nome de touts vos auters Subjects remercient tres humblement vostre Majesty, & prient Dieu vous doner en sonte bone vie & longe*.

Armed with all these instructions, Cromwell's House of Lords sat and waited. Nothing happened. Across the courtyard in St Stephen's Chapel the Lower House, liberated from Army control, had welcomed a strong intake of republicans. Pledged to single-chamber government by the Commons, they were even now debating the constitutional position of the new Upper House. Under the Lord Protector the House of Lords, they decided, could only be an appeal court. It could play no role in government.

The Commons also spent most of January 1658 quibbling about how they should refer to it. One member said that to accept a chamber called the House of Lords would spell enslavement, but on the other hand would have the advantage of leaving it in constitutional limbo; to call it, as Cromwell had, the 'Other House' was to recognize its existence. It was, in any case, as Sir Lislebone Long told them, 'not fit to be called a Lords' House', and any member of the Commons would tell them so.

In the Queen's Chamber by the river, Cromwell's lords continued to wait. 'Having no business to do', as one contemporary commentator put it, 'the House consumed a great store of fire to keep them warm at the public charge.'

At the end of the third week of January, Cromwell lost his temper and summoned both Houses to a joint session in the Banqueting House, where Charles I had been executed. He challenged them to produce a better alternative: 'Have you any frame or model of things that would satisfy the minds of men, if this be not the frame that you are now called together upon, and engaged in – I mean the two Houses of Parliament and myself?'

When the Commons asked for his speech in writing, he went further. The frame that would satisfy the minds of men was the Lord Protector and the two Houses, 'the House of Lords and the House of Commons'. This was an ultimatum, but it failed.

Inside the Commons the leading republican Sir Arthur Hesilrige listed the sins of the old House of Lords and attacked the notion of the new one. Outside, thousands of signatures were collected on a petition in support of single-chamber government, with the intention of presenting it to the House of Commons, ignoring the unfortunates waiting in the old room by the river.

To prevent this going any further, Cromwell dissolved both Houses and sent Black Rod to bring the Commons through to the Lords' Chamber. He praised his Other House for being so faithful to the public interest and for their readiness to carry on the government. Then, turning to the Commons, he told them he owed his present position to them, relying as they had on the 'ancient constitution'. He had only accepted it on the understanding that 'some other body might interpose between you and me to prevent a tumultuary and popular spirit'. This was his Other House, which he had summoned in the interests of Christianity and the nation to be a 'balance to a Commons House of Parliament'. Instead, the Commons had tried to overthrow the government, so that some 'tribune of the people' could seize power. He then sacked six members of his immediate staff who had refused to acknowledge the new House.

Later that year Cromwell died. Under his son, Richard, the Other House sat again from January to April 1659 but, with the Army against it, was once again dissolved. Within the year, the new Parliament, called under General Monck, sent for Charles II.

Monck's 'Convention' Commons immediately made its position plain: 'The single actings of this House inforced by the pressing necessities of the present times, are not intended in the least to infringe, much less to take away, that ancient native right which the House of Peers consisting of those Lords who did engage in the cause of Parliament against the forces raised in the name of the late King and so continued until 1648 had, and have, to be a part of the Parliament of England.'

At the end of April 1660, ten peers returned to the Queen's Chamber, apparently of their own accord, and composed an address to General Monck: 'The Peers in Parliament assembled' praised the General's valour and prudence in managing the great affairs entrusted to him, and thanked him for the intention he had expressed of restoring them to their ancient and undoubted right. They wished him success in achieving a well-grounded peace, according to the ancient and fundamental government of the nation, in which they promised to employ their utmost endeavours.

William Prynne, having spent most of the 1650s in prison again, retained his independence of spirit: at the service of Holy Communion for both Houses of Parliament in 1661 he was alone in refusing to kneel when he received the sacrament. But he now entered into his reward. Appointed Keeper of the Records in the Tower of London by Charles II, he sat with his cropped ears concealed under a Canterbury cap munching a piece of bread for elevenses, according to Pepys, and sipping at a tankard of beer. Anthony Wood, a young man who went to consult the records, said that Prynne received him 'with the old-fashioned compliments such as were used in the reign of King James I'. He continued to wrestle with the problem of the three co-ordinate estates. To be fully co-ordinate, on an equal footing with the Crown and the House of Lords, Prynne and the constitutional lawyers decided, the House of Commons needed to have existed 'from time immemorial', and time immemorial meant before 1189, the year of Richard the Lionheart's Coronation. After 1189 there were reliable records, charters and memorials. Any right established from time immemorial, or from time out of mind, was considered to be unwritten or 'customary' law. It would stand up in court unless written proof could be found to contradict it.

Both the monarchy and the House of Lords, Prynne decided, had been there before 1189, but the Commons was more doubtful. After trying to equate it with the Witan and various twelfth-century Great Councils, Prynne reluctantly came to the conclusion that it had begun in the thirteenth century, summoned by either the King or county sheriffs and was not, after all, co-ordinate.

During these thrilling and terrible years, new Horizonist constitutions had continued to appear in Army debates and in printed
pamphlets. Almost the last dream–Parliament was floated by John
Milton. Milton had been in trouble before the Civil War began as
a pamphleteer against the bishops, notably attacking Bishop Ussher
who had claimed that their order was specifically sanctioned in the
Book of Revelation, not as 'elders', but as 'the Angels of the Seven
Churches'. Now the poet devised a secular ideal. In *A Letter to a
Friend Concerning the Ruptures of the Commonwealth*, he suggested
two 'perpetual aristocracies', one military, one civil. The first would
be composed of senior Army officers, the second a Council of State.
In March 1660 he expanded these ideas in his *Readie and Easie Way
to Establish a Free Commonwealth*. There would be a Great Council
'of the ablest men in England, chosen for life by the people'. He
considered the possibility of a proportion retiring every year, but
rejected it. He disliked the idea of elections as they might bring
back the old system.

King, Lords and Commons were officially restored on 29 May
1660. With the Restoration, as one commentator put it, 'all these
airy models vanished'. The peers returned to the Queen's Chamber,
more outrageous and debauched than they had ever been under
James I. Their numbers were rapidly increased by the arrival of
royal bastards, and they were to play a crucial role in bringing about
the Glorious Revolution.

CHAPTER TWELVE

The Senate of Lilliput

In the Land of the Giants in *Gulliver's Travels*, begun in 1714 and finally published in 1727, Gulliver finds himself sitting in the palm of the Giant King's hand answering questions about the House of Lords. Living behind high rocky mountains in Brobdingnag on the west coast of Canada, the Giants have now become, according to Swift's first outline notes for the book, 'among the most virtuous people on earth', and their king is hugely amused by what he hears about the bishops who sit in the Upper House.

Swift's hero Gulliver, the Mr Pooter of his day, incapable of understanding irony, is happy to brag about the destruction he and his little countrymen can achieve with bombs and gunpowder. He is equally proud of the bishops. They were

> holy Persons whose peculiar Business it was to take care of Religion, and of those who instruct the People therein. These were searched and sought out through the whole Nation, by the Prince and his wisest Counsellors, among such of the Priesthood as were most deservedly distinguished by the Sanctity of their Lives, and the Depth of their Erudition, and were indeed the spiritual Fathers of the Clergy and the People.

The King of the Giants has his doubts. He asks Gulliver whether those holy lords he spoke of

> were always promoted to that Rank upon account of their Knowl-

edge in religious Matters, and the Sanctity of their Lives, had never been Compliant with the Times while they were common Priests, or slavish prostitute Chaplains to some Nobleman, whose opinions they continued servilely to follow after they were admitted into that Assembly.

This might seem fairly rich coming from the Reverend Dr Swift, Dean of St Patrick's in Dublin. He had himself, he was always ready to admit, entertained fantasies of becoming a bishop and riding in a coach and six, and his failure to do so was one of the bitterest disappointments of his life. But throughout the past fifty years the bishops, like Swift himself during his time in London, had become increasingly politicized. It was their last great period of real influence in the House of Lords and they had to figure in any satire on contemporary government.

When the Lords reassembled in the Queen's Chamber in 1660, the Bench of Bishops remained empty. All ten peers who returned to claim their parliamentary rights – Northumberland, Lincoln, Denbigh, Suffolk, Saye and Sele, Wharton, Hunsdon, Grey of Wark and Maynard – had fought on the Parliamentary side against Charles I. At their first joint session they met the Commons in the Painted Chamber, with the Presbyterian Earl of Manchester as Speaker.

They were then gradually joined by the rest: first by the 'young lords', those who had inherited their titles since abolition, then by the royalist peers, and finally, after a good deal of resistance and a personal request from Charles II, by the new peers created by his father during the Civil War. By June 1660, eighty of the 147 peers entitled to sit in the House had arrived. But there was still no move to reinstate the lords spiritual.

The following spring Pepys reported that there were people in the street chanting, 'No bishops, no bishops!', but in the interests of reconciliation a Bill for their restoration went through the Commons. It was stopped in the Lords, and now the tangle of interests began to show below the surface.

The bishops, it seemed, were being used as pawns. Ever since the Reformation, Catholics had been excluded from holding public office, though this ban did not extend to a seat in the Lords. According to the Lord Chancellor, the Earl of Clarendon, Charles II was in league with the Catholic Earl of Bristol to pass an Act of Toleration that would readmit Catholics to public appointments. Their plan, Clarendon believed, was to keep the bishops out until they had passed the Act. Clarendon threatened to expose this scheme, and the Act of Toleration was blocked. Instead the Act Restoring the Temporal Power of the Clergy was passed in 1661, the bishops' bench was pushed back into its old position alongside the Throne, and the bishops resumed their seats. Charles II ruefully thanked both Houses for 'restoring Parliament to its primitive institutions'.

Once back in the Lords, the bishops took a leading role in trying to reunite the country by force of law in religious uniformity. With their vigorous support, Act after Act was passed against 'nonconformists', whether they were Roman Catholics or Presbyterians. New laws were brought in prohibiting the building of chapels except in certain designated places, limiting meetings, and making it obligatory for anyone taking a degree from Oxford or Cambridge to be a full member of the Church of England, subscribing to the Thirty-nine Articles of Belief laid down in 1562.

When James II was crowned in 1685 they therefore found themselves leading the Lords against a secret nonconformist on the Throne. Wherever it was within his power to do so, the King appointed Catholics to positions of discreet power, and they included the Master and Fellows of Magdalen College, Oxford.

Seven bishops spoke in the Lords against 'Popery and Slavery', warning that the King intended to bring the country back into subjection to Rome. The bishops were imprisoned, tried and acquitted. It was therefore as heroes of the resistance to the threat of European Catholicism that the bishops played their role in the Glorious Revolution. The Bishop of London represented them in the Lords' delegation, led by Lord Nottingham and including Lord Lumley and the Earls of Danby, Devonshire and Shrewsbury, when they offered the Crown jointly to William of Orange, a grandson of Charles I, and to his wife Mary, the daughter of James II, both professed Protestants.

If the Glorious Revolution and the Bill of Rights were victories for the Bright Horizon, a man-made settlement and a man-made contract further establishing and limiting the role of the God-given tradition of monarchy, it was the old hierarchy, Lords rather than Commons, who had taken the initiative in bringing in the new King.

James II, who met a party of peers, many of them his supporters, before he fled to France, noted their resolve. 'You were all kings,' he wrote to his friend Lord Ailesbury, 'when I left London.' It was only in the days that followed that the House of Lords received the first of three specific blows that, it could be argued, weakened it for ever after.

In *Gulliver's Travels* Swift, looking back, treats the peers to the kind of ridicule familiar to any modern reader.

> They are [Gulliver squeaks up at the Giant King], Persons of the noblest Blood, and of the most ancient and ample Patrimonies.
>
> I described that extraordinary Care always taken of their Education in Arts and Arms, to qualify them for being Counsellors born to the King and Kingdom; to have a share of the Legislature, to be Members of the highest Court of Judicature, from whence there could be no Appeal; and to be Champions always ready for the Defence of their Prince and Country, by their Valour, Conduct and Fidelity. That these were the Ornament and Bulwark of the Kingdom, worthy followers of their most renowned Ancestors, whose Honour had been the Reward of their Virtue, from which their Posterity was never known to degenerate.

Again, the King of the Giants is sceptical.

> His Majesty consulting his Notes, proposed many Doubts, Queries, and Objections, upon every Article. He asked what Methods were used to cultivate the Minds and Bodies of our young Nobility, and in what kind of Business they commonly spent the first and teachable part of their Lives. What Course was taken to supply that Assembly when any noble Family became extinct. What Qualifications were necessary in those to be created new Lords; whether the Humour of the Prince, a Sum of Money to a Court-Lady, or a prime Minister, or a Design of strengthening a Party opposite to the public Interest, ever happened to be Motives in those Advancements.
>
> What Share of Knowledge these Lords had in the Laws of their Country, and how they came by it, so as to enable them to decide the Properties of their Fellow-Subjects in the last Resort. Whether they were always so free from Avarice, Partialities, or Want that a Bribe, or some other sinister View, could have no place among them.

This view of the Lords, as an effete and irrelevant institution, as it has regrettably been seen so often since, could well have been inspired by the constitutional farce that followed the flight of James II, and the first of the three hammer-blows to the Lords, in this instance self-inflicted. The farce turned on the loss of the Great Seal.

William of Orange had landed at Torbay on 5 November 1688 with a relatively small army of Dutch troops. James had joined his own army on Salisbury Plain, outnumbering the Dutch by four to one, had panicked and returned to London. There he had called for the Great Seal and, collecting his wife disguised as a laundrymaid and their infant son James Francis, had taken the old horse ferry across the Thames at Westminster and, pausing in midstream, had dropped the Great Seal in the river. Without this essential ju-ju object, the constitutional witch-doctors were powerless.

During the weeks of debate that followed in both Houses, it is possible to see the machinery of government – Crown, Lords and Commons – with the lid off, stopped and dismantled.

A contemporary commentator spotted the missing component. 'It is the Great Seal that is the dead spring of our government, as the King's presence, or the presence of any that are deputed by him, gives life to it.' The King was in France, the Great Seal was in the Thames, there was no lawful authority, no spring of government. Without a King there was no machinery for summoning a Parliament, both Chambers were deprived of power. No decision could become law and, more important, there was no income. Ireland was threatened by Catholic rebels. The complete set of King, Lords, Commons, Great Seal and all the rest of the theatrical effects were needed to raise the money to pay an army.

Sir Edward Seymour made the point to the 'Convention' that would, in the presence of the King and the Great Seal, have been the House of Commons: 'I should be glad to see us a legal Parliament, that we may have the people's hearts along with us, and then we shall be sure of their money.'

Both the Upper and Lower House continued to meet in the Queen's Chamber and St Stephen's Chapel. They consisted of the existing peers, including peers recently created by James II, and those MPs who had been elected to the last parliament under Charles II.

In the Upper House Dr White, the Bishop of Oxford, read

prayers. He included a prayer for King James II. Lord Halifax was heard muttering to those peers nearest him that this 'could not be', but he made no official protest. There was then a roll-call, and Lord Berkeley got up to say that there seemed to be a number of peers present who had not been introduced, in particular Lord Griffin. Griffin rose amid some uproar and said he had been created a peer by the King a few days before his departure for France. He assured their lordships that he had his writ of summons, and that his letters patent were 'at the door, waiting to be produced'. Lord Lovelace and Lord Delamer both bellowed at Griffin to withdraw, and a fierce argument sprang up. An anti-Catholic mob was chanting outside, anarchy threatened, the King of France was preparing for war, but the peers were more concerned, as was so often the case at times when their existence was under threat, with details of procedure.

Some said no peer could take his seat until he had been officially introduced by two supporters according to James I's ritual, others that peers created by Charles II in exile had sat in the House of Lords unintroduced after the Restoration. Still others argued that this was not a proper parliament anyway so the rules did not apply. Eventually it was agreed that Griffin should be formally brought in, with Lovelace and Delamer sulkily volunteering to act as his supporters. All the rigmarole was performed, with bows and nods and hat-doffing, and Lord Griffin was allowed to take his seat.

The peers were, admittedly, almost equally concerned about what form of words was necessary to conjure up a new king, and at this stage shot themselves in the foot. The scheduled debate on the State of the Nation, until then a subject that would have been held in the Upper House, was shifted, at the notional Lords' own suggestion, to the notional House of Commons. The Commons would discuss it first, a debate in the Lords would follow, 'by which time we should be able to gather some lights from below, that might be of use to us'. This infuriated Lord Nottingham, who foresaw the effect of this transfer of initiative. It was, he said, 'as if the Lords were only to take aim from the gentlemen below'. But the motion was passed.

The next day was spent in the Lords arguing about Prayers. Lord Halifax told the Bishop of St David's, whose turn it was to read them, that he was to leave out the prayer for King James II 'as improper at this time'. The Bishop refused, and Lord Halifax announced that prayers would be suspended altogether until further notice.

In the Commons, after hours of logic-chopping, it was meanwhile agreed by a substantial majority that James II had 'endeavoured to subvert the constitution by breaking the original contract between king and people, and, by the advice of Jesuits, and other wicked persons, having violated the fundamental laws, and withdrawn himself out of the kingdom, had abdicated the government, and the Throne was thereby vacant'.

The Bill was sent to the Lords, who spent another day arguing about the word 'abdicated'. 'Abdicate', they said, was not English, and in any case it was impossible for a king to extinguish his own kingship. The Throne could never be vacant. The monarchy, like the peerage, was hereditary and not elective. They therefore passed two amendments, changing the word 'abdicated' to 'deserted', and striking out the phrase about the Throne being vacant. This left the succession, whatever they thought about the legitimacy of the infant Prince James Francis – said to have been a fake smuggled into the palace in a warming pan to provide a Catholic heir – to heredity rather than the will of man, and sent the Bill back to the Commons.

On the same day in the Convention Commons they debated the Protestant succession. It was inconsistent with the safety and welfare of this Protestant Kingdom that it should be governed by a popish prince, and the argument, in this second hiatus in the monarchy when anything seemed possible, now turned on the ancient metaphysical point: what came first, the law or the King?

A majority of members of the Lower House agreed that it was the law. The idea of kingship was only there to sanctify the law. 'First make a settlement of the laws,' as one member put it, 'and then settle the Crown.' 'Will you establish the Crown,' another asked, 'and not secure yourselves?' Some, aware of time pressing and the danger of anarchy, were already alarmed at the length of the debate. 'If this takes so much time here, what will it do in the House of Lords?'

The Lords' amendments on 'abdication' and 'vacancy' now arrived, and conservatives in the Lower House appreciated the difficulty. If the Crown of England became elective, every throne in Christendom would tremble. There would, they said, be 'an earthquake'. The fragile thread of heredity that secured the monarchy that in turn secured the law had somehow to be preserved.

The old guard in the Commons remembered the execution of

Charles I forty years before. 'Abdicated' was reconsidered. What about 'forfeited' or 'forsaken'? Someone else suggested 'surrendered', as Richard II had surrendered the Throne to Henry IV. Sir Joseph Tredenham agreed that the Throne was vacant, but was it entirely vacant? Members groaned. Colonel Birch despaired. 'Poor England, for want of speaking one plain word, will be ruined!' He finally took his fellow MPs by the scruff of the neck, and made them face the truth. 'Say but where your power is, and the debate will end! It is here! Take it in your hands, where God in His providence has given it you!'

There were hours more of quibbling, but the Commons eventually took the power into its own hands, and was to keep it. The Bright Horizonists had won. The Crown was now to all intents and purposes elective, the succession decided by man rather than by God or by nature. William and Mary's reign, it was decided, would end with the death of the surviving spouse, and the Crown would then pass to Anne, James II's younger daughter.

The Commons now effectively controlled the monarchy, and had seized real power from the House of Lords. But there were two more humiliations to come for the Upper House.

In 1707, at the Union with Scotland, Scottish peers by all the precedents should have been entitled to a seat in the House of Lords. They were not. Fearful that the Upper House would be swamped by a tartan flood, the Articles of Union specified that all the Scottish peers should hold elections at Holyrood house in Edinburgh on the eve of every new Parliament and send sixteen of their number to Westminster as 'Scottish representative peers'.

In practice the first such peers required heavy subsidies to encourage them to come south, like the Earl of Home. 'He says,' his friend Lord Kinnoull wrote, 'the devil take him, if it were not for his circumstances that he had an old family to preserve, he would serve the Queen without asking a farthing, he has so good will to work. But he spent a great deal last time, and I believe some taken upon tick.' London journeys, another Scot wrote, did not agree with Scottish estates, and only one of the sixteen, the Marquess of Annandale, could afford to pay his own expenses. This inevitably brought accusations, in most cases justified, that the Scottish representative peers were lobby-fodder in the pay of the Government.

But what was more damaging to the old principles of heredity and the Shining Ladder was their lordships' uncomplaining acceptance that any member of the House should be elected. In that year Parliament laid it down as law that the right of a peer to take his seat in the Upper House was no longer purely dependent on anything Mr Justice Dodderidge might have defined as being fixed in the blood. He sat there by right of election to a quota system.

The third blow to the Lords was its vulnerability, vividly demonstrated in 1712, to the ruling party in the Commons. One of the Giant King's jokes, as he looks down at the pathetic little creature in the palm of his hand, is to ask him whether he is a Whig or a Tory.

These political parties had come into existence in the reign of James II. Both nicknames had originally been terms of abuse. The Whigs took theirs from the Whiggamores, Scottish traders who shouted, 'Whiggam!' at their ponies instead of the English 'Giddy up!' A Whig had originally been a Covenanter, a Protestant extremist. The Tories were called after the Catholic peasants driven off their land by Protestant soldiers and settlers. They had become outlaws in the hills, known in the original Gaelic as 'wanted men', men on the run, the ancestors of the IRA.

The Protestant Whigs led the opposition to James II and Catholicism, the largely High Church Anglican Tories opposed the Presbyterians and Nonconformists. As Sir John Percival, later the Earl of Egmont, wrote at the time: 'One party pretends we are in danger of tyranny and Popery, the other of anarchy and Presbytery, all of which is only to beguile the multitude and support their own interests.'

Whigs and Tories then, apart from being recognized as shifty politicians, were the direct heirs of the old Bright Horizon and the Shining Ladder, and would carry that tradition down to the end of the twentieth century. The Whigs would become Liberals and eventually Labour, the party of – until recently at least – equality, creating schisms and splinter-groups like the old Puritans in pursuit of Paradise on Earth. The Tories would remain, at least until Mrs Thatcher, the party of hierarchy and order, closely associated with the Church of England, which had taken over the ecclesiastical hierarchy from Rome.

By Swift's time the parties were already well established, and he brings them into the Lilliputian Parliament as Tramecksan and Slamecksan, the High Heels and the Low Heels, his code for the

High Church Party, the Tories, and the Low Church Party, the Whigs. But the King of the Giants' toughest question is about the possibility of one of these parties interfering with the constitutional independence of the House of Lords: 'whether', as the King asks, when men are ennobled and are made members of the House of Lords, 'the Humour of the Prince or a prime Minister, or a design of strengthening a Party opposite to the public Interest, ever happened to be Motives in those advancements'.

This could only have been read as a reference to Queen Anne's creation of twelve new peers in 1712 to push through the treaty of Utrecht with a Catholic king in the face of Whig opposition.

As in all his comments on the House of Lords in *Gulliver's Travels*, Swift is being decidedly hypocritical in the light of his own record. He had consistently worked for the Tory government as a pamphleteer, he was a close friend of many Tory peers, he had even drafted the Lords' Humble Address to Queen Anne in 1713, which by an even more convoluted irony included a condemnation of a pamphlet he himself had written criticizing the Scots. Far from condemning the Tories' creation of the twelve peers, described by Wharton as 'those mortal wounds which have been given to the bleeding constitution of this country', he actually recounts in his journal how he found his way through the Painted Chamber to congratulate three of them personally in the Lords' Robing Room.

In his *History of the Four Last Years of Queen Anne's Reign*, written within months of starting *Gulliver* in 1713, he entirely justifies the Government's action.

> The adverse Party [the Whigs] being thus driven down by open Force, had nothing left but to complain, which they loudly did: it was a pernicious Example set for ill Princes to follow; who by the same Rule might make at any time an Hundred, as well as Twelve; and by these means become Masters of the House of Lords whenever they pleased.

Swift's answer was that tough measures were necessary. 'Ill Princes' or bad rulers are not going to be concerned about finding precedents, and newly created peers will be as keen as old peers on preserving their liberties. The fine balance of the constitution between King, Lords and Commons sometimes requires a readjust ment of the equilibrium between the two Houses, and that anyway the Whigs have spent the past twenty years 'corrupting the nobility with republican principles'.

Even in the thick of Westminster politics, Swift argued for parliamentary reform, including the abolition of Rotten Boroughs that would not come for another hundred and twenty years, but his defence of the twelve peers was pure Tory propaganda. To accuse the Whigs of having spread republican ideas since 1688 was like the Whigs accusing the Tories of favouring the Roman Catholic Stuarts and supporting the Old Pretender. The threat of swamping the House with new peers would be used again, and the threat would always be enough for the government of the day to get its way.

The Lords counter-attacked, but without success. In 1717 the Earl of Oxford, responsible for the new creations five years earlier, was impeached. The Lords acquitted him, but they made every effort to restore their independence, and drafted a Bill in 1719 that would have re-established their old authority: the peerage of Great Britain should never be enlarged by more than six at a time.

Concerned with keeping out Scottish peers infiltrating their House under new titles as peers of Great Britain, they further proposed that the system of electing Scottish peers should stop, and that twenty-one hereditary Scottish peers should take the place of the elected representatives.

The Bill was passed by the Lords and, after a hold-up, reappeared in roughly the same form in the Commons, where it was rejected by 269 to 177, the Prime Minister, Robert Walpole, arguing quite openly that it would make the Lords independent of the Crown and of the Commons. He was, as Sir William Blackstone tactfully phrased it, 'desirous to keep the avenues to the other House as open and easy as possible'.

If a writer as remarkable as Swift should have become caught up in party politics, it was an indication of the power the new parties already had over both Houses. In *Gulliver's Travels*, looking at them from Ireland, he was able to turn them into a joke, but in real life the pattern was set, and power was already moving into the hands of the party, the cabinet and the prime minister.

When Queen Anne died with no surviving children, the Hanoverian George I in 1714, as grandson of Charles I, was the acceptable

Protestant heir. He was a German with at first very little grasp of English, and the King's ministers took more power, an inner core of politicians ostensibly chosen from one of the two competing parties. Such a cabinet was often largely composed of peers, but they were exercising their power as members of the cabinet, not as members of the Lords.

If, in the long view, you had to choose a moment when the real decline in the power if not the influence of the House of Lords began, it was in 1712. As the domination of the parties grew, breeding eventually leaders who would be rival claimants to the Premiership, so the power of the Lords as a senate began to dwindle. Implicitly acknowledging the supremacy of the Lower House and of the parties, individual lords who were not in the cabinet, many of them now richer and more prosperous than at any other time in their history, devoted themselves to controlling events through the Commons. In public, they acknowledged that the Commons represented the power of the nation; in private, they continued to control it, exercising what one foreign commentator rather melodramatically called their 'occult power' in the Lower House.

CHAPTER THIRTEEN

A Cushion down the Trousers

One morning, a few days after one of my tours of inspection with Peter Horsfall, I got a telephone call. It was from the Major himself, and he sounded worried. 'I've just seen Lord Ampthill and he seems to have heard about me showing you all round the building. "What's this I hear, Peter, about you giving Wells a tour of the Palace?" I think it'll be all right, but he'd like you to come and see him.'

I rang the general House of Lords number, listed in the Business and Services volume of the London telephone directory after House of Hanover of Hanover Street, House of Hardy Ltd, Fishing Tackle, and before House of Mirrors and House of Mistry Ltd, Natural Cosmetic and Homeopathic Remedies. I asked to speak to Lord Ampthill's secretary. She sounded only slightly severe, and said that Lord Ampthill would like me to come and have lunch with him.

I arrived in good time, as instructed, at the Peers' Entrance. The House was by now in session again, and downstairs by the Redcoat's desk a lot of visitors in advanced middle age were standing about looking like mourners at a society memorial service. The traditional drawl of the old aristocracy, sometimes referred to as 'Binkies' by the life peers, was relatively easy on the ear, involving a minimum of thought or lip-movement. The style adopted by some of the life peers, known by the hereditaries as 'the Day Boys', was in some cases more grating. Months of being bowed to and deferred to and having doors opened for them by former members of the Brigade of Guards calling them 'my lord' and treating them with exaggerated courtesy had obviously had its effect.

'It's not ker-white 'alf parse twelve, meigh watch is slow.'

This was, of course, the result of Ladderism. For centuries, successful members of the middle and even working class had bought or won their way into the Lords, and had aspired to be like them. Within a generation, or possibly two, hereditary peers, educated at Eton, had forgotten the way their father or grandfather had wrenched his jaw trying to get the accent right.

A tall good-looking American girl in a hat arrived with her husband and was greeted eagerly by an elderly hereditary she had clearly never met before in her life. He kissed her with great enthusiasm on both cheeks and told her that she was looking 'virry, virry nice'.

Another doorkeeper, playing, as always, the urbane head waiter in a black tail coat and horn-rimmed spectacles, was at his desk ticking names off his list as people came in. Another old hereditary tottered up and asked if his guest had appeared yet. 'Standing in front of you, my lord.'

The Day Boys and the Binkies were two distinct breeds, plump captains of industry and threadbare old gents of the old school, stringy-looking Etonians in dirty shirts with unwashed hair curling over their collars, funny ears, and bony, knobbly faces. The Day Boys were alert, efficient-looking, the Binkies dignified.

A party of high-collared vicars in their best suits had now arrived.

'Very kaind of you to entertain us today, my lawd . . .'

An old-fashioned spiv, grown grey in the used car trade, made an expansive gesture. 'Can I introduce you to my colleague, Ken 'enderson?'

A ringleted but entirely Anglicized party of orthodox Jews bowed and smiled to a noisy party of Italians. A few more elderly peers drifted through in a gentle daze, floating by on sticks. Then a doorkeeper came in, almost running. 'We've lost 'im! Lord Spens! You got 'im in there?' For a moment he seemed almost rattled.

A younger hereditary who was clearly basing his performance on some minor character in *Leave it to Psmith* breezed in and was hailed by a guest.

'Are you will?'

'Tirribly will, nauseatin'ly will.'

To my relief I saw Jo Grimond again, his huge blue eyes grown rather farouche in old age, beaming all over his face. 'Have they made you a lord? What a splendid idea!'

I explained that I had been sent for by Lord Ampthill. He shook his head. 'Oh dear, oh dear, oh dear. He's one of the prefects. You'd better stick a cushion down your trousers!'

Then the doorkeeper called my name and told me that Lord Ampthill's secretary would meet me at the top of the stairs. I walked up, past the heraldry and stone escutcheons, and she led me along the now familiar red-carpeted corridors to the office of the Lord Chairman of Committees.

Traditionally committees have always been part of the work of the House of Lords, as they have of the Commons. In earlier days, as at the time of Magna Carta or in the reign of James I, they could play a direct role in governing the country. More recently they have questioned witnesses, carried out investigations and chewed through business that would be indigestible in the Parliament Chamber. This last role was greatly increased as part of an exercise to make the Upper House more efficient at the end of the last century. Committees were seen as a means of lightening the workload on the floor of the House. Committees of one kind or another had continued to exist – meetings to decide everything from the books to be bought for the library to the future of some extinct peerage – but they were now used more and more on legislation. A small group of peers could investigate the practical advantages and disadvantages of building a new port. Arguments for and against new powers for the police that might clog up the Chamber for days could be digested and clarified in an upstairs committee room. The idea was revived and extended with the same idea in mind in 1969, and the Lord Chairman of Committees became a powerful figure. He was appointed by the Government, officially neutral, but had the job of encouraging peers to join, of balancing front- and back-bench representation, reactionaries and progressives.

Lord Ampthill was sitting at his desk, bespectacled and youthful-looking for a man of seventy. He gave me a warm smile, shook my hand and indicated a table in the middle of the room littered with black-and-white photographs of a West End show. Jonathan Miller and I had directed Leonard Bernstein's *Candide* in 1989. In the days before he inherited the peerage, Lord Ampthill, as Geoffrey Russell the impresario, had put on the first English production twenty-five years earlier. The photographs were by Tony Armstrong-Jones, now the Earl of Snowdon, the only peer in recent times created at the personal request of the Monarch, and showed the young Denis Quilley as Candide posing against sets by Lord Snowdon's uncle, Oliver Messel. This made surprising common ground, and by the time we had had a drink and gone down to lunch we were getting on like a house on fire.

Lord Ampthill, it turned out, had subsequently been general manager of Fortnum and Mason, and when he had first joined the Lords he had been elected chairman of the catering committee on the strength of it. Rumour had it that he had brought in his French wife to raise standards, but that the old boys had rebelled: they wanted the usual nursery food, requiring fewer teeth. There was now, he told me, a full-time catering manager, Mr Bibbiani, and he had a permanent staff of sixty, plus what Peter Horsfall had described as 'some permanent casuals', all on annual salaries, even though the House was closed for at least three months every year. Peter Horsfall had called them 'a very switched-on outfit', and told me that Lord Ampthill had been responsible for switching them on. The Commons, with twenty-six restaurants, snack-bars and cafeterias, employed a catering staff five times as large.

Lord Ampthill adopted a breezy and informal tone. 'The Lords don't drink so much. You can get pissed that end for thirty per cent less than you can this end. That's because they charge less. We charge the going rate. Catering in the House of Commons costs the taxpayer three and a half million in subsidies, the House of Lords only three hundred and fifty thousand.'

As well as reducing their losses, Lord Ampthill had dug them out an entirely new restaurant from what had been a cellar used for storing lumber. The Barry Room, where he took me for lunch, was vaulted in newly cleaned honey-coloured stone, had heavy, comfortable blue chairs and a thick blue carpet. It was noisy, trolleys full of puddings and cheeses were being shunted through the limited space between the tables, and it could have been any fashionable basement restaurant within a mile of Piccadilly. A friendly manager bowed us in. 'Your usual table, my lord?'

Lord Ampthill was proud of himself, as catering manager, for having poisoned a great many peers. 'Actually I very nearly knocked off eighty-four of their lordships!'

I asked him how he'd done it.

'With salmonella. I did it with the mayonnaise. They put it in all the sandwiches to moisten them up, so we had quite a whoopsy day.' He admitted that it would never have happened if the lorry delivering the eggs to the House of Lords that morning had not gone off the road and crashed. 'I was forced to borrow some eggs from the Commons.'

He had also made a revolutionary change in the arrangement of tables in his new restaurant. 'The peers used to eat by party, as they do in the Commons, you see. Then I introduced that long table' – he spoke with the proprietary tone of a zoo-keeper who had introduced some new piece of apparatus into the Chimpanzees' Tea Party – 'and now they all sit together very happily. First guy in at one o'clock and the next one that comes in sits next to him. Everyone knows each other here. It's pretty light-hearted. If I was sitting there now I'd be ragged unmercifully, being put through it by these old gents.'

He was also proud of the Lords' initiative in introducing television cameras. 'We had it first, as you know, and we had to go on at the Commons for five years before they put it in. We thought it might make them do a bit more work.'

He went on to talk about how the Chamber was run. With no official Speaker whose eye they could catch, the peers managed their own debates. I had become familiar with the routine from the press gallery. It did not always work. On rare occasions when the House was full, one peer would sit down and several others would hesitantly rise. They were so overwhelmingly polite they usually all sat down again. One courageous figure would eventually risk it, get to his feet and warble away, sharing the few thoughts he had jotted down on odd bits of paper. Occasionally two deaf or disoriented peers would rise and talk for a few moments simultaneously, and this produced a sort of well-bred growl of embarrassment that made one or possibly both of them sit down in confusion. Usually, though, it worked, and there were days when it could have been a session of any large city council. Except, that is, for the stage-set and the excessive good manners. Lord Ampthill said he sometimes regretted their legendary politeness. 'They waste a tremendous amount of time at the Other End shouting at each other. We waste time being polite, thanking each other for our great kindness in spelling out opinions we disagree with, and so forth.'

I asked him if there was any way of shutting people up.

'Well, occasionally the chief whip will say, "Do you realize, old boy, you've spoken three times this week?" and if he's a real sonofabitch you can glare at him.'

There had been an occasion when the last Earl of Longford had been so infuriated by Anthony Wedgwood Benn's father, Viscount Stansgate, that he had taken the ultimate sanction of proposing that 'the noble Lord be no longer heard', but that happened only rarely.

Yet despite the entertaining jokes I was aware that the lunch was not purely lunch for the sake of it. As the former manager of a successful grocer's, Lord Ampthill was selling me the House of Lords as an efficient modern business. 'The House of Lords costs twenty-three million a year to run, the House of Commons a hundred and sixteen million. The European Parliament, as a matter of interest, costs three hundred and ninety-one million.' But, as a former West End theatre manager, he was also selling it to me as a damn good show. There was backstage planning, to work out for instance a timetable for each session of Parliament. But what you saw in the Parliament Chamber was the Upper House At Work.

Over the very good asparagus soup he explained the general outline, the machinery of the plot.

Broadly speaking, the Lords had a far greater degree of individual initiative than members of the Lower House, a better chance of raising their own personal concerns and campaigns. In the Commons such initiatives were usually crushed by the pressure of government business.

As far as new legislation was concerned, Public Bills introduced from the front bench certainly took up most of their time. These were ideas hatched in the cabinet and then sent to a legislation committee to be drafted. The committee decided whether they would be introduced in the Commons or the Lords, but the weight of work inevitably fell on the Commons. Financial business always started there, and with most government ministers sitting in the Lower House, that was where, as Earl Jellicoe once put it, 'they liked to see their own babies learning to walk'.

But the leader of the governing party in the Lords, appointed by the Prime Minister, was also a member of the cabinet, and secured as much business as possible, usually the less controversial work, for the Upper House. This was principally to level out the burden of the Lords' work as a revising chamber: often they had nothing to do at the beginning of a session and could be buried at the end of it under hastily drafted Bills pushed through the Commons under the threat of the guillotine.

Stage-management was then in the hands of the leader, his deputy, the government chief whip, and the leader's secretary, who between them planned the timetable, kept the back-benchers informed, planned the shape of debates, and organised speakers in order of appearance. The whole programme was put on paper every Thursday. Sent out on Friday by the chief whip, it listed the following week's debates, outlined 'future business', and drew their lordships' attention to those occasions when their presence would be particularly welcome.

Back-bench peers might find themselves discreetly invited to do the Government's business. They could, in the technical language, propose a Motion to Take Note: this simply meant airing a topic, flying a kite to give the Government an idea of which way the wind was blowing. There was also a Motion for Resolution, which meant taking a snap vote on some topical issue, and there was a Motion for Papers, which if passed would oblige the Government to draw up a Bill.

They could also ask questions: so-called starred questions, of which there were usually four a day after lunch, but which can develop into miniature debates, required notice, and could produce valuable or embarrassing information. Private Notice Questions could be submitted by any peer before noon on the day. Ninety per cent were turned down as 'not urgent', meaning that the government spokesman had no time to get the answer, but those that got through gave peers a great deal more leverage with those in power than a letter to the *Times* or the *Daily Telegraph*.

But when they were not being employed by the chief whip on such business the same range of possibilities was open to them as individuals. With no Speaker's eye to catch and the old-fashioned courtesy of self-regulation, special interests could be aired, kites of their own devising could be flown, and frequently were. An individual peer's concern, for instance, for the welfare of badgers or buggers had a far better chance of becoming a Private Member's Bill than that of a Member of the Lower House.

But all of this was mere machinery. On stage the ceremonial reigned.

A Commons Bill, printed on yellow paper in a white cover and tied with a green ribbon, is carried along one of the red-carpeted passages. In the seventeenth century it would have been brought by the Speaker or a Member of Parliament, with the obligatory hat-doffing, but now it arrives at the Bar delivered by a Commons clerk. With it he brings the message that it has received three readings at what Lord Ampthill called 'the Other End'.

A Lords clerk, possibly the tall randy-looking one who had assisted at Mrs Thatcher's entombment, will then bow, accept it and carry it past the cross-benches to lay it on the Clerks' Table. It is formally announced by its short title and its objectives read out. That constitutes its First Reading. A date and time is then decided, at least two weeks later, for its Second Reading.

'That's when we have the chance to talk about it in general, and after that there are two more weeks before the Committee Stage.'

The House then resolves itself into a committee and the Lord Chancellor, as a minister, takes his seat on the government front bench. The Bill is picked over. Words and phrases may be amended, and if their lordships think it necessary, it can be referred to either a select committee or a joint committee of both Houses.

'The House is at its best on something like the Embryology Bill in 1989. Lord Walton of Detchant was a neurologist at the Hammersmith Hospital. He specialized in genetically transmitted diseases, and he was able to explain everything to the House in layman's language. Then there was the Archbishop of York, an ex-scientist – he was fascinating about the actual moment at which life begins.'

During the Committee Stage, Lord Ampthill explained, when he sat in an armchair in front of the Woolsack, their lordships could talk for as long as they liked, virtually until the cows came home. He had been criticized for speeding things up at the Committee Stage by what he called 'a bunch of dinosaurs' – 'Three hundred and eighty-four years between the five of them' – but was anxious to make it clear he was not ageist. He remembered Manny Shinwell at ninety-four, holding the House enthralled without a single note. But the Committee Stage is the time to be businesslike.

After that comes the Report Stage, with the Lord Chancellor back, when Lord Ampthill as Chairman of Committees has to report to the Chamber on what has been discussed and decided. Again the peers intervene, but they are allowed to speak only once.

This is followed by the Third Reading, after which the Bill goes off to be given the official Royal Assent and becomes an Act of Parliament – the law.

By now we had drunk most of a bottle of Crozes-Hermitage and were well into a breast of roast guinea-fowl.

In theory the Lords can propose improvements and clarifications to a Bill as amendments, and vote on them, at any stage after the Second Reading, the point at which they make their general reaction clear. If, as is almost always the case, they approve a Bill in general but have minor suggestions, it is carried without a vote. If they have major reservations about a large part of a Bill they can vote for a 'reasoned amendment', which means asking for a formal delay, to allow them more time to study the subject and think about it. This means that the Lord Chancellor, instead of proposing that the Bill 'be *now* read a second time' would say 'be read this time three months' or 'this time six months'.

A reasoned amendment is mildly irritating to the Government in the House of Commons, but is usually no more than a touch on the brakes. The Lords can also reject a Bill altogether. This happens rarely, but they did it in 1990 at the Second Reading of the War Crimes Bill. Since the two Parliament Acts of 1911 and 1949, they no longer have the power to 'kill' it and the Commons sent it back. When the Lords rejected it again in 1991, also at the Second Reading, it became law automatically later that year, twelve months after its original Second Reading.

This still allows the Lords to play their traditional role, which is to give time for mature consideration after the often impulsive response of the House of Commons. If the Commons is Caesar drunk, the Lords is Caesar sober. The delay allows the Opposition another chance to argue its case and, if public opinion changes, for the Commons to redraft the Bill in a way that will reflect the change in mood.

'We are a revising chamber. Our job is tidying up the messes they make at the other end of the building.' It is detailed and tricky work, requiring legal expertise. 'Drafting amendments is extremely difficult. There are only about twelve people in the country who can do it.'

Sometimes a government minister accepts an amendment without a vote, but if necessary the Lord Chancellor asks the opinion of the whole House. Those 'Content' say 'Content'. Those 'Not Content' say 'Not Content'. If the first bellow is not markedly louder than the second, their lordships may be asked to shuffle through the lobbies, those Content going to the left of the Throne, the others to the right. The doors of the red-carpeted corridors on either side of the Parliament Chamber are locked at the Bar end, the peers file through and are counted in by their tellers. When they have all voted and shuffled back in, the tellers report to a clerk at the table who in turn announces the vote to the Lord Chancellor. He then tells the House that the amendment has been 'agreed to' or 'disagreed to'.

With any amendments attached, the Bill is then sent back to the Commons. If, for instance, the amendment has corrected a piece of sloppy drafting, they might accept it. If the amendment frustrates government policy, they might not. In any case the Bill will then have to be sent back to the Lords and then back to the Commons again until both Houses agree precisely the same text. Towards the end of any parliamentary session, Bills are whacked back and forth like shuttlecocks.

The process also works in reverse. Some of the Bills that go through Parliament begin life in the Lords. Those are generally on less controversial subjects and less likely to involve party-political conflict, and it is always a struggle to secure a reasonable share of government Bills for the Lords. 'It means the government chief whip using his elbows in the Cabinet Committee.'

Relations between the Lords and the Commons depend on what Lord Ampthill described as 'a certain amount of delicate negotiation behind the scenes'.

In many cases, the Government argues that there is no need for the Lords to vote on an amendment. Merely raising a question during the debate in the Lords will persuade them to amend a Bill at its Third Reading in the Commons.

Each parliamentary party plans its strategy behind closed doors, but the Lords is a difficult place to manage. Those on the cross-benches owe no loyalty to any party, but even straight Conservative, Labour and Liberal Democrat peers are not easy to discipline.

'The big advantage we have is that we are here for life, unlike the MPs in the Commons. We are technically impervious to whips. Nor are we under any pressure from the electors, being far too old and decayed to put ourselves up for election. The only advantage I see to a three-line whip in the Lords, really, is purely theatrical, in that it produces what looks like a cast of extras selected by Central Casting rather than real people.' Lightning raids by 'backwoodsmen', Lord Ampthill insisted, were however largely precluded by the need to take the oath before voting.

I mentioned the 'ambushes' staged by the Liberal Democrat peers: under the direction of their whips' office and its dynamic secretary, Celia Thomas. They would calculate a time when the House was likely to be empty, conceal themselves, then spring out with what force they could muster to push through a division and win the vote. Secrecy was essential, and Celia Thomas herself was sometimes uneasy, as the conspirators spilled into the corridor outside their downstairs office, when she heard Lord Jenkins, boom 'When did you say you wanted us to come back, Celia?' But it was a valuable guerrilla tactic for a small party. How did Lord Ampthill feel about them?

He said he thought the Liberal Democrats had been 'silly'. What is needed from the Lords is not minor party-political advantage, but a sensitive response from a forum of independent-minded men and women.

'We are useful, rather than important. What we can offer is expert knowledge and there is no substitute for that. We have twelve Fellows of the Royal Society. There is no way you can handbag this house, as Margaret Thatcher has discovered. We make something like two thousand amendments a year to Public Bills. And of those 98.5 per cent are accepted.' A large proportion of these, he admitted, were initiated by the Government.

On the way out of the restaurant I asked Lord Ampthill why he did the job. Hereditary peers are not people you immediately associate with the nuts and bolts of parliametary legislation.

He thought about it for a moment. 'Well, I felt I ought to take it seriously, really, after all the trouble I'd had getting in.'

I asked him what he meant.

'My father died and I automatically assumed I would receive what is called the writ of summons, but when I rang up the office they told me my brother had already applied for it. I got on to my lawyer, who said, 'Leave this with me. I think we can have it straightened out in three weeks.' Then he rang me back and said he'd looked into the papers and it might take three months. In the end it took three years.'

I still hadn't made the connection and pressed him further.

'Well, you see, it was a bit complicated. My mother was a virgin when I was born.'

CHAPTER FOURTEEN

Wiser Councils Prevail

The great portrait of decadent aristocracy appears four years before the dawn of the eighteenth century, in 1696, in Vanbrugh's *The Relapse*. But it is a character that continued to be easily recognizable throughout the century.

Lord Foppington, formerly Sir Novelty Fashion, is an idiotic, entirely narcissistic Philistine who has bought himself a peerage. He believes that 'Thinking is the greatest fatigue in the world.'

> Well, 'tis an unspeakable pleasure to be a man of quality, strike me dumb! 'My lord.' 'Your lordship.' 'My Lord Foppington.' Ah, c'est quelque chose de beau, que le diable m'emporte! Why, the ladies were ready to puke at me whilst I had nothing but Sir Novelty to recommend me to 'em. Sure, whilst I was but a knight, I was a very nauseous fellow. Well, 'tis ten thousand pound well given, stap my vitals!

Lord Foppington is a far cry from Lord Byrhtnoth, but both enjoyed some irrational glamour. The House of Lords not only survived the so-called Age of Reason, it flourished in it. Whether this was due more to growing prosperity and stability in the country or to the romantic yearning for medieval antiquity that made Sir Robert Walpole's son Horace build his Gothick house at Strawberry Hill, the House of Lords somehow renewed itself in a Rococo fantasy of the old Shining Ladder. It was also accepted, both by serious students of politics from abroad and by theorists at home, as a perfect element in a piece of beautiful constitutional clockwork. 'If the supreme power were lodged in any one of the three branches separately,' the constitutional lawyer Sir William Blackstone wrote, 'we must be exposed to the inconveniences of either absolute monarchy, aristocracy, or democracy.' All three, it seemed, were dim but terrible memories of the century before. Now these three elements of the Constitution were rebalanced and retuned, combining virtue, wisdom and power.

In reality the role of the Lords as a 'Screen or Bank' between the King and the Commons had ceased to have any importance. The screen, as some of the more clear-minded peers recognized, was needed now between the Prime Minister and the people. The country was managed by the party, Whig or Tory, in power in the Commons, 'led and directed', as Lord Shelburne put it, 'by an administration consisting of four or five persons, and those again by one man'. The Prime Minister held the shared central power. He had become the elected monarch.

If the Lords tried to define their duty in terms of practical politics, it was as a mature senate, but when it came to a real crisis, like that with the American colonies towards the end of the century, it was not a role they played with any great distinction.

The sad story began in 1766 with the imposition of a duty on tea, and continued for fifteen years. In the House of Lords, informed, reasonable and maturely considered opinion was consistently ignored and voted down by Tory warmongers. Their conduct was summarized by Lord Camden, in 1777, during the debate on Chatham's motion to end the war, looking back over the past ten disastrous years 'You passed a law for laying a tax upon tea; but you could not collect it, because neither the importer, nor vendor, nor consumer could be found. You passed another law, which ministers flattered themselves would force the tax into operation. You gave the East India Company a draw-back on their teas exported to America. The teas were sent to America, particularly to Boston, where a large quantity was destroyed.

'What did we do? Without demanding reparation, without enquiry, without hearing the party accused, nay, even without proof of the fact, you condemned the people of Boston: you shut up their port; you annihilated private property; you reduced thousands of innocent people to beggary. You did not stop there: you resolved to punish the whole province as well as the town. You deprived them of their charter, you deprived them of the benefit of trial by jury.'

He went on. The Government had told them there would be no resistance: a file of musketeers could march from one end of America to the other without being molested. In case they were molested, they had sent General Gage out with four regiments, which 'were fully adequate for the purpose'. General Gage had camped outside Boston for twelve months, his army increasingly sick, inactive and taunted by Bostonians preparing to defend themselves. 'The next year we declared these people to be in rebellion; we prohibited them from trading with each other; we deprived them of their fishery; and a noble Lord in the other House pledged himself to that House that with an army of 10,000 men, which would reach America early in the summer, the conquest of that country would be certain.'

With their lordships' approval this army had sailed. Nonplussed by Washington's guerrillas, they had 'mouldered away', been starved and besieged, and been lucky to get back to their transport ships. Since then, their lordships had approved an army of 70,000, augmented by foreign mercenaries and a hundred warships. What, after all that, had they achieved? 'What part of America is your own? Just as much as you can command with the mouths of your cannon.'

It was an extraordinarily lucid speech, concluding with a practical account of the economic consequences: America had been driven into an anti-British alliance with France and Spain; trade routes were now so threatened by French and American gunships that British merchants found it safer and cheaper to use French cargo ships, of which there were at that moment twenty-six in dock in the Thames.

Chatham's motion to make peace was defeated, with twenty-five proxy votes on each side, by ninety-nine to twenty-eight. The Tory cabinet, backed by an obstinate George III, had had its way. Before the War of Independence began, Lord Townshend called the Americans 'a turbulent and ungrateful people', who given an inch would take a mile. Once the fighting had begun, Earl Gower told the House that the rebels were vastly outnumbered by loyalists who 'having tasted the difference between British liberty and American tyranny would gladly return to their allegiance'.

Once the time came to sue for peace, the Tories blamed everyone else. The settlement was a 'disgrace to the nation'. Richard Oswald, empowered to negotiate the line of the Canadian border with Benjamin Franklin, had allowed the wool to be pulled over his eyes, losing forts, trading-stations and millions of square miles of territory. The American Indians, whose sacred independence had never been considered during the blind drive to impose order on an insubordinate Empire, were now linked with the abandoned loyalists as the tragic victims of the peacemakers' folly. We had sworn inviolate friendship with them, Lord Stormont told the House, 'as long as the woods, the mountains and the rivers should remain'.

As a last resort, the Lords even debated a proposal by Joseph Galloway, the former Speaker for Pennsylvania, suggesting a House of Lords for the former American colonies. Many peers blamed their loss on 'that unmixed democracy prevalent in the plantations', and were convinced that hereditary honours, providing the basis for an American peerage, might have prevented all the trouble. Even now, Galloway promised them, an American House of Lords could 'restore imperial unity'.

From outside the Palace of Westminster, however, the system appeared to be working perfectly. The Dean of Gloucester, Josiah Tucker, in his *Treatise concerning Civil Government*, continued to feel complacent about the three-tier constitution of King, Lords and Commons as a rational machine. 'A government compounded of all three, and partaking so much of the nature of each, as shall make every part be a check and counter-balance to the others, without impeding the motion of the whole, seems to be the best.'

The explanation lay in its dignity, its existence as an image of order, a beautiful piece of political theatre.

The French playwright Beaumarchais, inventor of Figaro and the author of the famous line against hereditary power, 'What did you do for all this? You took the trouble to be born!', attended several Lords' debates when he was living in Sloane Street and working as a spy for the French embassy. One event he witnessed, and which was reported in the French newspapers, dramatically captured the spirit of the Lords' assembly.

Aware that the presence of foreign visitors like Beaumarchais in the public gallery of the Queen's Chamber meant that details of government business would appear within days in the enemy press in France, the peers voted to have all spectators removed. Only one man would be admitted by the doorkeepers to listen whenever he wished, a man 'to whom their lordships owed more than anyone else alive for the conduct of their debates'. It was the actor Garrick.

But even the pure theatre, the masque of order, was upset by the Gordon Riots in 1780. Horace Walpole wrote that the House of Lords had 'sunk from the temple of dignity to an asylum of lamentable objects'. In a sudden flare-up of the old Eurosceptic anti-Catholic mania, the mob attacked the Palace of Westminster, and several peers were injured in what Walpole satirically described as 'the holy hurly-burly'. Lord Hillsborough, Lord Stormont and Lord Townshend, all prominent Tories in the American debates, had their wigs torn off by the mob and arrived at the House 'with their hair dishevelled about their ears'. Lord Ashburnham was 'torn out of his chariot', the Bishop of Lincoln was jostled, the Duke of Northumberland had his watch stolen, and Lord Boston was all but trampled to death. When they 'diswigged' Lord Bathurst – 'a most feeble, awkward and puzzled speaker' but violently anti-Catholic – he was brave enough to shout at them. They shouted back, calling him 'the Pope and an old woman'.

The Lord Chief Justice, Lord Mansfield, who was deputizing for the Lord Chancellor, was less courageous. His glasses were broken in the mêlée and he took his seat on the Woolsack, according to Walpole, 'quivering like an aspen'.

What made the whole charade, whether dignified or farcical, so irrelevant was the peers' 'occult power' in the House of Commons. As 'borough-mongers', nominating their sons or dependents for parliamentary constituencies, the Lords literally owned or directly controlled more than half of the seats in the Lower House. One Tory seat was occupied for many years by a waiter at a gambling club, the previous member having put down his parliamentary seat as security and lost it on the turn of a dice. It was not until 1809 that a Bill was passed – and it was not the first of its kind – 'to prohibit the sale of seats in the House of Commons'. Of these seats, two thirds were Tory and the rest Whig, though the balance changed as William Pitt ennobled many of his more slavish Whig supporters among the two hundred-odd new peers he sent to the Upper House.

The landowning peers spent a lot of money on general elections, and wanted value from their successful candidates. Surviving budgets list party ribbons, banners and the rent of public halls, but most of the expense went on drink and shillelaghs. One peer, having emptied his cellar of port in such an exercise, was forced to start on his precious claret, only to have the mob turn against him for giving them 'sour port'.

But if the House of Lords often failed in its role as a wise senate and endangered the fair working of the Constitution by meddling in the Lower House, it was once again under threat as an institution from the Bright Horizonists. The old hierarchy might be prized by rational eighteenth-century minds who had revived the notion of the Great Chain of Being to explain the order of nature, but egalitarians had other ideas. Why should they respect an Upper House, an assembly seen as high above them on the Ladder, when they could form their own people's assemblies? The spread of these unofficial local 'societies' – what would become in France the Revolutionary Committees – questioned the whole doctrine of the Shining Ladder and the purpose of a House of Lords. These gatherings often began with modest and entirely unrevolutionary aspirations.

John Wesley, the founder of Methodism, whose parents remembered stories of the Civil War and shuddered at the mention of Puritans or Nonconformists, set out to take Christianity back to its primitive beginnings, and one of his methods was the creation of small 'self-regulating groups' or 'classes'. Like his brother Charles, he remained throughout his life a priest in the Church of England, but his work among the poor and his methods of political organization were bound to bring him into conflict with the hierarchical ideas of the established Church and make the emergence of the independent Methodists inevitable.

In the 1730s and 1740s Wesley took the poor and starving in the cities and put them into small mutually supportive groups of the kind later used by Alcoholics Anonymous. Members monitored, encouraged or criticized each other's behaviour, and contributed regular payments to enable them to create employment for each other. If they had no money, richer Methodists paid their share.

This pattern of organization also existed in more subversive political movements. The House of Lords and the House of Commons remained the official forums of debate, but others rapidly proliferated. These were the so-called Corresponding Societies. Looking back over the end of the century, the Earl of Liverpool wrote that the French Revolution had 'familiarized mankind with a system of [political] organization which has been justly represented to be as ingenious and appropriate to its purpose as any invention in mechanics'. That efficient new 'system of organization' was the intercommunicating network of political clubs, the Societies, and they had been in existence long before the French Revolution. They ranged from the London Corresponding Society and the Society for Constitutional Information and mechanics' institutes for self-improvement with carefully catalogued libraries and reading rooms, to gangs of desperate vandals in rags bent on murder and destruction.

The Societies were dangerous for two reasons. First, they spread the egalitarian Horizonist dogma, both by word of mouth at meetings and through the clandestine distribution of forbidden literature: one and a half million copies of Tom Paine's *Rights of Man* were sold in this way, to be hidden in the lining of their caps by persecuted believers. Second, they constituted a challenge to the established forms of government.

What so appalled Edmund Burke about the distribution of these pamphlets as 'ammunition and cartridges' was that the printing press was becoming 'the grand instrument of the subversion of order, of morals, of religion, of human society itself'. Human society was shaped politically by a number of inherited ideas, a kind of 'family settlement'. The hereditary House of Lords offered a paradigm. Our civilization, like the Upper House, depended on unbroken tradition, respect for the past combined with respect for the future. 'We transmit our government and our privileges. The institutions of policy are handed down, to us and from us, in the same course and order. We have given to the frame of polity [the shape of government] the image of a relation in blood, binding up the constitution of our country with our dearest domestic bliss.'

The Bright Horizonists, he believed, were bent on destroying this. He seized on the fact that their prophet, Jean Jacques Rousseau, loved the story of Robinson Crusoe. Crusoe was a man cut off, on a desert island. The hero of Rousseau's *Emile*, his treatise on ideal education, was an orphan. Rousseau wanted to begin from a *tabula rasa*. But Rousseau was scrapping tradition and the slow growth of institutions in favour of a model based on fantasy. His Golden Age, for instance, no longer had any Christian associations, but relied on something very close to the Garden of Eden. Primitive man was not a flesh-eating ape, he was an idealized figure living in a state of nature before 'civil society', the root of all evil. Life before 'civil society' was an idyllic commune.

> The first man [Rousseau wrote in his *Discourse on Inequality* in 1755] who, having enclosed a piece of ground, bethought himself of saying, 'This is mine,' and found people simple enough to believe him, was the real founder of civil society. From how many crimes, wars and murders, from how many horrors and misfortunes might not anyone have saved mankind, by pulling up the stakes, or filling in the ditch and crying to his followers, 'Beware of listening to this impostor: you are undone if you once forget that the fruits of the earth belong to us all, and the earth itself to nobody.'

This was bad news for the landowners of the House of Lords, and there were three English Horizonist prophets they had particular reason to fear. None openly advocated armed uprising, but all preached an ideal world that could only be achieved by the removal of Ladderist forms and institutions.

Joseph Priestley made his name as a scientist in Leeds with his pioneering work in the fields of electricity and oxygen. He was approached by the Whig peer the first Marquess of Lansdowne who, as second Earl of Shelburne, had been Prime Minister in the Commons: he offered Priestley a sinecure as his librarian to enable him to pursue his researches in comfort, with a house, rent-free, on Lansdowne's estate at Bowood, another in Hill Street, Mayfair, and £200 a year for life. Priestley asked him to make it £250, apologizing for his ignorance of 'things of a *political* nature, which he had not particularly studied'.

Living with Lansdowne, in Priestley's own words, 'as a friend', he had made up for lost time, leaving the gently liberal ideas of his host far behind. He met and talked with many leading political figures, including Benjamin Franklin, and became what Burke contemptuously described as one of the leading 'political theologians' of his age.

Priestley was genuinely religious in the more conventional sense of the word, a direct intellectual descendant of the seventeenth-century

Puritan Democrats. A Nonconformist, he had rejected the Church of England and the doctrine of the Holy Trinity in favour of a single God, Divine Reason. Human beings, he believed, had only to make use of their God-given intellect to achieve paradise on earth.

One major obstacle was the House of Lords. In his early *Essay on the First Principles of Government*, written in 1768, Priestley was prepared to tolerate it, although he saw the presence of the bishops as a hangover from the old days of the political power of Rome. Now, after the American Revolution, he believed that, in a holier and better world, the House of Lords would have to go. The hereditary system 'degraded' the rest of mankind: no one would ever realize their full potential until there was a state of perfect equality. In Priestley's earthly paradise there would be an indirectly elected national assembly of 1,000 members and a senate of 100 persons 'of superior wisdom' with limited powers of revision and delay.

The second airy model was floated by Tom Paine, author of *The Rights of Man*. As a corset-maker, schoolteacher and part-time customs official in Thetford and later in Lewes, he was angrier than Priestley and less cautious. The earthly paradise would have no lords and no king. The idea of hereditary legislators was as absurd as that of hereditary mathematicians. The law of primogeniture was 'the law against every law of nature' and made anyone who believed in it incapable of understanding 'distributive justice' let alone administering it. The lords, Paine preached, were inbred and degenerate, 'shrinking into dwarves' when set beside the true nobility of natural man. They might well trace their descent to the Normans: they were, he wrote, echoing the Levellers, French invaders who had enslaved the English people and had kept them in humiliating subjection ever since.

His practical alternatives were complicated. The Holy Trinity might be anathema to Priestley, but Paine found magic in the number. He suggested a single chamber of 300 members, with a general election every three years. At the end of each year, a third would stand down and there would be by-elections. To avoid the need for a revising chamber, he suggested that in discussing any Bill, the 300 members should divide into three, with two-thirds listening as the others debated it. Then all 300 would vote.

The third model was proposed by William Godwin. Described by one recent historian as the most dangerous 'solvent of tradition', he was out to melt the Shining Ladder in pure Reason. Like Priestley, he was close to the Whig Establishment, and when his expensively priced *Political Justice* appeared, Pitt is alleged to have stopped an order to prosecute him on the grounds that a three-guinea book could 'never do much harm' among those who couldn't spare three shillings.

It certainly scored a direct hit with the Romantic poets. Godwin's own son-in-law, Shelley, inflamed by his beautiful dream of everyone being equal and everyone being in charge, immediately planned to found such a 'pantisocracy' in America by the banks of the Susquehanna. Coleridge composed a sonnet praising Godwin's 'holy guidance'. Wordsworth wrote to say he was convinced that 'hereditary distinctions and privileged orders of every species' could only stand in the way of human improvement.

Members of the House of Lords, Godwin believed, were at a natural disadvantage, excluded by birth from facing the kind of challenge that generated ability or virtue and built moral muscle. They could never, as Lord Reith would have said, be 'stretched'. They were therefore inferior to other people, their potential stifled by being too rich to have to work. Worse, by hogging all the money and property, the Lords condemned ninety-five per cent of the rest of mankind to be beasts of burden, when they might have developed their minds to the advantage of society.

Godwin's new world would not only do away with hereditary rulers and the Lords, but ultimately with all government. Government might be necessary in rare circumstances, but it was always evil: it perpetuated past abuses and was always opposed to change. He quoted Paine's first book, *Common Sense*, blaming the invention of government on human wickedness, but went further: government, he said, was the major *cause* of human wickedness. Keen to limit it to a minimum, he proposed a single National Assembly. It would meet, except in the case of the direst emergency, for not more than one day a year. If its members were not sure of something, they would discuss it again and, if necessary again, until they agreed.

Like all Horizonists before and since, Godwin was sure that human wickedness, if not government, would wither away in the purifying light of the new dawn, in his case the rising sun of Reason: 'With what delight must every well-informed friend of mankind look forward to the dissolution of political government, of that brute engine, which has been the perennial cause of the vices of mankind.'

All three prophets described how their hearts beat high at the news of the French Revolution – a feeling even shared by many of the House of Lords who saw Monsieur Frog as the traditional enemy and considered the Versailles regime badly in need of constitutional reform – and all three published major works within months of it breaking out.

As the extent of constitutional change in France became clear, there was a clamp-down. Lord Eldon, the Lord Chancellor, took on the political clubs, instituting so many prosecutions for libel and high treason that as one satirical commentator put it, 'Foreigners must have been induced to think that society in England was on the point of being broken up.' Among the first he prosecuted was Thomas Hardy, the plodding and respectable secretary of the Constitutional Society.

Eldon had come, as we have seen, from humble beginnings and he had slipped into law almost by accident, having suddenly to support a wife after a whirlwind elopement. But no one was a more passionate believer in the Shining Ladder and he was prepared, in his imagination at least, to face martyrdom in its defence. 'I would rather lay down my life on the scaffold,' he once claimed, 'than be a party to any measure for subverting the ancient institutions of my country.' His condemnation of Thomas Hardy and the Societies went on for seven hours. Erskine, the future Whig Lord Chancellor, spoke for the defence, and the case was dismissed.

But tough government triumphed, and in 1795 the Treasonable and Seditious Practices Act was passed, in response to a stone or an early airgun pellet – nobody ever established which – that cracked the window of George III's carriage on the way to the State Opening of Parliament. The purpose of the Act was not only the 'ultimate suppression' of any literature that favoured 'the confiscation and division of the land, and the extinction of the funded property of the Kingdom'. It also envisaged the destruction of the Societies. Except for university lectures, the Act banned any meeting of more than fifty people, unless it had been publicly announced at least five days in advance, the notice bearing the signatures of seven householders – which provided the authorities with seven property-owning hostages. If fifty or more people did meet, the magistrate had his instructions: he was to tell them that their Sovereign Lord the King charged and commanded them immediately to disperse themselves and peaceably to depart to their habitations or to their lawful business on pain of death, concluding with the words 'God save the King'. If more than twelve were still there at the end of an hour they were to 'suffer death'.

Death was also specified for anyone hindering the magistrates, and if anyone was killed or maimed in the crush the magistrates bore no responsibility. There were heavy fines on any house or room that was used for political meetings.

The Societies were also under heavy attack by the patriotic 'Church and King' mobs. On 14 July 1791, Joseph Priestley took the chair at a dinner organized by the Birmingham Constitutional Society to celebrate the fall of the Bastille, held early to avoid trouble, after which the Society's members went home. Finding them gone, the mob rioted for three days, wrecked Priestley's Unitarian chapel and burned his library, shouting, 'Death to all abettors of the French rebellion!' 'No Olivers!' and 'God save the King!'

The Terror in France shook the faith of all but the most devout Bright Horizonists. Tom Paine was actually a member of the French Assembly, working with a permanent interpreter, and nearly went to the guillotine. Many of his supporters, while opposing British intervention in France as reactionary, were still appalled by the news from Paris. Aristocratic heads and, more terrifyingly, twenty times as many middle- and working-class heads falling higgledy-piggledy into the basket at the foot of the guillotine were not part of the holy vision promised by the prophets, when Reason would reign supreme.

The third Earl of Stanhope, the eccentric peer who preached republicanism even in the House of Lords and liked to sign himself Citizen Stanhope, was chairman of the Society for Commemorating the English Revolution. In 1789 he had been sent to Paris with a congratulatory address to the National Assembly. Now he was less sure. Having given up his carriage at the Fall of the Bastille to be on an equal footing with the people, he was now persuaded by his wife to buy a new one, but insisted that there should be no armorial bearings on the panels.

Lord Lansdowne, who had welcomed the end of the 'Orders' in France – the old hierarchy of King, Lords and Commons – and believed that French peers would make more impact in an elected assembly, began to receive distressing letters from his friend the Abbé Morrelet. Everyone he knew, Morrelet wrote – whole families, people he had loved all his life, those with whom he had hoped to spend his old age – was dying on the scaffold, martyrs to Horizonist fanaticism.

With the resumption of war with France, the Horizonist faithful faded away, and by 1800 both the Societies and the radical political theologians were silent. When the war ended, they were back, more alarming than before. Priestley, Paine and Godwin were reprinted, their ideals expressed by Jeremy Bentham as 'the greatest happiness of the greatest number'.

It did not promise much happiness for the hereditary few.

CHAPTER FIFTEEN

Port In A Storm

Of all the great debates in which the Lords have argued for their right to exist, by far the most dramatic and theatrical was the Second Reading of the Reform Bill in October 1831. Its climax, at the end of five astonishing days and nights in the unbearably stuffy atmosphere of the overheated White Chamber, was a speech by the Lord Chancellor, Henry Brougham. It went on for two and a half hours and ended with the Lord Chancellor collapsing on his knees, blind drunk.

The Lords were now in a new home. In 1801, to accommodate the new Irish representative peers at the time of the union with Ireland, they had moved from the Queen's Chamber into what was known as the White Hall or the White Chamber, lying parallel to the river and joining the west end of St Stephen's Chapel to the west end of the Painted Chamber.

It had been repainted in dark red; it was eighty feet long and forty feet wide, with round-topped windows high up under a barrel-shaped roof, and there was a grandiose new velvet canopy at the north end over the Throne, supported by slender gilded columns. The Hall had been extended at one end, and it was hung with the famous Armada Tapestries that since James I's day had hung in the Painted Chamber. There was a fireplace in the middle of one wall to the right of the Throne.

The remaining benches were arranged as today, facing each other across the Chamber, with a block of cross-benches opposite the clerks' table, the Woolsack and the Throne. Behind them, below the Bar, there was standing room for about a hundred and fifty people. At night Lord Grey described it as 'lit by the glimmering of a sepulchral lamp to the dead'.

The crisis that brought Brougham to make his great speech was the climax of a long series of troubles. At the end of the Napoleonic Wars there had been a slump. There was already mass unemployment brought about by primitive new technology, steam power and machines in the factories. Soldiers, whose limbs had been torn off by cannon or paralysed by musket fire, risked imprisonment for begging. Petty theft was regularly punished with seven years' transportation to the floggings of Botany Bay.

In such an atmosphere the Societies revived. Huge protest rallies were organized and there was mass refusal to pay taxes. Haystacks were set on fire, machines were smashed, Bristol was sacked, and Birmingham, which thirty years before had rioted for Church and King, armed itself for a workers' revolution. Rioters broke the windows of both Houses of Parliament.

Mysteriously, though, the House of Lords attracted little printed criticism: the focus of the people's rage was the House of Commons.

Most political theologians, perhaps because of the religious excesses by Horizonists in France, were less extreme than they had been before the war. Re-examining, in the now less reliable light of Reason the old structure of King, Lords and Commons, they came to the conclusion that the Ladder served a useful purpose in maintaining public order. The machine need not after all be scrapped. It had a fault, but the fault could be repaired.

The three parts of the machine, the rationalist political mechanics decided, had become entangled. Monarchy and the Aristocracy were recognizably everything they had been intended to be, although they might not be to everyone's taste. Democracy, on the other hand, the Commons, had lost its independent popular drive. It betrayed the influence of the other two estates, particularly of the Lords. As Swift had pointed out a hundred years earlier, the depopulated medieval boroughs – the example always quoted was Old Sarum, then a heap of stones, which returned a Member of Parliament – put unjustifiable power in the Commons into the hands of the peers who owned these so-called Rotten Boroughs. In many constitutencies there was often no contest. When Brougham won the county of Westmorland for the Whigs in 1818, it was the first election there for fifty years.

Many defended the status quo. John Wilson Croker said that aristocratic influence in the Commons gave the system 'a certain elasticity, which has acted like springs, and prevented violent collision with the Crown and the House of Lords: take away these springs and we must run the risk of jostling and destroying each other'. Not so the Lords. When it came to reforming the House of Commons, they almost welcomed calls for redrawing constituencies and redistributing seats. Demand had been building steadily for more than a century, but successive Tory governments had refused to do anything about it. When Pitt had tried in 1785, the Bill had been thrown out. Even in the terms used by the Birmingham Political Union, founded in 1830 by Thomas Attwood, the reforms seemed harmless enough to the House of Lords. The Union planned 'to obtain by every just and legal means such a reform in the Commons House of Parliament as may ensure a real and effectual representation of the lower and middle classes of the people in that House'.

At first only a few reactionaries in the Lords saw the danger, expressed by John Wilson Croker to Peel in 1822: 'The day which reforms the House of Commons, dissolves the House of Lords, and overturns the Church.'

The run-up to the great debate had begun in 1820, when the first Reform Bill was debated in the Commons. Many members of the Upper House encouraged their minions in the Commons to support it, and the Bill went through, despite Tory derision, by a majority of one. Then the penny dropped. It was only as the Bill's clauses were picked over in detail before the Lords' committees that the Tory peers began to realize how much they stood to lose. All the boroughs in Schedule A, in which many owned land and enjoyed the right to appoint their own man to the House of Commons, would 'cease to return any member or members to serve in Parliament'. Cities like Birmingham, now apparently brimful of Bright Horizonists, would send representatives to Westminster for the first time. The Lords rejected the Bill and the Government fell.

More riots followed: petitions were delivered on rolls of paper so huge that they had to be brought into the Parliament Chamber in wheelbarrows. The Whigs deselected those in the party who had voted against the Bill and replaced them with their allies. Some opponents of reform actually sold their seats back to the Whig whips who resold them at a higher price to reformers, using the profit to run the election campaign. With a strengthened majority, the Whigs brought in a second Reform Bill which, after forty nights in committee, was approved in the Commons by a majority of 109. They sent it to the Lords for their approval.

In declaring they would resist reform, the Tory peers had now succeeded in turning themselves from a generally tolerated, even respected institution into the focus of national hatred. They were under real physical threat: the Birmingham Union claimed it had the men and funds to raise an army twice the size of Wellington's at Waterloo, and was not alone in its determination to defeat 'the oligarchy'.

Brougham, the new Lord Chancellor, came to the debate with a reputation as a brilliant Edinburgh lawyer who had defended Queen Caroline thirteen years earlier. Then he had spoken to the Lords in a way that, had they taken the trouble to think about it, might have seemed disparaging. 'Save the country, my lords,' he had begged them at the trial, 'from the horrors of catastrophe. Save yourselves from this peril. Rescue that country, of which you are the ornaments, but in which you can flourish no longer, when severed from the people, than the blossom when cut off from the roots and stem of the tree.'

Until then, any self-respecting member of the aristocracy might have thought of himself as an ornament, but never as blossom. The peerage, together with the monarchy, had always been the roots and the stem of the tree: why else the endless insistence on the spiritual relation, the links with the past, the unbroken succession, the authenticity of old families? But Brougham had turned the image of the family tree the right way up: authority no longer flowed down from above through the upturned roots and into the trunk, it came from below. The House of Lords represented decorative but vulnerable display, dependent on the economic vigour of the whole tree, and with memories of the French Revolution thirty years before, images of blossom being lopped were alarming.

As a young man, too, Brougham had been known to have 'strong republican feelings'. He was said still to be signing himself 'Henry Brougham' rather than 'Brougham', and these suspicions must have been confirmed when, later in the debate, he named his supporters, like the Duke of Bedford and the Duke of Devonshire, as 'my friends John Russell and William Cavendish'.

Above Brougham, on either side of the chamber in anticipation of a historically important debate, the draped wooden galleries brought in for the trial of Queen Caroline had been reinstalled. As Brougham looked up, he could see faces crammed together, listening and watching in the stuffy heat from the winter furnace. But his real audience, he knew, was a million times larger, waiting to read his words in the press and the parliamentary reports, circulated through the Societies. It was that audience, primarily, whom he was addressing. Both Holland and Grey described his speech afterwards as 'superhuman'.

Brougham faced a House that had panicked itself into an attitude of extreme reaction. The Earl of Carnarvon, who had at first welcomed reform, told the House that his noble friend Earl Grey's new allies, the 'twopenny trash' – the Birmingham Union and the working classes in general – would form the bulk of the electorate, and that this would lead inevitably to the seizure of their lordships' estates. Dr Allen, the Bishop of Bristol, accused as a younger man of feathering his nest from lucrative livings, said that the Bill was a dangerous infringement of the rights of ownership. Once started on that road, no property would ever be safe. The first Lord Wynford – once thought of as a liberal judge but now an ultra-Tory, who organized meetings of the Grand Orange Lodge inside the Palace of Westminster – said the Reform Bill meant universal suffrage, and universal suffrage meant universal plunder.

Lord Grey, who introduced the Bill, was seen by the ultra-Tories as another dangerous radical. As a young man in the Commons at the time of the French Revolution, he had belonged to a society called the Friends of the People, and had spoken against the Seditious Practices Act. 'If grievances are complained of, remove them, and all idea of sedition will at once be removed.' He was now sixty-seven and Cobbett accused him of bringing in the Bill 'under the stupid, the silly, the foppish, the childish, the coffee-house-club pretence of following "the spirit of the age".' According to an eye-witness he looked sick and nervous, and had gone down in his first sentence to the roars of the Tory lords. Their cheering, one Tory peer said afterwards, was 'thundering, and in a compact volley'. Not more than a handful of Whigs on the government benches had summoned up the energy to shout back.

But Grey had remained dangerous. When Dr Allen of Bristol had interrupted to accuse him of inflaming the people against the bishops, Grey had 'spoken to him in a tone of the most contemptuous severity, and, when he rose to interrupt, told him to be silent, as if he was speaking to a noisy child'. He had talked of the Rotten Boroughs as 'this gangrene of our representative system', and reminded the House that they had been debating their abolition for eighty years.

Lord Mansfield, heir to the Lord Chief Justice who had sat trembling on the Woolsack with his glasses broken fifty years before, another ultra-Tory, described by his friends as 'occasionally languid', answered. As a loyal Shining Ladderist, he compared the proposed reform to Henry VIII's dissolution of the monasteries. The Church had rights to its own land and the King had no business to 'parcel it out to his favourites'. Their right as landowners to send members to the Commons was equally sacred.

The Duke of Devonshire, a deaf, bookish bachelor, one of the richest men in the country who, as things stood, directly controlled five seats in the Commons, was one of the Bill's steadiest supporters. He presented a petition from Derbyshire in favour of reform and there was an ugly scene when the Marquess of Londonderry, famous for having once punched a wet-nurse, jumped up and shouted that one of the names on his petition appeared twelve times. Another was that of a child of three. The Duke denied it: some enemy of reform bent on discrediting the petition had tried to persuade a child of three to sign it, but the child had refused.

There was another prolonged squabble between the Catholic and very dim Duke of Norfolk, also presenting a petition in favour of reform from Worksop, and the Duke of Newcastle, who said, again true to the Shining Ladderist tradition, that it had been signed 'by Catholics and Protestant Dissenters'. Not so, said the Duke of Norfolk. The first signature, as it happened, was that of the Anglican vicar of Worksop.

After that the Duke of Wellington spoke. What he called the 'Close Boroughs' protected the landed interest against the commercial and manufacturing interest, and must be retained.

There then came two most poignant performances, both from very old men. They had both had dinner with the Duke of Cumberland, and Charles Greville in his *Memoirs* describes them before the debate began as being drunk 'not as Lords and Gentlemen sometimes are' but more 'like porters'.

The first was the ancient Lord Wynford. He had spoken in the earlier debate, and he was determined to speak again. He apologized for his 'poor and feeble efforts', but he was convinced that 'in the present great and dreadful crisis, it was the duty and the business of every man in the Empire to employ what little talents he might possess against this measure, which was 'pregnant with destruction to the best interests of the country at large'. Here Lord Teynham, present holder of the peerage bought for ten thousand pounds from James I and a reformer, interrupted to suggest that Lord Wynford 'on account of his infirmities' might be more comfortable if he addressed the House sitting down, but despite further concerned interruptions, the old man continued for another eleven columns of *Hansard*, his ancient legs giving way only three columns before the end.

Lord Eldon, who followed him, was so drunk that he forgot to take his hat off. He was now eighty, reputed to have made a fortune out of his years on the Woolsack, and spoke in a low mutter. Only a small circle of peers sitting nearest to him, Wynford and his host at dinner, the Duke of Cumberland, could hear more than a few sentences of what he said. According to the parliamentary reporter, sitting nearer than those on the government side who complained, he was saying that he thought that on the score of age and infirmity he was entitled to still more indulgence than Lord Wynford, but he could not go to his grave without giving his opinion. The measure was most destructive to this country and was calculated to reduce, by its consequences, this, which had hitherto been the most glorious of all the nations upon earth, to that state of misery which now afflicted all the other countries of the world. 'I may be wrong,' he concluded. 'No man is more likely to be so from infirmity of mind, produced by the infirmities of age.'

Despite such longueurs, the Tories thought the debate was going their way. They had, they thought, 'much personality and violence of language and a good deal of talk about broken windows'.

It was now Brougham's moment. Where he spoke from remains

a subject of controversy. For the constitutional purists, he can only have spoken as Lord Chancellor from the left of the Woolsack. Eye-witnesses insist it was from the government front bench. If that was the case, he would have faced, on the opposition benches, the more moderate Tories: Wellington and the ultras would have been on his right, on the cross-benches facing the Throne, in all 199 Tory peers who were fierce defenders of the old House of Lords and its 'occult' power in the Commons. Behind him, in addition to an estimated hundred and fifty-odd Whigs and more broad-minded Tories, there were ranged, according to a poster in Bond Street, twenty-two million who wanted reform. Whether he would achieve it some of them were doubtful.

'The fact is,' one radical journalist wrote, the 'Chancellor goes down to the House of Lords to have some fun with the old ladies, to tumble about their robes, to disport with their gravities. He appears like a young Pickle [he was fifty-three] quizzing his great-grandmother and great-aunts, making sport of their antique habits, upsetting their revered china and roasting the parrot; and after he is tired, and the public somewhat scandalized at his amusing himself thus, out he comes with a sermon, professing his duty, and profound reverence and respect.'

This time he had taken the precaution of arming himself with two bottles of port mixed with spice and slices of lemon, which he entrusted to his friend Earl Bathurst who sat beside him. Bathurst's job throughout the speech was to refill Brougham's glass.

Brougham was not entirely sober when he began, in high oratorical style. The House of Lords, he said, stood 'on the brink of the most momentous decision that ever human assembly came to at any period of the world.

'If I had foreseen in my earliest years that I should live to appear here, to act as your adviser on a question of such awful importance, not only to yourselves, but to your remotest posterity, I should have devoted every day and every hour of that life to preparing myself for the task which I now almost sink under.'

He then adopted his Pickle tactics and went for the old ladies. It was the first stage of his plan, which was to isolate the reactionary peers as a remote, arrogant, hopelessly outnumbered caste, drawing their confidence from an entirely irrational religious faith. Few Lord Chancellors can ever have been so offensive to the Lords to their faces. He compared the Tory peers to cooks struggling to get into the kitchen; he mocked their use of Latin tags and supercilious epigrams; he analysed their voting record. Most of the opposition to reform, he told them, did not come from the ancient families who could trace their titles back to the Norman Conquest – though even Norman blood came in for a certain amount of ridicule – but from jumped-up recent creations of the kind Pitt had 'rained down in scores' on loyal party hacks in the House of Commons. More offensively, he compared them to the Nabob Wallajh Cawn Bahauder, who could buy an estate in the country and a British Member of Parliament to go with it. Most offensively of all, he asked for their sympathy. He had abandoned a lucrative career in the law and a respectable Yorkshire seat in the Commons to come and work in what he implied was a second-rate institution.

His main attack, though, was on those who controlled the Rotten Boroughs. Without the Lords meddling in the Commons, Brougham told them, the slave trade would have been abolished years sooner, and we should have made a better and an earlier peace in the American War of Independence.

'Talk now of the principles of property, the natural influence of great families, the sacred rights of the aristocracy, the endearing ties of neighbourhood, the paramount claims of the landed interest! Talk of British duties to discharge, British trusts to hold, British rights to exercise!' What was to prevent any foreign prince like the Nabob with sufficient money – 'a heap of star pagodas too massive to be carried along' – from buying the title deeds to a few long-abandoned villages which retained the right to return a Member to the Commons? Its gates, Brougham assured them, would 'fly open to receive his well-disciplined band'.

Like the Nabob, peers commanded 'well-disciplined' Members of Parliament who would always vote exactly as their masters told them. He attacked one noble family who had commanded Members in the Commons so well disciplined that they could switch from one party to another and back again: such small forces, he said, sometimes decided the outcome of a battle. He took perhaps the greatest risk in the entire speech by suggesting that the Duke of Wellington might have lost the battle of Waterloo if Grouchy had arrived in time.

Many peers present that night, he reminded them, had been such well-disciplined but far from gallant MPs, voting as Mr Pitt had told them to: 'Service without a scar in the political campaign, constant presence in the field of battle at St Stephen's Chapel, absence from all other fights, from Blenheim to Waterloo, but above all steady discipline, right votes in right places, these are the precious, but happily not rare, qualities which have generally raised men to the peerage. For these qualities the gratitude of Mr Pitt showered down his baronies by the score, and I do not suppose he ever once so much as dreamt of ennobling a man who had ever been known to vote against him.'

These insults out of the way, he went on to answer their lordships' objections to the Bill. They had argued that it would unleash revolution. Brougham told them it would not unleash revolution, it would prevent it. It was not hasty; he quoted Swift, as a Tory like themselves, demanding the same reforms more than a hundred years before. He twitted Lord Wharncliffe, a famous bore, who had been quoted in the press as saying that he had gone into every shop in Bond Street and not found a single shopkeeper in favour of Reform. One had later explained that this was inevitable, as 'wealthy customers preferred that all things should remain as they were'. As soon as Lord Wharncliffe's words had appeared in the press, every shopkeeper in Bond Street had signed a petition in favour of the Bill. Wharncliffe had then been quoted as saying he had not meant Bond Street particularly, the same was true in St James's. This had produced an immediate denial in the press from all the shopkeepers in St James's. Brougham suggested that if Wharncliffe wanted to find a street with no friends of the Bill he would have to find one that was uninhabited.

Having abused their lordships for an hour, he refreshed himself with another swig, and took on a more conciliatory tone. He talked of the ancient Constitution. Had it been a fundamental principle of the ancient Constitution to have members without constituents? Boroughs without members? A representative Parliament without electors? He saw himself not as a reformer, but as restorer of those ancient rights.

He remembered the words of the Archbishop to George IV at his Coronation: 'Restore the things that are gone into decay; maintain that which is restored; purify and reform what is amiss; confirm that which is in good order.' He hinted that he had had a close friendship with the King, and said he had frequently reminded him of those words. He would restore, but he would also tell those who wanted to change too much, 'I have also sworn to maintain.'

He then returned to the attack. If they did not pass the Bill, there would be trouble. He accepted that they were within their constitutional rights to throw it out, but if they did so there would probably be a revolution, and all order would be destroyed.

At a time when horror stories were appearing in the press about explosions on early steamships, boiling the skin off the bloated pink bodies that were found floating among the debris, he offered the image of a reformed House of Commons as a safety valve: 'Where no safety valve is provided for popular discontent, to prevent an explosion that may shiver the machine in pieces, where the people are without a regular and systematic communication with the Legislature, refused a voice in naming those who make the laws they must obey, impose the taxes they must pay, where they feel the load of such grievances, and feel too the power they possess, moral, intellectual, and let me add, without the imputation of a threat, physical, then, and only then, are their combinations formidable. When they are armed by their wrongs, far more formidable than any physical force, then, and only then, they become invincible.'

This was the second part of his plan: having set up the Tory peers as a tiny, vulnerable minority of boobies, he was threatening them with 'the people', an ungovernable mob who would burn down their houses, drink their cellars dry, steal their silver, rape their wives and daughters and probably their lordships themselves. If the peers refused to pass the Bill, then Brougham – 'without the imputation of a threat' – would whistle them up and set them to their frightful work.

If they turned down the Bill now, they would lose the support of the country for ever. 'What, my Lords, the Aristocracy set themselves in a mass against the people? They who sprang from the people, are inseparably connected with the people, are supported by the people' – and, just when they might have expected some derisory reference to themselves as froth or blossom – 'are the natural chiefs of the people? They set themselves against the people, for whom Peers are ennobled, Bishops consecrated, Kings anointed?'

'The people' were a source of constant menace throughout his speech. Where did the unions and workers' movements come from, these 'musterings of men in myriads'? 'What power engendered these uncouth shapes, what multiplied the monstrous births, till they people the land?' That power was the same power that had engendered armed resistance in Ireland, that had torn the old empire in half and lost America. It was the power of justice denied, of rights withheld, of wrongs perpetrated. They could not go on treating nineteenth-century Englishmen like children, like barbarians, like natives in the South Seas.

Brougham's sense of fun never deserted him. At this point, he took another sip of negus, and put the tumbler down on the bench behind him, next to Bathurst. He had just begun to speak again, when it seemed suddenly to occur to him that it might be drunk by someone else, and he turned round, to general laughter, to retrieve it and put it more securely on the table in front of him where he could see it.

He then moved on to the third part of his assault, talking over the heads of the lords to those Brougham knew were their real masters, and his.

In threatening the Tory peers, Brougham employed a certain sleight-of-hand. Even at the height of the troubles police reports had identified a clear division: it was, as one cynical correspondent reported from Yorkshire, 'the war of No Property against Property'. Those with property were on the side of order and could ultimately be counted on to support the existing Establishment. Brougham's trick was to lump Property with No Property and call them 'the people'.

The people of No Property, having served their purpose as a bugaboo to frighten the Lords, Brougham now discarded as 'the populace' or 'the mob'. Was he a man, he asked their lordships, to bow down before that great Juggernaut? No, he was not. Then he switched the cards. 'But if there is the mob, there is the people also.'

One or two peers must have blinked at this, but it passed without interruption.

'I speak of the middle classes, of those hundreds of thousands of respectable persons, the glory of the British name, the wealth and intelligence of the country, the most numerous, and by far the most wealthy and important order of the community.'

Now Brougham produced his master-stroke. No Property, the 'populace', was against them, but so was Property.

When he talked about invincible armed combinations 'far more formidable than any physical force', he was not talking about starving men smashing windows, though he had managed to conjure them up in their lordships' imaginations as his shock troops: what he was talking about was the great grovelling middle class, which he was at that moment summoning up with bugle blasts of outrageous flattery to oppose their old masters. What was more, he was about to prove why they were invincible.

Put their lordships' castles, manors and broad acres in a pair of scales and weigh them against the 'vast and solid riches of the middle classes', Brougham roared, and the scales would tip with a crash in favour of 'the people'. The price, as he put it, would kick the beam.

It was a horrifying and obscene thing to have done. No amount of mockery, of stripping peers of their titles like the Gordon rioters stripping them of their wigs, could equal that effrontery. To reduce centuries of mystical and sacramental tradition to pounds, shillings and pence, to prove that the despised bourgeoisie could buy them up without noticing it was both terrible and prophetic.

Economically, the day of the House of Lords was over. Never again, in crude financial terms, would they be able beat the middle class, and they would be well advised to swallow their pride and join them. Joining them, of course, would mean welcoming even the lower-middle class to the voting booth, and that the Tory lords were showing themselves very reluctant to do. Householders owning property worth £20 a year they would accept; not, as the Bill was drawn up, worth £10.

He noticed that 'the master-key that unlocked the sluices of indignation on the Tory benches, and let loose the wildest cheers' was the idea that the Reform Bill would open the right of voting to vast numbers and interfere with the monopoly of the few. Would they begrudge the vote to householders with property worth £10 when that would give the vote, in a city of 18,000 inhabitants, to 300 men?

The temperature had now reached a stifling eighty-five degrees, and he was approaching the end both of his speech and of his second bottle of negus.

He conjured up finally the image of the Sibyl appearing at their gate and offering to sell them two volumes, Wisdom and Peace.

The price was reasonable, the restoration of the old constitution, a truly representative House of Commons. If they sent her away she would return with pages torn from both those volumes by lawless hands, and scrawled with blood. Then the price would be higher: Parliaments every year, universal suffrage, votes for the million. If she came back again who knew what she might take? Perhaps even, Brougham shouted with a wild gesture towards the Throne, the Mace from the Woolsack!

The House of Lords was the highest court in the land. He begged them to think before passing judgment on the Bill. 'As your friend, as the friend of my order, as the friend of my country, as the faithful servant of my Sovereign, I counsel you to assist with your uttermost efforts in preserving the peace, and upholding and perpetuating the Constitution.' He had finished the second bottle of port, and was, as one observer termed it, 'almost mad'.

'By all you hold most dear . . . I solemnly abjure you, I warn you, I implore you, yea, on my bended knees' – and here, after two and a half hours, his knees finally hit the floor – 'I supplicate you, reject not this Bill!'

They rejected it by 199 votes to 158, a majority of 41, of whom 21 were bishops.

Two days later a mob smashed all the windows of Londonderry House, and another burned down Nottingham Castle. One arms manufacturer was said to be offering to supply the Birmingham Union with 10,000 muskets at fifteen shillings each, and there were hourly rumours of a march on the capital.

According to Grey, Wellington's response to such threats was 'Ah, bah!'

Grey himself went to the King and asked him to create enough new peers to pass the Bill. Under this threat the peers passed it, but then wrecked it at the committee stage by voting an amendment by Lord Lyndhurst which would have meant indefinite delay.

Challenged to create the new peers, William IV havered, and Grey resigned. The King did however write to Wellington, Lyndhurst and other Tories offering the prospect of 'the Reform Bill with an addition to the peerage, or the Reform Bill without it.'

Called on to form a government, Wellington pledged himself for the first time, and very reluctantly, to introduce some kind of constitutional change. For five days the country was on the verge of war, and when Wellington proved unable to form a government, the King recalled Grey. When it came to the vote at the Third Reading in the summer of 1832, Wellington and a hundred other Tories walked out and the Reform Bill became law.

One Tory predicted that the reform movement would now gather pace, and sweep away the House of Peers within ten years.

CHAPTER SIXTEEN

A Turner Sunset

We were standing in front of a wall-painting in the Royal Gallery showing *Alfred in the Danish Camp*, a scene reminiscent of the battle of Maldon. Our guide was Lord Hesketh, plump, youthful and rosy-faced in a bright blue suit, well-polished shoes and red socks. As Tory chief whip in the House of Lords at a time when the post-Thatcher government was pursuing an openly pro-European policy, Lord Hesketh made no secret of his own alarm at the power of Brussels, and looked ruefully at the bearded Danes with their battle-axes, demanding the Danegeld. 'Early Maastricht stuff, what?'

Our tour of the whole Disney-theatrical set had been arranged, suitably enough, for an actor, Dan Aykroyd, the star of *Ghostbusters*. We had arrived at the Peers' Entrance, approached the doorkeeper, and said, almost in unison, 'We've come to see Lord Hesketh.' It sounded like a line from *The Wizard of Oz*.

We had reached his office by the little lift that spares elderly and infirm peers the effort of the climb up the stone stairs. The room was wood-panelled and Pugin-wallpapered, like every other room in the building, but full of cases of wine, and there were photographs on the walls of the Hesketh racing bikes – but 'Fatty' Hesketh owed his friendship with Dan Aykroyd, himself no wraith, to a shared interest in guns, weaponry and Unidentified Flying Objects.

Squelching along with the flat-footed delicacy associated with the overweight, Hesketh induced confidence in the way that only hereditary peers can. On the way through the book-lined corridors of the Lords, he greeted everyone we passed by their Christian name as if they were much-loved old servants or shooting chums. But Dan Aykroyd created the sensation. Doorkeepers and policemen who let dukes go by without a second glance stared goggle-eyed at the star of *Ghostbusters*. Doors flew open and little knots of people gathered behind us on the red carpet as we passed, whispering.

The Royal Gallery, where we stood, was designed by Barry as a tribute to the beauty of the old St Stephen's Chapel. Gilded statues of former kings and queens stand on carved marble plinths, sheltered by decorative wooden canopies of intricate Gothic design. Elaborately wrought gilded pillars rise to support carved and curving pillars under the gold-coffered ceiling. High stained-glass windows are filled with heraldic devices, and the floor is a rich mosaic of coloured tiles.

Hesketh waved an elegant hand over the gold pillars and tracery. 'This is all gold paint at the moment, redone after the war, and it's due to be restored with gold leaf. It'll look splendid.' During the Second World War a German bomb had destroyed most of the Commons Chamber. Lady Elliott, whose father had been born before the Reform Bill, could remember standing among the dust and fallen timbers the morning after and looking up at the sky. Painting the Royal Gallery gold had been considered important enough to be part of the emergency work, restoring the dignity. 'You see the Royal Gallery is really for ceremonial. You have to picture me in Wellington boots, a waistcoat, and a long frock coat, with this helmet with plumes on under one arm, and in the other hand I have a silver-knobbed cane.' He retold the story of the State Opening. Dan Aykroyd listened, as if to a director outlining a comic scene in a costume movie.

The Royal Gallery is built roughly on the site of the old Painted Chamber, where the first division of Lords and Commons had occurred in 1341, and where joint sessions of the first English Parliaments had met at dawn to hear the Speech from the Throne and to consider the requests of the Lower House.

Of the many ghosts said to people the new Palace of Westminster, most hover about the site of the old Palace. In October 1987 in the West Front Corridor of the Lords, somewhere near the site of the White Chamber where Brougham made his great speech, a tough old Scotsman on patrol reported a 'drifting grey figure'. In March 1993 a horse's head, 'white, with a haze round it', started out of the wall of the darkened crypt of St Stephen's Chapel before the widening eyes of a security man whose torch had gone out. It was followed by the whole horse, bearing a spectral rider in a leather jerkin and boots, exuding the smell of sweat and hot leather.

There was a mischievous spirit at the Commons end, which is built on a concrete raft over what used to be the Thames, who produced an alarming drop in temperature and kicked a security man in the seat of the pants, not to mention the 'bald-headed little man in Elizabethan costume sitting on the roof of the Victoria Tower writing in a book with a quill pen' who so terrified a sandblaster during the restoration work that he abandoned the job unpaid and returned to Birmingham.

Lord Hesketh would probably still have been standing in the ancient chamber, looking up at the medieval paintings of saints and angels in the coffered roof, if it had not been for the complacency of both Houses of Parliament in 1789.

Westminster Hall had been extensively rebuilt at the end of the fourteenth century, raising the level of the walls and fixing a line of heraldic shields just below the new hammerbeam roof, built of English oak. The inside had accumulated bookshops, law-stationers, dress shops and even toy shops, as well as the enclosed King's Bench and Chancery Courts. All were vulnerable when the Thames flooded.

Outside the walls of the old Palace stood a jumble of buildings. The earliest were of timber, wattle and daub and thatch, the later ones in brick and tiles, but all had been added on, like modern Portakabin extensions, to answer some immediate need. All were heated by open fires, with flues fitted into crevices in the old stone walls and cut through rotten wooden rafters in the palace roof.

In 1789, a committee of architects was appointed to make a thorough survey of the Palace. They condemned the entire range of buildings. Westminster Hall, St Stephen's Chapel, the White Chamber, the Painted Chamber and the Queen's Chamber were beyond repair and too dangerous to use for fear of fire. They recommended total demolition, the building of two new debating chambers and more practical accommodation for the offices of government. Nothing happened.

James Wyatt was employed to extend St Stephen's Chapel.

He hacked out panelling at the west end to reveal medieval wall-paintings of extraordinary beauty, preserved from the light for centuries. He immediately gave orders for them and the walls they were painted on to be demolished. Shocked, architects and antiquarians rushed to make coloured sketches of them. Some showed knights in armour with coats powdered with *fleur-de-lis* kneeling in *trompe-l'oeil* niches. Others, more primitive, showed the King and his court on a floor of geometrical coloured tiles. Those at the west end showed scenes from the Old Testament with three angels displaying beautifully patterned cloths.

For the first time, artists and aesthetes seemed to realize the value of the old Palace. St Stephen's Chapel, beneath its seventeenth-century panelling by Sir Christopher Wren, they now knew to be a medieval shrine in brilliantly painted plaster and glazed tiles.

Wyatt's extension was built in concrete and composition stone to save money, incorporating a new west window in a vaguely Gothick style, and two mock-medieval turrets, also in composition stone. Purists denounced him as a Philistine.

But despite the growing awareness of many educated Englishmen that both Houses of Parliament and much of the civil service were billeted in a treasure-house, nothing was done to move government offices or to secure them against damage. In 1834, in the wake of the Reform Bill, efforts were being made to overhaul some of the legal work done by the House of Lords. There was to be a new and entirely separate Court of Bankruptcy, and the only available space was in the Tally Room of the old Court of Exchequer. It was stacked with flat sticks about eighteen inches long, known as tallies, which had been used in medieval times as primitive cheque-stubs, split in half to be matched against the missing section when a debt was repaid to the Exchequer.

On 16 October that year Irish workmen had cleared out the tallies and were burning them in a furnace that heated the Queen's Chamber. More were stacked nearby, which began to smoulder.

Later that morning visitors to the Queen's Chamber complained of the floor being alarmingly hot, and at half past three in the afternoon the housekeeper, Mrs Wright, found the room full of smoke. The workmen told her what they were doing, which reassured her, and at half past six she locked up and went home. Within minutes the old building exploded in flames. By seven most of the Queen's Chamber and the roof of the Painted Chamber were burning with what one journalist called 'irresistible fury'. Soon after seven the roof of the White Chamber fell in with a crash audible from the other side of the Thames. A wind was blowing, and the fire spread rapidly, reaching St Stephen's Chapel with its Wren panelling and ancient timbered roof. By half past seven the core of the old Palace was a wall of flame, sweeping back and forth in the wind, scattering sparks high into the clear sky, with the moon showing only fitfully through the smoke.

By this time a train of carriages and carts was turning into Old Palace Yard, and everything that could be rescued in the way of records, furniture and pictures was thrown down from the upper windows and carted away.

On the other side of the Thames, Turner arrived with an easel, watercolours and a pad of paper, and began painting what he saw: the river in front of him a brilliant reflection of the furnace-flame, the bridges crowded with people watching, smoke drifting towards him, the silhouette of the old medieval Palace showing through. To the north, and still untouched by the flames, was the long roof of Westminster Hall, and beyond it the towers of Westminster Abbey, glowing red in the light of the fire.

Pugin thought it was 'a glorious sight' to see Wyatt's 'composition mullions and cement pinnacles flying and cracking', while 'the old walls stood triumphantly amidst the scenes of ruin'.

The most dramatic scenes took place inside Westminster Hall, lit by the blaze through the high south window: long ladders buckling under the weight of soldiers and firemen climbing upwards with buckets, as others strained over handpumps, spraying water upwards on to the great hollow barrel of the roof-timbers.

With the exception of Westminster Hall, every part of the old medieval Palace was gutted.

When Parliament met again three months later in February 1835, William IV offered the Commons Buckingham Palace, but the Prime Minister thought the size of its rooms would encourage too many spectators, and they continued to meet among the boarded-up ruins under tarpaulins and makeshift roofs. Sir John Soane actually began work on a scheme to restore the old buildings, completing a new Lords' Library and a ceremonial stairway near the river.

A joint committee decided that architects should be asked to compete for the design of an entirely new palace: the new building should be either 'in the Elizabethan or the Gothic style'. They had to look at nearly fifteen hundred drawings from Greek temples to Renaissance palaces, any one of which could have shaped our democracy for centuries to come.

The winners were Barry and Pugin. During the twenty-odd years it took to build the new Palace, rumours ran wild about whose was the real mind behind it, but it seems safe to say that Barry, with his architectural skill and knack with committees, was responsible for the building, and Pugin for the design and decoration. Their original scheme was simpler than the building that was finally completed. The site was cleared, leaving only Westminster Hall and the Jewel Tower. Between them there began to rise Barry and Pugin's fantasy of medieval Gothic. It was rich in gargoyles, battlements and coats-of-arms, and owed a lot to Sir Robert Walpole's son Horace and his early-eighteenth-century romantic house at Strawberry Hill.

By 1842 the building was far enough advanced to consider the decoration, though Arthur Hallam complained that Barry 'had so bescutcheoned and encrusted the Houses there was little room for painting'. Another competition was staged to find suitable painters, with Prince Albert chairman of the judges. No one was more cruelly disappointed than Benjamin Robert Haydon, the original starving artist of Victorian London, who had dreamed all his life of painting great patriotic subjects. As early as 1812 a pupil remembered him jumping up to point with his umbrella at the wall of Westminster Hall and shouting, 'This is the place for Art!' In 1819 he made sketches. Soon after the fire he called on Lord Melbourne, suggesting murals for the new House of Lords. Melbourne laughed and said there was no sense in painting 'a room for deliberation', but Haydon persisted. His plan was to 'rouse the people, showing the best government by exhibiting the consequences of the worst'.

His scheme for the House of Lords embraced Anarchy (Italian Banditti, Despotism), the Burning of Rome, Revolution (the Tumbrils), then turned to Moral Right, the Jury System, and Limited Monarchy (King, Lords and Commons). Melbourne didn't like the idea of the French Revolution as it would offend the French government. When the competition was announced Haydon threw himself into work, torn between a picture of the Black Prince and one of Adam and Eve, cheering himself on to patriotic fervour. While 'steaming' the cartoons he scalded his foot, and limped down to Westminster

Hall to deliver them. They were rejected. He was generous about *Alfred in the Danish Camp*. It was by Daniel Maclise, an Irishman who had graduated from the Royal Academy fifteen years earlier with a reputation for big historical subjects.

The first painting to be started was Dyce's *The Baptism of St Ethelbert*, which occupied the centre panel of the south wall of the Parliament Chamber, above the present vacuum cupboard and behind the Throne.

Prince Albert was convinced that all the paintings should be in fresco, painted on wet plaster, and Daniel Maclise was commissioned to make one for the Parliament Chamber of *The Spirit of Chivalry*. This showed a woman in white holding a laurel wreath, and surrounded by symbolic figures: War, a king in full armour wearing a coronet, and Religion, an archbishop consecrating a statesman representing Civil Government. The young woman was defended by the Spirit, a young knight, his belt embroidered with the oath *A dieu et aux dames*. Fresco had been thought of as a lost art, and had only recently been revived. Maclise was soon in trouble. Used to working in oil on canvas, he used too much paint, which formed a crust vulnerable to the air, and mistakes could not be corrected. Cracks formed between each day's work, making the whole effect look like a patchwork or mosaic.

Haydon, whose view was perhaps jaundiced, found the experiments in fresco disappointing. 'All the flesh looks as if dipped in a tan-pit. There are no reflections, and the effect is hot and offensive, and dirty; black, sooty, as if painted with boiled fish-eyes.'

Defeated, Maclise suggested oil on wooden panels, but Prince Albert was set on fresco. Oil would shine, and was too perishable. Wood warped and twisted. Fresco was made to last a thousand years. He sent Maclise to Germany to study the 'stereochromic' method of a Dr Fuchs in Nuremberg. Maclise went, then travelled on to Berlin to watch experiments with zinc oxide and a solution of flint.

That was by no means the end of his troubles. The stained glass in the vast windows of the Parliament Chamber had already been put in: on cloudy days he could barely see what he was doing; in bright sunlight he found his painting patterned with the colours from the glass.

The Royal Gallery had wall-paintings connected with military victories, the Queen's Robing Room with chivalry and knightly virtues, the Conference Chamber with the noblest exploits in connection with the acquisition of our colonial empire. Those in the peers' refreshment rooms illustrated the chase during the Plantagenet period, when hunting was a baronial amusement. As they were completed, the purpose of all this scenery became clear: it might look like an early exercise in Walt Disney Ruritanian kitsch, but it was a shrine to the Shining Ladder.

The new Palace was built during the 1830s and 1840s, a time of continuing social unrest which culminated in the European Year of Revolutions in 1848. On the part of those in power at least there was a strong sense of nostalgia for what Richard Trench had called the spiritual relation, the romantic vision of a pre-industrial world, the imagined security of a legendary past in which everyone knew their place. It celebrated continuity, its family crests in stone, stained glass and carved wood emphasizing the unbroken link with an imaginary age of gold, the guarantor of order. 'One day's devotion to the frescoes of Westminster under a tolerable guide,' *The Times* wrote when the new Palace was opened, 'will make any member of the public quite learned in the principal events which have fashioned the institutions and given the deciding stroke to the destinies of his country.' He would see 'the sturdy Norman chase', chivalry and devotion, 'the quarrelsome Plantagenets and their Baronial Wars', the evolving role of the Crown, the Church and the Commons. He could look up at British heroes 'fighting battles which have decided the fates of empires, now making discoveries which have thrown the light of civilization over barbarous lands'. He would see Britain 'instructing the savage, abolishing barbarous rites and liberating the slave'.

Against that, the ground plan of the new building was laid out in a way that would appeal to any good Horizonist or believer in horizontal order. Beneath the ornamentation, it was a remarkably efficient and functional public building, concentrating what had been a rabbit-warren of semi-detached courts, halls and houses into a single block of offices and committee rooms arranged round the two council chambers.

Lord Hesketh, our own easily tolerable guide, saw it as a well-designed piece of constitutional machinery. He was, by inclination, an engineer. His passion in life was motorbikes, and he had always been controversial. Questioned privately at a time he was Heritage

Minister – one of the few ministers to sit in the Lords – about a quarry he was opening in some environmentally sensitive area on his estate, he amused his friends by throwing his arms in the air and shouting, 'New policy! Fuck the environment!' He also raised eyebrows, a few years earlier, when he was quoted by the journalist Tina Brown as having said that 'you could tell an English gentleman by the quality of his drugs'. He later denied this.

Stepping back now from the wall-painting of *Alfred in the Danish Camp*, he asked us to look north, through the big doors into the Prince's Chamber, situated directly behind the vacuum cupboard and the Throne. On our left, he told us, was the haunted West Front, facing Westminster Abbey, running from the Chancellor's Gate near the Victoria Tower past the Peers' Entrance, with the triangle of parked cars in front of it, to Westminster Hall and the statue of Oliver Cromwell. On our right was the East Front with its famous façade, the terraces overlooking the river, ending in the Speaker's House, Big Ben and New Palace Yard with its £2.5 million underground car park, five levels deep, dug out in the early seventies, and the restored medieval fountain found during the excavations.

The new building, he explained, laid out with absolute constitutional logic, was Parliament as described in the constitution: King, Lords and Commons. Behind us was the Queen's Robing Room, and we were standing in the Royal Gallery. This was the constitutional power source. In front of us were the Lords and the Commons. In theory, with all the doors open, you could sit on the Throne in the House of Lords with the red opposition benches on your left, the red Government benches on your right, the red cross-benches in front of you and, looking through the Lords' Lobby and the Central Lobby, see the Speaker's Chair with the green Government benches on your left, the green opposition benches on your right. The arrangement at the core of the Palace, with the two Chambers end to end of the Central Lobby, Lord Hesketh said, was exactly like a flat-bed horizontal accelerator.

I found the image almost as stimulating as that of the Vacuum behind the Throne: ideas accelerated by the oratory at both ends encased in Bills tied with green or red ribbon whizzing to and fro, transformed by a process of political physics into law by the shared power source, and plugged into the Throne. Knowing him to be an expert on motorbikes, I didn't think of asking him what a flat-bed horizontal accelerator was. Later, when I rang the Science Museum to ask, they said they'd never heard of such a thing. 'It's like a flat-bed horizontal accelerator,' he repeated confidently, 'with the energy coming from both ends and creating an explosion in the middle: Commons at one end, Lords at the other, between them the Central Lobby.'

Lord Hesketh took us next to the wide windowless passage that runs parallel to the Lords' Chamber, and which, when the Division Bell rang, had its decorative Gothic doors locked at either end to transform it into the Government Lobby. Into this the peers shimmer to register that they are 'Content'. Walking through it just after the doors are reopened is like passing through Harrods' scent and body-spray department. 'This,' Lord Hesketh said, 'is where I work. I suppose there are about a thousand peers, of whom four hundred ever turn up. Actually four hundred is the highest ever except on very special occasions, but I think it may have something to do with the recession and daily allowances. If you attend regularly and you live outside London you can make a hundred and forty pounds a day. Only about two hundred and forty peers really vote.'

He stood at the end of the Lobby, the film director conjuring up the scene. 'I have two clerks who stand *here* and *here* writing down the names, and I stand *here* with a clicker and an ivory rod, going click, click, click.' The clicker and the clerks were relatively recent introductions. There had been a famous moment in 1680, during a division on Habeas Corpus, when Lord Norrey and Lord Grey were acting as tellers and things got out of hand. Lord Grey saw a peer infinitely fatter than Lord Hesketh waddling past him and, for a joke, counted him as ten. Somehow this was included in the final tally and the vote went the wrong way. 'We're meant to be in here for six minutes, but the only official means of knowing is a Victorian egg-timer, and in hot weather I can tell you the sand runs very slowly indeed.'

We set off along another corridor. Suddenly and dramatically Lord Hesketh pressed a section of Pugin wallpaper, which swung open to reveal the Lords' Tea Room. Painted on the walls were the Scenes of the Chase, making it look like the tea room of an old-fashioned seaside hotel. There was a dim murmur of conversation, some family parties, and a well-known Eurosceptic beauty canvassing the support of a notoriously randy old peer, Lord Jay. Cheery waitresses in black dresses, white aprons and white caps bustled between the tables, licking bits of pencil and writing orders on little pads. To my amazement our waitress did not recognize Dan Aykroyd but was all over Lord Hesketh. She was Irish, and she suggested the full tea with the legendary House of Lords crumpets, square for some reason rather than round; she particularly recommended what she called the an*chovy* toast.

It was shortly after the first separation of the Prince and Princess of Wales, long before any revelations had appeared in the press about Diana's private life, and another young hereditary peer leaned over to whisper to Hesketh in a voice that carried half across the room, 'You do realize that carnal knowledge of the Princess of Wales is High Treason? The Tower, chopping block, the whole business!'

Lord Hesketh's eyebrows shot up in innocent Bunterish surprise. 'Why are you telling *me* that?'

The other glanced round the room. 'Well, one of the chaps here is bound to take a crack at her some time and I thought you ought to know.'

Hesketh said he would look into it, and met my eye unflinchingly. 'I suppose you think I paid him to come up and say that.'

The waitress returned with an armful of tea things which she banged down on the table. The an*chovy* toast was off, but they had some very nice scones, would his lordship like those? His lordship said he would, and the conversation turned to life on other planets: Aykroyd's real interest, beyond guns, was Flying Saucers.

In 1979 the House of Lords became the first and last legislative chamber on earth to discuss Unidentified Flying Objects. The debate had been scheduled for half past seven in the evening, a traditional time for eccentrics to speak to the empty red benches when everyone else has gone off for a drink before dinner. On this occasion the Chamber was packed. When Lord Hewlett stood up to try to pour rational cold water on their airy dreams he was – by the standards of impeccable good manners obtaining among the lords – almost howled down. Like the early Shining Ladderists, who believed in the orders of angels, they were passionate. He described himself 'a veritable Daniel in the lions' den of UFO Believers', and he was given, as he himself protested in *Hansard*, 'a very rough time'.

The debate had been introduced by the Earl of Clancarty, a

member of the Ancient Astronaut Society, who was alleged from time to time to whisper to himself in a voice too soft to be heard. He was, he said, communicating with Higher Beings. He called on the Government to take action in exposing what he believed to be a concerted cover-up by London, Moscow and Washington. Before they were elected, Eisenhower, Johnson, Ford and Carter had all sworn to make public the secret records when they took office: each had broken that promise on becoming President.

Lord Clancarty recalled that Flying Saucers had been mentioned in a papyrus during the reign of Tutmose III in Egypt in the sixteenth century BC. He reminded their lordships of the bright cigar-shaped ship that had terrified peasants in the Middle Ages. He described nine gleaming crescents flying at high speed over the State of Washington in 1947, seven Flying Saucers buzzing a BOAC transatlantic flight in 1954, watched aghast by the pilot and many passengers. He spoke with real dread of a large glowing thing over Teheran in 1976 that had immobilized the controls of fighters sent up to intercept it. He demanded what he called an intra-governmental investigation.

Lord Trefgarne was more sceptical. He did not like the idea of other universes inhabited by other races. He was not aware 'that there was any suggestion in the words of Christ or in the words of the Almighty, as recorded, that we must share his goodness with people from another universe'. But he certainly took exception to a learned professor he had heard that morning speaking on the wireless. 'Anyone who believes in UFOs,' the professor had said, 'is a loony.'

The Earl of Kimberley, soon afterwards to marry for the sixth time, felt the need to declare an interest: he was director of a company that was to make an Unidentified Flying Object, to be identified as the Thermo Skyship. None the less, he had to remind them that the medieval monks of Byland Abbey had been terrified by a huge silver disc. UFOs, he said, 'defied worldly logic'. He had approached the Ministry of Defence. They had told him that UFOs were the responsibility of the BBC and the Post Office, and he found this unsatisfactory.

He was followed by a garrulous Welshman, Harold Wilson's former Parliamentary Private Secretary, Harold Davies, now Lord Davies of Leek. Just before he came into the Chamber, he said, he had been informed that a green ambassador eight feet six inches tall with webbed feet had asked whether he could park his flying saucer in the Lords' car park. Some of the older peers began to suspect Lord Davies of Leek of irony at their expense, but he went on to reassure them. Ordinary people had been laughed at, like the man in Pascagoula who fainted when he saw a chap with one leg jumping towards him with a wizened and wrinkled face, pointed ears and crab claws for hands. He himself had attended a scientific lecture in one of their lordships' committee rooms where a scientist had proved conclusively the existence of the Loch Ness Monster.

The Bishop of Norwich opened with a joke. What was a bishop doing, he asked rhetorically, 'moving among the various parts of this chequered chessboard'? He told them. Backing his arguments with lengthy quotations from Holy Scripture, he regretted what he called 'the religious aspects of the UFO situation'. There was a danger that interest in such things might obscure the central truth of the Christian story. He quoted from St Paul's Epistle to the Colossians: 'All things in heaven and earth, visible or invisible, whether thrones or dominions, or principalities or authorities [another version of the orders of angels] were created through him and for him.'

Lord Trefgarne got up to interrupt. What did he think about having to share God's love with other races?

The Bishop was not sure. God might have other plans for other worlds.

It was now nearly half past eight, and Lord Gladwyn rose to apologize that he would have to leave them shortly. He had entered into an obligation for the evening from which he found it difficult to escape. This did not stop him from filling five columns of *Hansard* with his random thoughts. Even travelling very fast indeed, he mused, creatures from the nearest galaxy would have been 'cooped up in their small machines' for something like five years. Would they come all that way to play some sort of cosmic joke on us?

The tail-coated attendants came and went, stooping to deliver urgent messages to the peers, and the theological debate rambled on. Lord Kings Norton mentioned a UFO in the Book of Ezekiel, coal-fired, stabilized by gyroscopes and crewed by cherubim, and complained about being lobbied by a religious group who thought, like the Bishop, that UFOs were anti-Christian. He quibbled with Lord Clancarty's demand for an 'intra'-governmental study. It should be 'inter'. 'Intra' meant 'within', and 'might smack of a secret probe'.

His place was taken by Lord Rankeillour, an even more devout believer. He described a 'fantastic air circus' that had been witnessed by the police and emergency services above Farmington, New Mexico, in 1950, when 'countless saucers performed aerial acrobatics at speeds of a thousand miles an hour, showing incredible handling, and acute control in split-second timing in their ability to avoid collisions'.

Then the Earl of Halsbury got up, grandson of the old Lord Chancellor. He was a distinguished scientist in his early seventies, and he admitted that as a child he had seen an angel. He dazzled their lordships with his extensive knowledge of astronomy and optical illusions. He told them how to create a mirage with a bunsen burner and a tray of sand, he discussed C. S. Lewis's ideas on other races in the cosmos, some tempted and fallen, some tempted and unfallen, but he won all their hearts when he told them his own theory about nature's mysteries: 'I have always thought that just as Mother, when baking bread, leaves a little of the dough over in order that the children may make funny little men with raisins for tummy buttons and put them into ovens and bake them alongside the bread or the cake for the day, so possibly on the day of creation a little of the Divine creative power was left in reserve for the lesser seraphim and cherubim to use, and they were allowed to make funny little objects like the Abominable Snowman and the Loch Ness Monster, and therefore by the grace of God since this is an orderly universe and a home is provided for everything, so the snows of Tibet were created for the benefit of the Yeti, and Loch Ness was created for the Monster.'

After that the debate had gone downhill. Lord Hewlett, an old-fashioned Horizonist, was listened to with impatience as he talked about the ten thousand pieces of broken-up space rockets known to be in orbit, the eight thousand million meteorites of one kind or another that entered the earth's atmosphere every year, and the constant vigilance of Jodrell Bank that had reported nothing but natural phenomena.

The Shining Ladderists, still convinced of the existence of higher orders of intelligence 'up there', accused Jodrell Bank of a cover-up.

Dan Aykroyd and Lord Hesketh were clearly of the same opinion. We finished our scones, drank our tea, our host settled the bill and, bowing graciously to tables left and right, led us off to complete our tour of the building.

He led us out through the Robing Room, with its squat oriental throne made for Queen Victoria as Empress of India, where all the peers assembled during the Second World War, having ceded the Parliament Chamber to the bombed-out Commons, and showed us his *pièce de résistance*. It was in David Cholmondeley's dark-wallpapered Lord Great Chamberlain's Room, and strictly, Lord Hesketh promised us, out of bounds. He laid a finger to his lips and opened another door. Inside, looking rather like the oriental throne in the Robing Room, was a squat little seat. Lord Hesketh lifted the mahogany lid and revealed the blue and white flower-patterned bowl of Queen Victoria's own private lavatory.

CHAPTER SEVENTEEN

A Naked Absurdity

By the beginning of the twentieth century most people believed that the old House of Lords, like comparable aristocratic survivals in Hungary and Spain, had had its day. In the preamble to the Parliament Act of 1911 the Liberals gave a solemn promise that all hereditary peers would be excluded from the Upper House 'within the term of the present government'. The debate on the Parliament Bill took place on the hottest day for seventy years. The red benches were packed. The Tories divided into the 'Hedgers', those prepared to compromise, and the 'Ditchers', led by the eighty-seven-year-old former Lord Chancellor, Lord Halsbury, who were prepared, they claimed, to die in the last ditch.

There were echoes of 1832, but what had then been a nightmare was now a reality. Brougham's threatened People had the vote in their millions, they exercised their power legally, and the middle classes, apparently satisfied that the Stock Exchange index rather than the old Shining Ladder represented order in society, were urging the People to destroy the Lords. Bright Horizonism, if not actually the ruling creed, was the orthodoxy to which even the peers were required to pay lip-service. It was the climax of a twenty-year campaign against the House of Lords, fought under the slogan 'End it or mend it.'

The young Winston Churchill had powerfully urged the second option. His mended House of Lords would be a senate of 250, nominated by each of the political parties for the term of each parliament, their party strength exactly matching the composition of the Commons. This, he wrote, would exclude 'frivolous, lethargic, uninstructed or disreputable elements', and would rebalance an Upper House that had become dominated by the Tories.

Until then they had been so frivolous, uninstructed and above all lethargic that it was a toss-up whether the House of Lords would come to a violent end or simply peter out: 'The pleasant walk across the lawns of St James's Park, the comfortable crimson benches inviting repose of body and mind alike, the certainty of getting home in good time to dress for dinner, and a season of immunity from her ladyship's notes and telegrams,' wrote the Liberal Whip, Lord Ribblesdale, about the brief parliamentary season, 'became matters of agreeable habit with an average of fifty to seventy peers.' Bagehot had warned the Lords in 1867 of the danger in being 'an assembly which did not assemble', but even seventy peers was just under 15 per cent of those entitled to take their seats. Most of those who came treated it more like school chapel than the Debating Society. It was a place to listen rather than to talk. 'There are,' the political correspondent of *Punch* wrote in the 1890s, 'some half-dozen whose opinion is looked for. This given, it remains only for the rest to vote. In the Lords, only the big men speak, and when they have had their say it is all over. If any outsider wants to make a speech, he finds himself without an audience, and so desists.'

Of all the 'big men' who controlled debates in the House at that time the biggest was the Tory Prime Minister Lord Salisbury. Bald, bearded and six foot two, he seemed to be living proof that the hereditary peerage worked. He was a Cecil, directly descended from Elizabeth I's first minister. Lying back on the Tory front bench, domed head gleaming, hirsute chin sunk on his chest, fist clenched, he dominated the scene, still grimly determined to defend the old system, with a cabinet largely composed of hereditary peers.

It was a battle he had been losing for many years. As a young minister in the Commons, he had written a series of articles opposing the Second Reform Bill of 1867, which planned to double the number of those allowed to vote and would include working men in the cities. His argument was that it would give power to what he called 'mere numbers'. In 'a healthy state of feeling', the community looked to an aristocracy to govern it. Any extension of the vote would reduce the role of the House of Lords to insignificance, and eventually to extinction. He justified the existence of the House of Lords partly on old-fashioned Ladderist principles. It was the remote and mystical focus of loyalty. It was, with the monarchy, the only force in society capable of stopping democracy 'splitting the country into a bundle of unfriendly and distrustful fragments'. But he was also prepared to redefine the meaning of 'aristocracy' in the light of what had happened to the House of Lords since 1832.

The qualifications for belonging to the aristocracy, he wrote, were 'always wealth, in some countries birth, in all countries intellectual power and culture'. The Lords had 'every right that superior fitness could confer'; they were the class that had contributed so much to the greatness and prosperity of the country; they were 'undefiled by the taint of sordid greed'; they were above corruption. He was describing not so much an aristocracy as a plutocracy, even a meritocracy. Few of the peers of ancient creation would have recognized themselves, but he was not writing for them. Salisbury in 1867, like Brougham in 1832, was buttering up the bourgeoisie – those who dreamed of a peerage as the final accolade after a lifetime of collecting money, those who could be relied on to underwrite the survival of the existing social structure and the House of Lords. The logic of numbers, he told them, meant that 'any battle between employers and employed would end in victory for the workers'. The less educated the voters were, the less responsible they were for property, the more likely they were to make the wrong choice and the wrong decision. Power and responsibility, he predicted, would be separated. The rich would pay all the taxes, the poor would make all the laws. How long the rich would remain rich under such laws he did not choose to consider.

Since 1832, the House of Lords had been looking for allies. Initially, the Reform Bill seemed to have tamed them. The Earl of Aberdeen described the Tory peers as standing 'self-degraded, scarcely daring to execute authority'. There had even been a move to drop the bishops: twenty-one out of twenty-six had voted against reform. In 1836, when a new diocese was created at Ripon, the Commons was alarmed at the prospect of even one more bishop, and a Bill was drafted to exclude them altogether. A compromise was finally reached in 1847, with the creation of another new diocese at Manchester. A Bill was passed by 44 votes to 14 in the Upper House limiting the number of bishops to twenty-six. The Archbishops of Canterbury and York, the Bishops of London, Durham and Winchester were assured a seat: the remaining twenty-one would join in order of seniority, and junior Bishops would have to wait their turn.

Reluctantly the Upper House had approved the abolition of slavery. But they were, as one Tory peer put it, 'very much displeased' at having to consider public opinion: 'It is not easy to make men feel that they are of no consequence in the country, who heretofore had so much weight, and still preserve their properties and their stations in society and their seats in the House of Lords.'

This was really the crux. When the dust settled in 1832 the old estates were intact, the rich man was still in his castle, the poor man at his gate and still without the vote. Salisbury in 1867 was simply recognizing the natural alliance proposed by Brougham, of the aristocracy and the middle classes, Property against No Property.

Immediately after 1832, Property found itself facing a weakened opposition. Political organization needed money and those who championed No Property were as broke as those they championed. Joseph Parkes of the Birmingham Political Union explained: 'I had rather go to Botany Bay than go through the sacrifices and labour of the last eighteen months. I have read no books; I have not slept enough; I have collected no money. I have neglected my business. Actually eight leading middlemen of the Union have gone "broke". And as I do not choose so to injure my utility and comfort, I don't mean to give so much time to our political plough.'

This gave the Lords breathing space, and they used it to hamper the Bright Horizonists and to slow down the pace of social progress. When Lord Ashley, later Lord Shaftesbury, brought in his Bill to keep children out of the mines it was passed in triumph in the Commons. In the Upper House Lord Londonderry, who owned a great many coal mines, painted a romantic picture of seven-year-old trap-boys sitting happily for long hours in the pitch darkness hundreds of feet underground, singing songs and chalking pictures on the coalface. The Bill was amended by the Lords to the children's disadvantage, and Ashley prayed afterwards that he might be spared as long as possible from inheriting his father's seat in the House of Lords, 'which would put an end to my public usefulness'. He had never, he wrote, seen 'such a display of selfishness, frigidity to every human sentiment, such ready and happy self-delusion'.

Money Bills, to raise state finance and set the level of taxation,

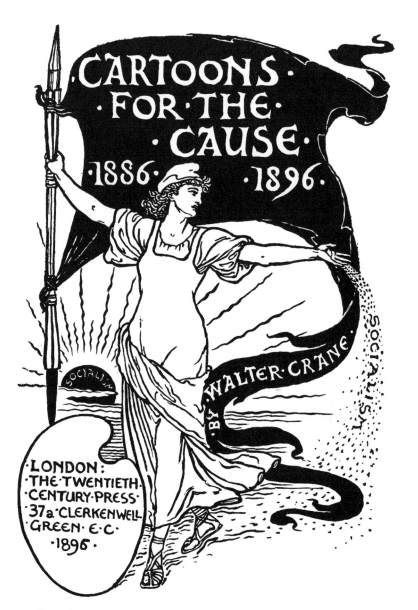

The Bright Horizon. A 1896 Marxist poster by Walter Crane illustrating the faith that
came to replace belief in the Shining Ladder, with distressing consequences for the
House of Lords. Mankind was capable of creating heaven on earth, a democratic
paradise was waiting just over the skyline.

Hatred, ridicule and contempt: Pitt's generous distribution of peerages provokes satirical comment on the recipients' merits.

The White Hall in 1831. The Lords moved here to accommodate Irish peers after the Union with Ireland thirty years before. It is seen in this cartoon on the eve of the Reform Bill.

The Rising Tide of Democracy. Brougham as Lord Chancellor (top L.) proposes change.

After the Flood, Fire. Irish workmen burning tally-sticks in 1834 inadvertently destroy both Houses of Parliament.

The Great Cartoon Competition. Westminster Hall, the only part of the Old Palace saved from the fire. Prince Albert encourages British artists to propose uplifting murals for the new Houses of Parliament.

A Punch Joke: Mr. Punch fails to take the Competition seriously.

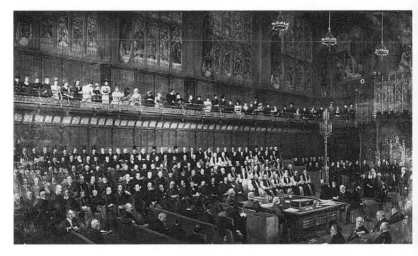

Dignity restored. The Lords in their new Parliament Chamber.

The Ladderists hit back. Painted in the decade of European revolutions, the murals of the new Palace express a hankering for the safe old days of hierarchy and the "natural order". Fiendish Roundheads assault noble Cavaliers.

JOHN BULL'S IDOL!

THE LORDS MET FOR THE DESPATCH OF BUSINESS.

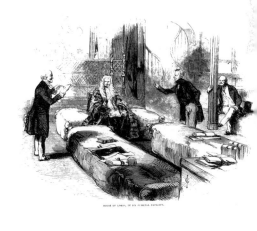

HOUSE OF LORDS, IN ITS JUDICIAL CAPACITY.

The Dwindling of Deference: Cartoonists of the 1840s ridicule the social esteem accorded to the peerage and the dignity of the House of Lords either as Senate or Court of Appeal.

THE CHALLENGE.

SENTRY SALISBURY. ": WHO GOES THERE?"
FRANCHISE BILL. "FRIEND!"

1884

WILL THEY BELL THE CAT?

"The mice resolved, in solemn conclave, to hang a bell
about the neck of the cat, as it had become a matter
of 'grave importance' to set a limit to her
persecutions. But—

19

THE CHANCE OF A LIFETIME.

OUR MR. ASQUITH.–"Five hundred coronets dirt-cheap!
This line of goods ought to make business a bit brisker.
What?"
OUR MR. LLOYD GEORGE.–"Not half. Bound to go like
hot cakes."

1907

"THE FIERY CROSS."

Chieftain C.-B. "GUID SEND THE RAIN DOESNA
COME ON AN PIT IT OOT!"
[The Liberal campaign in Scotland against the House of
Lords is announced to begin on October 5th, on which da
the Prime Minister is to address a meeting in Edinburgh

19

End them or mend them: With the extension of the vote to the lower middle class in
1884, the Liberals under Campbell Bannerman plot and lead the assault on the Lords
as the last stronghold of privilege. Asquith and Lloyd George finally push through the
relatively mild reforms of the Parliament Bill of 1911 under the threat of creating five
hundred new peers.

DISAGREEMENT ABOUT THE ADDRESS OF THE GUILLOTINE

1948

1955

1955

PAY-DAY IN THE HOUSE OF LORDS

1956

Execution suspended: Labour is divided between abolitionists and reformers. The Tories offer Life Peerages, women in the Lords and daily expenses. Gaitskell, Morrison and Atlee see the advantages of a quiet retirement home for Nye Bevan, coming as it now does with a small pension.

1962

"IT ALL HAPPENED SO LONG AGO."

1990

Wedgwood Benn's long struggle to renounce his peerage. Home and Hailsham are free to bungee-jump in and out of the Commons in pursuit of their political careers. Despite spectacular victories on the side of the angels, the reformed House continues to attract criticism and demands for more radical reform.

"REDUNDANT, AND NOT A SINGLE WORD ABOUT RETRAINING!"

Premature ejaculation, 1967

had been accepted for centuries as the exclusive business of the Commons, and made so by law in 1678. Unless the Lords could prove that other legislation had been improperly 'tacked' on to them they had to let them go through. Other Bills they could reject in extreme cases, but it was by amending them that they made their power felt. This was their major weapon. It created delays and frustrations; it made the party in power feel powerless; it sapped public confidence; it could, in extreme cases, bring down the Government. But Bills could come back from the Commons, and as in 1712 the Prime Minister could always ask the Crown to nominate as many new peers as he needed to overrule the existing majority in the Lords. With a reformed Commons, that threat loomed larger.

After 1832 the official constitutional doctrine, accepted by the Duke of Wellington, was that the House of Commons held the initiative and the power. If a policy was in a party's manifesto at the time that party was elected, then the Lords had no right to reject it or to distort its intention. It represented the manifest will of the people. If, on the other hand, a government was trying to bring in measures not approved by the electors, the House of Lords could block them, and even force it to call a general election to obtain a new mandate. Sir Robert Peel was convinced that this worked. 'The popular assembly exercised tacitly supreme power. The House of Lords, to avoid the consequences of collision, declined acting upon that which was notoriously the deliberate judgment and conviction of a majority.'

The doctrine might have succeeded if the House of Lords had been a properly balanced senate. In fact the Tories always had a comfortable majority. Until 1868, when the ancient system of proxy voting was provisionally suspended and never reintroduced, peers did not even need to go to Westminster to influence the outcome of a debate. A friend could cast a vote on their behalf. This permanent majority in the Lords, the Tories realized, offered the possibility of maintaining their 'occult' control over the House of Commons.

In his *Memoirs*, Charles Greville saw what was happening early in the reign of Queen Victoria. With the Tories in power, the House of Lords slumbered and the Commons governed unimpeded as a single chamber. When the Tories were in opposition, 'they placed the House of Lords', Greville wrote, 'in the new position of an assailant of the Queen's Government, frequently thwarting their most important measures.' It was, he believed, a significant change in the constitutional function of the House. Greville thought it a risky course, and Lord Grey, normally a cautious commentator, foresaw that if the Lords persisted, they would be 'swept away like chaff'.

By 1837 the Horizonists had got their breath back. The London Working Men's Association produced the People's Charter, pressing for the removal of duty on imported grain. The 'Chartists' represented the real People, and their Charter contained everything that Brougham had mentioned to terrify the Lords, including universal suffrage and salaries for MPs, so that ordinary wage-earners could stand for Parliament. Those advocating the repeal of the Corn Laws made it clear that if the House of Lords stood in their way it would be crushed.

Advised by Prince Albert to 'keep the peers straight', Wellington wrote to individual Tory members of the Lords, urging compliance. There was, he told them, a widespread and understandable impression that they had a personal interest as landlords in retaining the protectionist surcharge on foreign grain. He sympathized, but the main objective must be to preserve public order. Directly threatened by revolution, the Lords acted wisely and let the legislation through. But while the rest of the political machine continued to respond to the threat by gradual constitutional reform, putting more and more Commons' seats within reach of organized labour, the unreformed Lords increasingly concentrated on the protection of property and capital.

This was even true of their long struggle against change in Ireland that reached its climax in Gladstone's Home Rule Bill. Irish elected peers were clinging to their estates in Ireland, resisting any measures to help the Irish tenantry, and English peers, often believing themselves to be defending the rule of law against the bomb and the gun, supported them.

But the 'mere numbers' against the House of Lords continued to build up. Salisbury's arguments against the Second Reform Bill had no effect. Brought in by the Tories themselves after decades of unrest and the disasters of the Indian Mutiny and the Crimean War, it was passed in 1867. As intended, it doubled the number of those qualified to vote. In 1884 the vote was extended to agricultural labourers. These vast numbers were now led against the Lords by two men: Gladstone, who respected the peers as 'dominant influences' without whom the structure of society would be weakened, but who opposed their suicidal obstinacy; and Lloyd George, Gladstone's more extreme fellow-Liberal, seen in the Tory press as a 'dangerous demagogue' who despised them.

Many of Gladstone's Liberal peers seemed ready to accept reform. They had supported Liberal governments in the Commons in the gradual emancipation of Irish tenants. They had persuaded Tory peers to pass Bills establishing parish councils and county councils that challenged the power of English landowners. This, given the conservative nature of English society, had not proved too painful: a peer had often found himself democratically elected as chairman for life of a county council where he had ruled before by right of inheritance. What changed things was Gladstone's Home Rule Bill.

The young Liberal peers should on paper have supported him. Henry James describes one of them in *The Portrait of a Lady*. Seen through the eyes of the heroine, Isabel Archer, Lord Warburton is a hero:

> He was a nobleman of the newest pattern, a reformer, a radical, a contemner of ancient ways. He had enjoyed the best things of life, but they had not spoiled his sense of proportion.

Another character, Ralph Touchett, sees Warburton in a rather different light.

> He's a man with a great position who's playing all sorts of tricks with it. He doesn't take himself seriously, he regards himself as an imposition, an abuse. Great responsibilities, great wealth, great power, a natural share in the public affairs of a great country. But he's all in a muddle about himself, his position, his power, and indeed about everything in the world. He's the victim of a critical age; he has ceased to believe in himself and he doesn't know what to believe in. He can neither abolish himself as a nuisance nor maintain himself as an institution.

Ralph Touchett's father, representing the older generation, is more cynical.

> There's a considerable number like him round in society; they're very fashionable just now. I don't know what they're trying to do – whether they're trying to get up a revolution, but when you come

to the point it wouldn't suit them to be taken at their word. I don't think many of them would find it as pleasant as what they've got. Their radical views are a kind of amusement, these progressive ideas are about their biggest luxury. They make them feel moral and yet don't damage their position.

The old man was right. In 1886, when the Liberal peers saw their own interests threatened by Gladstone's first Irish Home Rule Bill, they deserted him in shoals. They formed a new party, the Liberal Unionists, and within a few years had joined the Tories. As his successor Lord Rosebery wrote, Gladstone 'threw the great mass of Liberal Peers into the arms of the Conservative majority'. In all the official court appointments made by the party in power, Lord John Manners recalled that Gladstone 'could not find a duke who would allow his wife to become Mistress of the Robes'.

The effect on the permanent Tory majority in the Lords was ludicrous. Ten years before, Earl Granville had told Queen Victoria that it was between sixty and seventy. By the early 1890s it was nearer four hundred.

Gladstone's policy for Irish Home Rule was far from popular, but the Lords' rejection of it was infinitely less so. Suddenly, after decades of relative peace, they had drawn attention to themselves. Keir Hardie made abolition of the Upper House part of the first manifesto of the Independent Labour Party, and Rosebery, as Liberal Prime Minister, told the Queen that many of his cabinet agreed. 'Nearly if not quite half of them is in favour of a Single Chamber.'

When the Liberal Government fell in 1895, the Tories in the Upper House should have reverted to their traditional slumber, allowing their party to govern from the Lower House. Instead they went on to infuriate the workers: the Lord Chancellor Lord Halsbury, representing the House of Lords as the final court of appeal, ruled against the trade unions in the Taff Vale case of 1901. The unions, the House of Lords decided, were responsible for compensating the employers for any damage resulting from a strike.

When the Liberals came back to office in 1906, the Tories virtually gave notice that they intended to govern from the Lords. Salisbury's nephew Arthur Balfour, as leader of the opposition, gave his assurance to Tories in Birmingham that 'whether in power or whether in opposition, the great Unionist Party should still control the destinies of this great Empire'. In an exchange of confidential letters, Balfour plotted with Lord Lansdowne, the Tory leader in the Upper House. The opposition might be 'lamentably weak in the House of Commons' but it was, as always, 'enormously powerful in the House of Lords'. They must work together, not as separate armies but with a common plan of campaign. Extreme Liberal legislation would be kept in check. The House of Lords, Balfour liked to think, would become 'the theatre of compromise'.

They had underestimated the Liberals. F. E. Smith warned the new Labour Party that if they ever took a bath, which he thought very unlikely, Winston Churchill would certainly 'steal their clothes'. Lloyd George did exactly that. As Chancellor of the Exchequer in a weak Liberal government he set out to harness the energies of revolution. The House of Lords made a perfect objective for attack. Addressing Welsh nationalists who were pressing for greater autonomy in Wales, he told them they had other priorities. The Liberal government was 'moving its artillery into position for making an attack on the Lords, and Welshmen who worried them with any other problems would find themselves in the guardhouse.

Lloyd George's plan was to provoke the House of Lords into overstepping its constitutional rights, which would give the Liberals a pretext to go to the country with a Bill to muzzle them. The will of the House of Commons must prevail within the lifetime of a single parliament.

The Tory lords, controlled by Balfour, manoeuvred with some skill. Lloyd George prayed that they would throw out the Trade Disputes Bill, which reversed Taff Vale. They passed it, but mangled an Education Bill that planned to withdraw state funding from Church of England schools and would benefit Nonconformists.

Then the Lords became unexpectedly compliant. They passed a Coal Mines Act, reducing the working day to eight hours; a Trade Boards Act, establishing a minimum hourly rate for piecework in what were called the 'sweated trades'; a Workmen's Compensation Act, which made employers responsible for accidents at work. They resisted the Old Age Pensions Act. One peer said it was 'so prodigal of expenditure as likely to undermine the whole fabric of the Empire' and another that it would be 'destructive of all thrift'. But it was officially a money Bill, so they had to let it through.

Balfour might have been on his guard against Liberal provocation, but he was always alert to the possibility of catching the Liberals with their trousers down when he could let his lords off the leash. He saw his chance with the Licensing Bill. Under pressure from their loyal supporters in the Temperance Societies and the Nonconformist churches, the Liberal government introduced a Bill that, over a period of fourteen years, would have closed thirty thousand pubs.

Confident of pleasing the brewers and drinkers, Balfour declared this to be 'an attack on property'. Amid scenes of low farce, he summoned his Tory backwoodsmen. Lord Lansdowne, looking round at the Tory benches crammed with bewildered old peers some of whom had mistaken his house in Grosvenor Square for the Parliament Chamber, welcomed 'a great number of noble Lords who had not often honoured us with their presence'. They went on to give the Bill 'a first-class funeral', but their appearance, blinking in the unfamiliar light of Westminster, was a cruel reminder to the general public of the Tories' permanent majority in the Lords.

It was Lloyd George's budget of 1909 that really did the trick. What made it so beautiful for him, as he drank toast after toast to the Lords rejecting it, was that it was a money Bill and the Lords could not touch it. He had also made the Budget as provocative as possible. At a public meeting in Shropshire he made what he later admitted was 'a bad joke' about 'having to rob somebody's hen-roost': 'I must consider where I can get most eggs, and where I can get them easiest, and where I shall be least punished.'

The House of Lords did not think he was joking, and neither did *The Times*. It called the Budget 'robbery of everyone who has anything to be robbed of '.

As Chancellor of the Exchequer Lloyd George needed a lot of money for defence, as he planned to build eight dreadnoughts. But he needed twice as much for the newly introduced old-age pensions. Income tax would start at ninepence in the pound, rising to one-and-eightpence for those with an income of more than £5,000 a year. There would be death duties. The rich would be hit by new charges on cars and petrol, and there was an additional tax of 20 per cent on what was called 'unearned increment' from land, with a further small annual charge, in the days before ecology was invented, on land that remained undeveloped.

Conservatives everywhere were appalled: Sir Edward Carson saw it as 'the beginning of the end of all rights of property'. But it was the House of Lords from which the shrillest cries of protest emerged: the Liberal government were 'piratical tatterdemalions'. The Duke of Beaufort said he would 'like to see Winston Churchill and Lloyd George in the middle of twenty couple of dog hounds'; the Duke of Portland announced that he would have to lay off household staff; the Duke of Buccleuch cancelled his annual subscription of a guinea to a local football club, pleading poverty. William Joynson-Hicks, a Tory lawyer concerned for the survival of the Upper House, criticized them for 'squealing' and said he wished every duke could be locked up until the Budget was over.

The masses, irritated by the new duties on alcohol and tobacco, were at first cautious. Then, during the ten weeks of all-night sittings in the Commons, with Tories arguing over every sentence and Winston Churchill appearing in the House late at night to rib them in his pyjamas, the electorate began to smell blue blood. Lloyd George whipped them up. When Lord Rothschild spoke against the Budget, Lloyd George said that he could think of countries who would not allow their politics to be dictated by great financiers. He addressed open-air meetings of thousands of workers. He talked of the eldest sons who inherited peerages as 'the first of the litter', he accused the Lords of being 'descended partly from plunderers who came over with William the Conqueror and partly from plunderers of the poor at the Reformation'. 'An aristocracy,' he told them to roars of laughter, 'is like cheese: the older it is the higher it becomes.'

He preached the pure essence of Horizonism: 'Should five hundred men, ordinary men chosen accidentally from among the unemployed, override the judgment – the deliberate judgment – of millions of people who are engaged in the industry which makes the wealth of the country?' Who ordained that a minority should own the land of our birth? How could one man spend his life in grinding labour and only obtain a pension of eightpence a day by threatening bloody revolution, while another man who never had to work received 'every hour of the day, and every hour of the night, whilst he slumbers, more than his neighbour receives in a whole year of toil?

'Where did the table of that law come from? Whose finger inscribed it? The answers are charged with peril for the order of things the peers represent; but they are fraught with rare and refreshing fruit for the parched lips of the multitude who have been treading the dusty road along which the people have marched through the dark ages and are now emerging into the light.'

The 1909 Budget was passed by the Commons and, even though it was a money Bill, rejected by the Lords. Believing that they could rely on the brewers, the Church of England and the middle classes, 'who knew and cared nothing for constitutional law', Lansdowne said that they were not justified in giving their assent 'until it had been submitted to the judgment of the country'. One Liberal, Lord Balfour of Burleigh, said this amounted to a referendum on the Budget. It would be a disastrous change in the constitution: it would destroy the supremacy of the House of Commons; it risked destroying the power, the prestige, the usefulness of the House of Lords. He was ignored.

Sensing triumph, the Liberals called an election. If the Lords rejected a Bill to reform them, the Liberals would swamp them with five hundred new peers. 'The people in future,' Asquith told a meeting of ten thousand supporters in the Albert Hall, 'when they elect a new House of Commons, must be able to feel that they are sending to Westminster men who will have the power not merely of proposing and debating, but of making laws.'

'This ancient and picturesque structure,' the Liberal leader Herbert Asquith told an audience in Hull shortly before the General Election, 'has been condemned by its own inmates as unsafe. The parricidal pickaxes are already at work, and constitutional jerry-builders are hurrying from every quarter with new plans.

'There must be something to put in its place, something – it does not matter for the moment very much what – but something which will be called a Second Chamber, with a coat, however thin, of democratic varnish.'

There had already been a few half-hearted attempts at reform. In 1888, the Earl of Dunraven had tried to introduce a Bill that would have involved 180 'Lords of Parliament' elected from their own ranks by the hereditary peers. The others would have been nominated by the government of the day, either as life peers or as senators, serving for a limited number of years. But apart from a measure that had been passed by both Houses to exclude peers who had been declared bankrupt, nothing had happened.

Then Lord Newton had suggested an elected second chamber, with hereditary peers only allowed a seat and a vote if they could produce some proof that they were qualified for the job. This alarmed Arthur Balfour, who reverted to orthodox Ladderist theology: 'Avoid the fatal admission that the ancient ground of hereditary qualification is insufficient to qualify for the Upper House. If it is not sufficient qualification it is no qualification at all. I think it is a fact that the accident of birth is more easily defended on what some call its naked absurdity than birth plus services.'

A Lords' committee was even appointed under the Liberal leader, the Earl of Rosebery, to draft a Bill based on Newton's proposals. A second chamber, they decided, was integral to the British Constitution but a peerage would no longer give a man the right to sit there or to vote. A minority of representative hereditary peers would be elected by the peers themselves; the rest of the members would be elected from local government.

Rosebery urged the Lords to accept it: in doing so they would be performing for their country the greatest service since the Barons had wrested the liberties of England from King John at Runnymede. They had a choice, he reminded them: either they could 'cling with enfeebled grasp to privileges which have become unpopular, to powers which are verging on the obsolete', or they could delay and face demands from those who wanted single-chamber government for their own extinction, while 'the ancient House of Lords may be found waiting in decrepitude for its doom'.

None of that cut any ice with Lord Curzon. He told the peers that in India the House of Lords was regarded with veneration and respect because its composition rested on a basis familiar throughout Indian society. The Archbishop of Canterbury, in frivolous mood and on pretty dubious historical evidence, assured the other peers that his title to sit in the House was six hundred years older than anyone else's. Earl Cawdor, who like most of the peers was against any reform at all, said how much better they were than the Commons at 'representing the mind of the people'.

Balfour himself, watching like a puppet-master, was sceptical. He was prepared to believe that an Upper House composed partly of hereditary peers and partly of elected Lords of Parliament 'might stand at any rate for fifty years', but was not convinced that such proposals would provide usable ammunition for Tories fighting an election in Yorkshire, Lancashire or Scotland against Liberal candidates campaigning for abolition.

Then, after only a few hours' illness, Edward VII died. Haley's Comet blazed in the sky, and a superstitious dread of change spread through the reformers.

A new constitutional conference was summoned, made up of four Tories and four Liberals. The Earl of Crewe offered to put them up at his place in the country, but Lansdowne was afraid they would be 'softened' by the excellence of Crewe's champagne and 'the other attractions of a hospitable and luxurious country house'. After six months they gave up without having reached any real conclusions.

Lansdowne and the more intelligent Tories now grasped the point: ask any number of individuals to reform the House of Lords and they would produce the same number of different schemes. For the Bright Horizonists the Shining Ladder would become the Tower of Babel. The Tories began therefore, while the reformers squabbled, to move the focus of attention away from what was called 'organic reform' to small tinkerings with the Lords' constitutional powers of delay.

The prospect of five hundred new peers had become the joke of the year. At a fancy-dress ball at Claridge's on the eve of the debate on the Parliament Bill, attended by Asquith, Balfour, and the Speaker of the House of Commons, Waldorf Astor, a Tory MP, turned up in a peer's red robes and a coronet. Stuck in the top was a label saying, '499 – still one more vacancy.'

Behind the scenes, the new King, George V, was caught in a crisis of conscience. His father, Edward VII, had first agreed, then hesitated, and finally refused to create the new peers. It has since been argued that this saved the old House of Lords. Sure of their new peers, the Liberals could have demanded real reform. Without them, they spent months agreeing a cautious compromise with the Tories.

Asquith did his best to release the King from his dilemma. 'The part to be played by the Crown in such a situation as now exists has happily been settled by the accumulated traditions and unbroken practice of more than seventy years. It is to act upon the advice of the Ministers who for the time being possess the confidence of the House of Commons, whether that advice does or does not conform to the private and personal judgment of the Sovereign. It follows that it is not the function of a Constitutional Sovereign to act as arbiter or mediator between the rival parties and policies; still less to take advice from the leaders of both sides, with the view to forming a conclusion of his own.'

George V was not satisfied with this. He talked to his own private secretary, Sir Arthur Bigge, and his father's old secretary, Sir Francis Knollys. Both agreed that it was his constitutional duty to do nothing. Bigge, a Tory, told him that if he agreed to five hundred new peers he would be seen as partisan and would damage the monarchy: giving the Liberals 'contingent guarantees' or hypothetical support would be intervening on the side of 'the Irish and Socialists'. Knollys was more cautious. The Liberals had been returned to government with a reduced majority, and the main worry was whether the King should support a weak government on such a controversial issue. Edward VII had asked him whether the Tories would be able to form an alternative government if the Liberals fell. Knollys had said, 'Yes.' When George V asked him the same question his answer was 'No'. In other words the King should probably back Asquith, the Irish and the Socialists. George V gave his consent: if necessary he would create five hundred new peers.

Meanwhile, in the shadow of the Parliament Bill, the Lords desperately reconsidered Lansdowne's earlier proposals, which went far beyond anything now being prepared in the Commons. Lansdowne envisaged an Upper House of 350, of which 100 would be elected hereditaries who had held public office, 120 elected from the provinces by MPs, and 100 nominated by the Government to match party strengths in the Lower House. Royal dukes and the archbishops of Canterbury and York would have a seat, plus five elected representative bishops and sixteen law lords who would sit for life. The rest would serve for twelve years, a quarter of every category retiring every third year. According to Lansdowne, this would reduce the Tory majority in the Upper House to eighteen.

The Lords rejected it lock, stock and barrel and turned their attention to the Parliament Bill which, by comparison was barely threatening at all. Liberals on the left in the House of Commons were 'almost aghast at their Government's moderation'. The Parliament Bill, 'a moderate but definite advance towards political equality', would allow all the hereditary peers and the bishops to stay but their powers of delay would be reduced to two years. Even this did not satisfy the House of Lords. During the committee stage they made amendments allowing them to interfere in financial measures. The Liberal Lord Morley called it 'tearing up the Bill'. The Commons rejected all the Lords' amendments *en bloc*.

The Liberal government now broke the news to Balfour that the King had agreed to create five hundred new peers, and the Tory opposition split. Curzon, who had until then believed that the story was a bluff, took over the leadership of the Hedgers, ready for compromise. The young foxhunting peer Lord Willoughby de Broke, together with the ancient Lord Halsbury, both still sceptical about the threat of new creations, rallied two hundred other peers prepared to 'fight and die in the last ditch'.

Balfour believed the Ditchers were being 'essentially theatrical', and their language largely 'for music hall consumption'. He conceded that 'the music hall attitude of mind' was 'too widespread to be negligible', and had no objection to the battle 'provided it did not swamp the House of Lords'. The Lords must retain its independent identity to be of any constitutional use.

In the debate there was much adoration of the old Shining Ladder. When Lord Willoughby de Broke said that at such times they could not entertain that affection for representative government which they ordinarily extended to it, his voice was drowned by a passing aeroplane.

Then, at a suitably dramatic moment, Lord Morley, speaking for the Government, fished in the pocket of his morning coat and produced the letter from the Palace. 'If the Bill should be defeated tonight His Majesty would assent – I say this on my full responsibility as the spokesman of the Government – to a creation of peers sufficient in number to guard against any possible combination of the different parties in Opposition by which the Parliament Bill might again be exposed a second time to defeat.'

One or two old reactionaries stood firm, including Lord Londonderry, who said that they should have stood firm in 1832. At the last minute the Archbishop of Canterbury, 'with a ring of leadership in his tone', said he was appalled by the levity and callousness of the Ditchers, and was joining the Hedgers to vote with the Government.

The Parliament Bill passed the Lords by 131 votes to 114. The

Ditchers, one said afterwards, had been beaten 'by the bishops and the rats'.

The political consequences were minimal: the House of Lords now had slightly less power to delay legislation from the Commons. It was still a powerful revising chamber. It could be argued that the delay the Lords imposed in the following session on the Irish Home Rule Bill, exacerbated by the lapse of the war years, both of which gave Ulster the time to arm and find its more extreme Protestant identity, was a major contributing factor in the Troubles that lay ahead. The overwhelming Tory and Unionist majority in the Upper House remained almost untouched.

What had changed was the public's perception. The battle had confirmed the worst caricatures of the Lords drawn by Lloyd George. They were inbred hooligans, the children of privilege, undeserving plutocrats. They were obsolete and must be replaced. But among the critics of reform were some highly intelligent politicians, and as early as 1895 the *Labour Leader* had seen the writing on the wall:

> The House of Lords is a body which cannot be permanently tolerated in a democratic country, but it is easily possible to conceive of a more dangerous second chamber. After all, the collective intellect of the peers is an insignificant factor, while their collective stupidity is of abnormal dimensions. And further, it is always possible to coerce them into submission. But a House of Lords composed of 'captains of industry', of subtle financiers, and of stock-jobbing Jerry Diddlers, would be a far more dangerous body than the landed aristocrats who compose the majority of the present chamber. The more cunning upholders of privilege realize this; hence the anxiety to reform the House of Lords.

It presented the Horizonist enemies of the House of Lords with only one real option, and that was abolition.

CHAPTER EIGHTEEN

Incomplete Relations

It was only when I was looking through the newspapers for references to the House of Lords after the First World War that I understood Lord Ampthill's words about his mother having been a virgin when he was born.

The story of the Russell Baby case is a bizarre one, and revealing of the lottery of primogeniture and the plight of hereditary peers in the twentieth century.

The story began during the First World War, in 1915, when 'Stilts' Russell fell in love at a wartime dance with Christabel Hart.

The war seemed the final catastrophe for the Shining Ladder. When it was recruiting its young officers, the Army, the last home of rank and hierarchy, instinctively turned to those who had led it into battle for centuries: men with ancient names. They personified the spiritual relation and were cut down by heavy machine-guns, the industrial principle in action. No class, proportionately, lost so many.

Stilts, the future Lord Ampthill, survived by serving underwater, though at six foot four he was an awkward height for a man working in submarines.

Christabel's upbringing had been fairly louche. She and her sister had been brought up for six months of every year in Paris, in the Latin Quarter. Their mother, a colonel's widow, believed it to be cheaper than London.

Her sister studied music with La Suggia, the glamorous Italian cellist immortalized by Augustus John, and Christabel appeared in 'exhibition dances' in a café in the rue Notre Dame des Champs, where she earned money teaching young men the tango. Her two great passions were dancing and riding.

When war broke out the family came home. Christabel was nineteen, considered 'fast' for shaving under her arms, and volunteered for war work at Woolwich. She was happy, working at a lathe all day and dancing every night. Stilts was only one of many who fell for her, and after their first meeting in 1915 she forgot all about him.

Men pursued her in swarms, and she began to refer to the lobby on the left of the revolving doors of the Strand entrance to the Savoy Hotel as her 'Proposal Room'. Among so many, Stilts succeeded. When they met again in 1917, she agreed to be his wife.

Shortly afterwards she broke off the engagement, telling him she was 'not a marrying sort'. A day or two later she left for Gretna Green with his best friend, 'Flick' Bradley. For some technical reason the quick marriage they had had in mind was not possible and Flick went back to his unit. Within a fortnight Christabel's passion for him seemed to have cooled.

A year later she wrote to Stilts, offering to be his wife if he was still interested. He sent back a single-word telegram, 'Yes', and they were married at St Jude's Kensington in 1918 while he was on leave from the Navy. His parents were appalled and refused to come to the wedding.

On the night before, Christabel made Stilts swear a solemn oath that in the first years of their marriage there was to be no question of children. He gave her his word and he returned to his submarine with his marriage unconsummated. He grew wistful underwater, and when the submarine docked at Greenock he sent his wife a copy of Marie Stopes's *Married Love*, containing tips on love-making and birth control.

Christabel reacted badly to this: she wrote back saying she hated the thought of 'being one', as described by Marie Stopes, and did not like the idea of contraceptives.

> I am afraid pandering to the *lower* side of nature would in no way make me fonder of a person, and there is nothing more distasteful to me than the feeling of being as *one person* with anyone. One's separate soul is the thing to aim at, and I'm afraid all the 'beauty' which is attributed to the sex relationship in *Married Love* is camouflage and self-justification.

In the winter of 1919, with Stilts still in the Navy, Christabel went to spend several months skiing in Switzerland with her mother. The letters she wrote to her husband in his submarine cannot have reassured him.

> Darlingest old thing, I am so in love with a Dago young man. You'd have spotted him as my future fate the moment you set eyes on him. He looks very ill, his hair is beautifully marcel-waved, his clothes fit like gloves, he is very slim and has lovely hands. Your very naughty wife, C.

As soon as he got leave in March 1920 he went out to join her, to find that the room they were to share had two narrow bunks, one above the other. He asked her if they could move into another room, but Christabel refused.

When Stilts left the Navy, he found a job at Vickers in Victoria Street. They moved into a small house in Chelsea, Christabel still insisting that she had her own room. She went out practically every night and, as Stilts did not enjoy dancing, always with someone else. One of her favourite dancing partners was her old flame Flick Bradley, who frequently joined her and Stilts with other friends for the weekend at her mother's house in Sussex. It was there that Stilts, on his own account at least, came nearest to losing his temper. He arrived to find that Christabel had gone out with Bradley in his car. When the pair got back he took Bradley aside, or so he claimed afterwards, and asked him, 'Are you playing hanky-panky with my wife?' Bradley said he wasn't, adding mysteriously that 'it would be much better if Chris had children'. Stilts agreed, but from then on Christabel refused to let her husband so much as kiss her.

After a few months Stilts lost his job, and the future Lady Ampthill took a dressmaker's shop in Mayfair, designing and cutting, sewing and fitting from ten in the morning until six or seven at night, when she went out dancing. The couple moved into the flat above the shop, Stilts only allowed into his wife's room to take her breakfast in bed, which he obediently did.

At such times she would tell him with whom she had spent the previous evening and whom she was having dinner with that night. If she was not back by breakfast time, she said, it was because she was staying at her mother's flat in Earls Court, to which she had a key.

In the spring of 1921, when they had been married for just over two years, Flick Bradley rang Stilts at nine one morning to say that Christabel had spent the night at his flat in Knightsbridge. Would he bring her a change of clothes? The same year she spent a weekend in a hotel in Somerset with a Captain Cross of the Royal Artillery, who was training a horse for her. The two subsequently went to Paris, sharing a sleeper in the train on the way back.

By May that year Stilts was living with his parents at Oakley House in Bedford. Old Lady Ampthill wanted the marriage annulled, and Christabel's mother, conceding that their children were not living together in any sense as husband and wife, agreed. Then, in June 1921, on Christabel's twenty-sixth birthday, Stilts risked his mother's rage and sent his wife fruit and flowers. She wrote to thank him, and suggested they should meet for lunch. There was something she wanted to tell him. The news was that she had been to a clairvoyant who had told her that her future appeared very inter-esting: she was 'five months gone'. Since then she had been exam-ined by a doctor, and it was true. They were expecting a baby.

This at first puzzled Stilts. When could the child have been conceived? They racked their brains, then Christabel reminded her husband of a time when she had found him wandering in Curzon Street in his pyjamas in the middle of the night, fast asleep. He had no recollection of it, but she assured him that she had taken him back to bed. He had probably made love to her in his sleep.

Stilts was bewildered but very happy. Before he caught the three fifty-five back to Bedfordshire he stopped at the St Pancras Hotel and wrote her a hurried letter. He must have been 'mad' the night he had gone sleep-walking. If he had known he was capable of such insanity he would have chained himself to the bed. He suggested that the Duke of Bedford should be godfather. When he got home and broke the news to Lady Ampthill, she hit the roof: Christabel's story was 'moonshine'; he was to begin divorce proceedings the following day.

As far as the public image of the aristocracy went, it was an unfortunate divorce. But it was one of many cases that confirmed the impression in the public mind that the aristocracy was everything that P. G. Wodehouse was telling them it was, only more sordid and decadent.

Talking about the forthcoming divorce, Christabel confessed to a friend that she 'longed for the fray'. 'Do think of the rows of co's' – co-respondents – 'lined up for trial!' The baby Geoffrey was born in October, weighing a remarkable ten and a half pounds, and the divorce case began at the Old Bailey in the summer of 1922. The Ampthills engaged Sir John Simon and Christabel was represented by Patrick Hastings. Of the 'rows of co-respondents' she had imagined, only three were cited: Flick Bradley, Captain Cross and a 'man unknown', in whose flat she was accused of having taken baths.

During the prosecution's opening account of Christabel's married life a lady in the jury came over faint and asked to be excused, and the trial continued with a new jury of eleven men and one woman. Absurd legal exchanges took place as to whether or not the baby Geoffrey constituted an 'exhibit'. In an earlier case a child had been examined for family resemblances by 'an eminent sculptor', but his judgment had subsequently been dismissed on appeal to the House of Lords as 'loose and fanciful'.

On the question of the sleepwalking episode in Curzon Street, Stilts's ancient nanny was called to give evidence. She said that he had never walked in his sleep as a baby. A brother officer swore that he had never walked in his sleep in the submarine.

Sir John Simon humiliated Christabel by asking her to write down on a piece of paper, in silence and before the whole court, the names of any men, other than Captain Cross, with whom she had stayed in hotels in separate rooms. He quoted a line from a letter she had written to her friend Maud Acton: 'I've been so indiscreet all my life that he has enough evidence to divorce me about once a week.'

This produced such a roar of laughter that the judge threatened to clear the court, but that did not stop him and Sir John Simon trying to raise a few laughs at the expense of Mrs Naismith, the clairvoyant, who preferred to describe herself as a 'psychological expert'. She had sensed that Christabel was pregnant, she said, from 'the vibration of the hormones'. Sir John asked her if that was Latin or Greek, and she replied, 'It is a very good word. It has to do with a very deep subject; it has to do with psychology and physiology!'

When Sir John queried, amid laughter, if this 'psychological science' could tell them who the father was, she answered, 'It could, in time.' Until then, Sir John concluded, they would have to depend on the verdict of the jury.

This seemed a foregone conclusion.

When Patrick Hastings stood up, for Christabel, he immediately produced a fascinated silence in court by asking Stilts how he would feel if he could prove to him that the child was his own. Then he surprised the jury by telling them that, after leaving Woolwich, Christabel had been with an engineering firm, Whitworth's, where she was directly in charge of two thousand workers. He asked them to compare her achievements with those of her husband. From what they had heard so far of his eerie tolerance towards his wife, he said, they must have been asking themselves, 'Is this a man or a jelly?'

He also produced photographs of Stilts at a ball, dressed as a woman and in full make-up. When questioned, Stilts admitted he dressed like that 'quite frequently'.

Sir Ellis Hume-Williams, representing the co-respondents, lent more support to Christabel. The idea of men dressing as women might have upset the court, but he now risked far greater trouble by shifting the argument to women taking the role of men. 'The war', he told them, 'has produced in women effects which would undoubtedly have astonished and perhaps would have shocked our ancestors. Women did men's work during the war, they dressed like men, they worked in conditions in which sex was subordinated and forgotten. That had a profound effect on their manners, though not on their morals. No woman who lived that kind of life in the war can entirely shed it when she comes out of it.'

Patrick Hastings proceeded to demolish the rest of the case against the 'co-respondents'.

The night Christabel had slept at Bradley's flat; she and Bradley had been out dancing with their friend Captain Cross. They had dropped Cross at his hotel, and only discovered when they got back to her flat in Curzon Street that she had no keys. They had banged on the door but had been unable to wake Stilts, who slept in a room at the back. Bradley had suggested that Christabel should stay at her mother's in Earls Court but she had no key to the front door of her block of flats, which was locked at night. It was now three o'clock in the morning, her mother was ill, and she didn't want to bring her down four flights of stairs.

At Bradley's flat in Onslow Place she had slept in the bed and he had dozed on two chairs in the sitting room. They were both in their evening clothes, and the housekeeper gave evidence that she had been asked in the morning to go into Bradley's bedroom where Christabel was asleep and find something for him to wear. There was no telephone in the flat, and he had then gone downstairs to a public call box to ring Stilts and ask him to bring some clothes for his wife.

In the case of Cross the relationship seemed equally innocent, if even less discreet. He was two or three years younger than Christabel, his interest in her seemed genuinely confined to dancing with her. He had had a girlfriend at the time whom he had since married. When he and Christabel stayed at a hotel in Salisbury they had had rooms on different floors, and in Paris she had slept in the cheap room on the top floor she used every time she went back to see her old friends. He took a more expensive room downstairs. The sleeping car had been a mistake, booked by the hotel porter. They had tried to get separate compartments but the train was full, and neither of them took their clothes off.

The bringing in of the 'man unknown' showed just how desperate the Ampthills were, Patrick Hastings said, to make Christabel look like a prostitute. The man turned out to be an Edgar Mayer, a divorced American with British citizenship she had met in France, and who had invested in her dressmaking company. When she and Stilts had been moving into Curzon Street he had suggested that they could have baths in his flat in Half Moon Street until the plumbing in theirs was connected. In fact, neither had taken advantage of the offer, and Christabel remembered going to his flat only once in connection with the business.

Stilts now readily admitted to Patrick Hastings that he had never suspected his wife of being physically unfaithful to him until she became pregnant. She was given, he agreed, to the wildest forms of expression in everything she said or wrote, but was otherwise 'absolutely moral'.

None of this would have cut much ice with a cynical jury, had not several Harley Street specialists been called who examined Christabel during the fifth and sixth month of her pregnancy. They all found her to be technically still a virgin. She had never, they all agreed, been penetrated by a man.

If this took the jury's breath away, worse was to come for the Ampthills. Maud Acton, once an intimate friend of Christabel, was called as the Ampthills' star witness. She had given them the letter about the 'rows of co-respondents' and claimed that Christabel had told her that Stilts was not the father of the baby. Under cross-examination by Hastings she became less confident, and admitted that Christabel had often talked of 'Hunnish scenes'. Stilts had repeatedly tried to rape her, but had failed. Something occurred which was described in court as 'incomplete intercourse'. 'He attempted to effect penetration,' Christabel told the court, 'but I would not suffer it.'

If others found this surprising, doctors to the aristocracy did not. One story in circulation at the time concerned a peer who had complained to his physician that his sexual enthusiasm had been blunted over a long period of time by his failure to achieve penetration. He eventually revealed that he thought access was to be obtained through his wife's navel.

One doctor told the jury of a case in which a husband had called him out in the middle of the night, believing his wife to be dying of a mystery illness. A few hours later she had given birth to a child.

More conclusively, the doctors unanimously agreed that conception was easily possible from semen spilled over the entrance to the vagina in the way that was being hinted at by the lawyers.

Stilts admitted to the 'incomplete relations'. Like his wife, he had no idea that such activities could result in pregnancy and also conceded – and this was finally the core of the case – that shortly before Christmas 1920 he and Christabel had shared a bed at Oakley when she again remembered 'Hunnish scenes'. This would have extended her pregnancy to just over ten months, but all the doctors considered this possible.

Sir John Simon then made what Hastings correctly identified as a hurriedly planned counter-attack. If, as they now discovered, Christabel had tolerated Hunnish scenes with her husband, was it not likely that she had also tolerated Hunnish scenes with Bradley, Cross and all the men whose names she had written on the piece of paper? If such 'incomplete relations' were capable of producing pregnancy, what proof had she that Stilts was the father of the child?

As Patrick Hastings was quick to answer, she needed none. Every precedent in English law confirmed that the burden of proof was on her husband: any child born in wedlock must be presumed to be his.

After a speech from Sir John Simon that lasted three hours and forty minutes, the jury dismissed the evidence against Christabel in connection with Bradley and Cross with costs, but disagreed about the possibility of her having committed adultery with the 'man unknown', Edgar Mayer. The judge therefore ordered a re-examination of this issue, which was alleged to have resulted in the birth of a child.

The Ampthills were not rich, but they spent a large amount of money on detectives as well as lawyers and returned to court the following year, in March 1923, with a second writ against Christabel for adultery with a 'man unknown'. To confuse matters further, they added a second co-respondent: Edgar Jaquard Mayer. This time they engaged Sir Edward Marshall Hall, a highly theatrical barrister who would enter the courtroom with a crash, preceded by a clerk carrying pills, smelling salts, nose and throat sprays, a green instrument-case filled with compasses, rulers, a magnifying glass, an air cushion and an adjustable footstool. Christabel was again represented by Patrick Hastings.

The second trial was, if anything, more lurid than the first. An unmarried lady on the jury, asked by the judge whether she would care to withdraw before it began, said she 'might be better employed elsewhere'. That, Mr Justice Hill replied to general laughter, was probably true of everyone in the court. The final jury again consisted of eleven men and one woman.

New witnesses were called, including a man named Crane, a porter at Half Moon Street, who described having seen Christabel 'lying on a sofa, being fed by Mayer with sweets', and a maid there who said she had found cigarettes burning at either end of the bath, as well as powder and hairpins. Both proved untrue. Crane, Patrick Hastings revealed, was known in the flats as 'Christopher Sly' and had a criminal record; the maid's story collapsed when Christabel showed that she had had an Eton crop at the time and never used hairpins. The maid herself then admitted that her memory had never recovered from the shock, some years before, of finding 'his lordship, the Marquess of Milford Haven, dead in bed'.

Stilts, called into the witness box, admitted that the family had spent at least £500 on detectives, and the implication was that they had spent more on Crane and the maid. But the case turned, Stilts insisted, on the succession to the peerage. He had even offered, had that been possible, to let the title pass to his younger brother. He had 'an honourable name he meant to keep untarnished'.

Hastings tore into him, asking what he thought he and his family were doing to Christabel's honourable name. 'These people have the insolence to pester this lady again and again with this sort of nonsense.' A barrister friend of his who had never met her but who happened to live in Curzon Street, he said, went in dread of the Ampthills citing him as a co-respondent. The girl couldn't go to a dance without being accused of adultery.

Later, Christabel made the same point. Perhaps her idea of honour was different from her husband's, but she would never have allowed private letters to be read out in court.

Old Lady Ampthill did her best to defend her son's habit of going out in drag as 'a bad joke', and Lord Ampthill himself bewailed the expense of the case, which had cost them over £10,000. He admitted suggesting to Stilts that he should put a notice in the paper disclaiming all his wife's debts.

This made Hastings very cross indeed. Christabel had no debts, and far from 'eating up every penny Stilts had', as Ampthill had claimed, she actually had to support him. The only money he had was his gratuity from the Navy, and he had spent that on the divorce.

At this second trial, Christabel was much more her amusing self. She revealed for the first time that she had often allowed Stilts to share her bed, and that he had once wrapped his legs round a loaded shot-gun, put his toe against the trigger, and threatened to shoot himself if she wouldn't let him penetrate her. He had also threatened to shoot the cat. She made a great many jokes, and at one point put on a funny voice: Marshall Hall asked her 'Are you acting now?', and she said, 'I'm imitating you!' Over-confident, she was tricked by Hall into finding resemblances between the baby Geoffrey and three pictures of a baby he suggested was Stilts, but which in fact were of three other children.

But the most damaging evidence came from Stilts, about the so-called 'Hunnish scenes' at Oakley ten months before the birth of the child. He had once tried to kiss her, she had told him she was revolted by the way he tried to take advantage every time she was nicer to him, and after that he had made no further attempts to be affectionate. Patrick Hastings said that this was inadmissible evidence, but the judge brushed his objection aside. In winding up, Hastings again asked the jury's compassion for the 'little fellow': Christabel Russell might not have been perfect, but it was hard to sympathize with Stilts when his wife did all the work and he did all the grumbling.

Marshall Hall let loose his final tirade: he bitterly resented the attacks that had been made on the Ampthills and on John Russell. His wife was contemptible. 'I am not suggesting,' he boomed, 'that any man had had complete possession of her. I am suggesting' – and the slur was obscurely phrased – 'that this woman was willing, at a price which she was prepared to pay, to accept the attentions of these scores of men.' Charitably, his words could have been interpreted to mean that she was prepared to pay the price of making her husband miserable to buy the admiration of other men, but in the context of whether or not she had been 'completely possessed', it made her sound like a prostitute. He ended on a fine flight of rhetoric, ridiculing the story of the clairvoyant and the sleepwalking, appealing not for sympathy for the child but for the 'breaking of a bond between two young people who were husband and wife in nothing but name.

This woman is abnormal. She is the super-sexless woman who glories in having a train of men always dancing attendance on her. I ask you to free this young man from what he hoped would prove a bond of pleasure, but is now nothing but a rusty chain which burns into his soul.'

Whether it was the effect on him of Christabel's high-spirited performance in court or Marshall Hall's oratory, Mr Justice Hill clearly felt the need to influence the jury against her. He asked them to consider which was the stronger character: if Mrs Russell was bent on having her own way, she usually got it. Her letter about the rows of co-respondents suggested a frivolous attitude to adultery. He asked them to imagine her in the arms of a more persistent Hun than her husband: 'If the respondent gave herself to another man, is he likely to have stopped short of complete possession?' This, in view of the unanimous findings of all the doctors of her technical virginity, was scandalous misdirection.

The jury found Mrs Russell not guilty of adultery with Mayer but guilty of adultery with an unknown man, which had resulted in the birth of a baby. The Ampthills got their divorce, 'the little fellow' Geoffrey was officially a bastard and would certainly never take his seat in the Upper House as Lord Ampthill.

In 1911 no legitimate heir to an hereditary peerage would have expected a seat there, but the Horizonists' zeal had been cooled by the experience of the war, and particularly by the experience of winning it. As the old hierarchy collapsed in a defeated Germany, the Shining Ladder survived in England as a symbol of patriotism.

Like Irish Home Rule, the exclusion of hereditary peers from the Upper House had been put off for the duration of the hostilities, but as early as 1917 a full conference on the future of the House of Lords was assembled under the Liberal peer Lord Bryce, a constitutional lawyer and historian. Bryce had never been a passionate Horizonist. As a minister in Asquith's government he had given lectures at Yale on the dangers of pure democracy. The number of Englishmen who could read and write, he told his audience, had increased twenty times in the space of seventy years, but the percentage of those who thought before they voted had not kept pace with that expansion. Natural Average Man, he believed, was a let-down. He was, therefore, keen to preserve what could be preserved, and by 1917 he found the mood gentler. Lord Lansdowne had made a famous speech at the height of the slaughter pleading for more wisdom in the use of British troops, and the Lords had unpicked and straightened out many hastily drafted wartime Bills from the Commons. The Socialist J. H. Thomas, who had been in favour of abolition, noted the 'curious and ironic fact that during many stages of the war the real guardians of the people's liberties were to be found in the Upper House'.

Once again the difficulty for reformers was what one peer called the paralysing perplexity of so many alternatives. J. H. Thomas wanted a senate either directly elected on a geographical basis or by a standing committee of members of the Lower House. Beatrice and Sidney Webb, alarmed at the threat of cabinet dictatorship, wanted a hundred senators, elected on a basis of proportional representation by Members of Parliament from 'persons of ripe wisdom and judgment, known to and respected by the public for their personal qualities; not representative of any one class or interest'. Shortly after this, Sidney Webb became a hereditary member of the unreformed House of Lords as Lord Passfield.

Ramsay MacDonald now identified a new danger, frequently called to mind since by abolitionists, that any elected second chamber would challenge the power of the Commons. MacDonald's ideal House of Lords would therefore have no power. It would be a 'non-political council', and would come trailing a few wisps of William Morris-influenced Shining Ladderism. It would be elected by 'guilds and unions, professions and trades, classes and sections', and would ensure, at least, that the Labour Party was properly represented on the red benches.

Unable to reach any real agreement from his conference, Bryce put forward the least unpopular scheme, on the lines of Lansdowne's 1911 Reform Bill. In addition to the law lords, who would form the permanent Appeal Court, there would be 324 members, of which 243 would be senators elected from thirteen regions by the local MPs. There was no lower limit on age or income; members would serve for twelve years, a third retiring at the end of every fourth year. Eighty-one seats would remain for representative hereditary peers, but the system by which they were to be elected had grown more complicated.

First, all the hereditary peers were to choose an electoral college of five of their own number. Then the Speaker of the House of Commons was to nominate five more hereditary peers, and the resulting committee of ten would choose the eighty-one to represent their order in the Lords. Over a period of time the number of hereditary peers would be reduced to thirty, and the fifty-one seats that became vacant taken by more elected senators.

The principal drawback was that no one outside Westminster seemed to care. Reform remained government policy, but the Government was not prepared to say when it would come.

Whatever its reputation during the war, the Lords was now a low-key affair, compared by Herbert Asquith to a second-rate rural district council. The aristocracy had run out of steam, and came to debates even less frequently than they had before the war. If many families had lost their sons in the trenches, many more had lost their money, and the composition of the unreformed House chillingly confirmed the worst predictions of the *Labour Leader* thirty years before. The Jimmy Diddlers had arrived.

Large contributors to 'party funds' were rewarded with peerages, even by Gladstone, but Lloyd George's sale of ermine, culminating in the notorious Birthday Honours List of 1922, called the ripest days of James I. Sir Joseph Robinson, Bt, paid for a peerage as chairman of the Robinson South African Banking Co. Ltd, and was to be ennobled for 'national and imperial services'. As Lord Harris pointed out in the Lords, Robinson South African Banking had gone into liquidation in 1905. The King himself wrote to Lloyd George: Sir Joseph's presence would be an insult to the peerage. Lord Donaldson was therefore sent to explain that the deal was off. He found Sir Joseph at home, mumbled a few words of apology and returned his cheque. Sir Joseph, who was deaf, assumed that Lloyd George wanted more money and rewrote the cheque for double the amount. He remained a baronet.

Other Jimmy Diddlers became alarmed. Sir Joseph had offered good money: could Lloyd George be trusted to deliver the goods? The shrewdest, a whisky manufacturer called James Buchanan who wanted the title of Lord Woolavington. He therefore postdated his cheque, signed it Woolavington, and entered the House of Lords in 1922. He later made a generous contribution to the restoration of St George's Chapel.

But however they got there, such men were now dominant: as a Labour Party pamphlet explained:

> The men who sit on the red benches are great financiers, like Lord Rothschild and Lord Swaythling; captains of industry like Lord Leverhulme and Lord Pirrie; great magnates like Lord Vestey of the meat trust, and Lord Inchcape of the P. and O. combine; and

finally newspaper proprietors like Lord Beaverbrook and Lord Rothermere.

Newspaper barons could now make and unmake governments.

1911, the Left now recognized, had been 'a sham fight'. The House of Lords, as a vestige of feudalism, no longer represented Norman blood or ancient titles.

> But though the representatives of Big Business have captured both the Commons and the Lords, their power does not reside there or depend upon this capture. Just as the King, the Sacramental Man of the Middle Ages, lost all his personal power and became a mere façade of the structure of government, so the whole Parliament has become a façade behind which go on the operations of finance capital and the real government of the country. Were the workers' representatives to gain a majority in the House of Commons and abolish the House of Lords, they would only have captured the outworks. The real struggle would still lie before them.

But the Lords remained loyal to the Ladder. Parliament had passed the Sex Disqualification (Removal) Act, but the House of Lords were not convinced it applied to them. If sexual disqualification had been removed, the Horizonists argued and there was evidence that there had been women in the Anglo-Saxon Witan surely peeresses in their own right should sit in the House of Lords. Viscountess Rhondda accordingly applied for a writ of summons in 1922. She argued that women in the Lords would change public attitudes. Their exclusion was damaging: 'It helps to form the opinion men hold of women, it helps to form the opinion women hold of themselves. It helps to make both men and women expect less of women than of men, less courage, less balance, less judgment, less public spirit.'

The Committee for Privileges found in her favour. Then Lord Birkenhead, formerly F.E. Smith, packed the Committee with like-minded old men and reversed their decision. 'The removal of a disability,' he pronounced, 'does not create a right.'

Bryce's Bill, when it finally came, was a flop. His proposals had been chewed over in a leisurely way by a cabinet committee, some of whose members had been on extended leave at the League of Nations, and their report had been a long time coming. When it reached the Lords the suggested reforms were extremely tame. The royal dukes, bishops and law lords would stay, and so would a proportion of the hereditary peers, elected like the Scots and the Irish: the rest would consist of directly or indirectly elected members from outside the existing House, and members nominated by the Crown. Election would be for a fixed period, but members could be re-elected or reappointed for further terms. With only four Labour peers in the Upper House, most of the speeches in favour came from Tory Jimmy Diddlers, who believed that a reformed Second Chamber stood a better chance of survival as a restraining influence on any future Labour government. Lord Crewe, uncannily echoing the imagery of Charles I and the role of the Lords as a 'screen or bank', questioned whether it could ever play such a role: 'You will never do it by setting up a privileged body of persons, whether you call that body the House of Lords or anything else, with the idea that you can arrest the onrush of the flood by a breakwater of that sort.'

But the majority remained firm against change. The Bryce conference had been a complete waste of time; the present proposals were too vague to be worth debating. In general, the peers saw cause for self-congratulation: the high tide of revolution was past, the Bright Horizonists were in retreat, the Shining Ladder, with some slight modifications, was safe. Lord Charnwood gave all the credit to the Parliament Act: 'To my mind the most striking thing about this whole question of second chambers is that now, since the Parliament Act – not, I venture to think before that Act – this House enjoys an universal respect and confidence enjoyed by no other chamber in all the world, and is probably able to maintain and safeguard that satisfactory and proud position. The authority of your lordships' House, which I believe greatly increased by the restriction of its former powers, is a growing authority.'

The Ampthill case had attracted a great deal of condemnation. *The Times*, while bewailing the filth that newspapers found themselves compelled to print until some legislation was brought in to prevent it – a law was actually passed two years later to restrict divorce reporting – cast serious doubt on the wisdom of the jury.

Christabel reinvested her costs in an appeal to the High Court. It was heard by the Master of the Rolls, who was near to death, and two other Lord Justices, and it turned on the question of the admissibility of evidence from a husband or wife about whether or not they had had sex together. According to a judgment dating from the eighteenth century, such evidence was neither decent nor moral. The dying Master of the Rolls couldn't see any objection on those grounds 'since most evidence given before the Divorce Court was positively loathsome', and the appeal was dismissed with costs. Geoffrey was still a bastard.

Then, in the spring of 1924, Christabel scraped together all the money she had and appealed to the House of Lords. Mounds of old law-books were produced: their lordships conjured up the ghosts of long-dead adulterers, impotent husbands and frigid wives; there was cautious discussion of 'access', of complete and incomplete sexual intercourse; and they returned to the admissibility of Stilts's evidence about whether or not he had been Hunnish in bed before Christmas at Oakley.

Finally, everything turned on a judgment given by the first Earl of Mansfield, who had sat on the Woolsack with his spectacles smashed in 1791. Lord Mansfield was not always a popular man – his house was burned down by the mob during the Riots – but he was always reasonable. He had once dismissed charges against a witch who had been accused of walking upside down in the air, saying that there was no law against walking upside down in the air and anyone who had seen her doing it was at liberty to do the same. He remained the authority on the evidence of husbands and wives about what passed between them in private: 'The law of England is clear that the declarations of a father or mother cannot bastardize the issue born after marriage. It is a rule founded in decency, morality and policy that they shall not be allowed to say after marriage that they have had no connexion and therefore the offspring is spurious.' Despite the intervention of Sir Douglas Hogg, later the first Viscount Hailsham, on behalf of the Ampthills the Lords' committee supported Lord Mansfield and the appeal succeeded.

The child Geoffrey bore the name of Russell, was deemed to be legitimate, and was declared so under the Legitimacy Act of 1924. The Ampthills were bankrupt. Christabel continued to be sensible with money, earning enough to pay for a good education for Geoffrey and for her nieces and nephews.

In 1974, on Stilts's death, Geoffrey Russell applied to the House of Lords for his writ of summons as eldest son and heir to the title. He was told that it had already been claimed by his younger half-brother, the Hon. John Russell. The nub of John Russell's case was that Geoffrey was still illegitimate.

The matter was considered by a Committee for Privileges, consisting of Lord Wilberforce, three law lords and five lay members of the House, in a room dominated by large oil paintings of George V and George VI. If lay peers were banned from hearing appeals, Committees for Privileges were still open to them.

The climax came when John Russell's barrister, Harry Law, flourished a bundle of faded medical records. Geoffrey Ampthill's counsel, Sir John Foster, a florid, boozy and socially confident figure with more than one mistress in aristocratic circles, asked Law what they were.

'Blood tests!'

'That may be,' boomed Foster, 'but I don't want them!'

When pressed, Foster argued that to admit such records would be putting his client 'into an Agatha Christie situation'. Old Lord Ampthill's blood had been taken at a time when blood samples were not admitted in legitimacy cases, and the records 'might have been tampered with or mixed up in the laboratory'.

Harry Law protested. Lord Wilberforce and his fellow law lords agreed with Sir John.

Harry Law, a stranger to the companionable old-school world in which he found himself, confessed himself stumped. It was, he said, a 'chicken and egg situation'. The case had been taken to the House of Lords on appeal forty years earlier, at the time of Geoffrey's birth, and the Lords had ruled that Geoffrey was legitimate. Now their lordships insisted that the previous judgment could only be overturned if Law's client could prove fraud. How could he prove fraud if they would not admit the evidence of the blood tests?

Lord Wilberforce explained that the Lords had given their judgment in 1924 and Geoffrey Ampthill had been registered as the legitimate heir under the Legitimacy Act of 1924. If ever there was a case for closing a chapter of a family's history this was it.

In 1974, when Christabel was eighty and Geoffrey inherited his peerage, she sold the castle she had bought herself in Galway, where she had been a proud figure on the hunting field riding side-saddle in a top hat and a veil, and invested in a second-hand van, which she drove overland to Australia. The van, she discovered on the way back through Central Asia, was neither taxed nor insured, and she had no driving licence.

CHAPTER NINETEEN

A Man in Space

If Geoffrey Ampthill had trouble getting into the House of Lords, it was nothing to the trouble Anthony Wedgwood Benn had in getting out of it. His eventual escape revealed a great deal about the political forces shoring it up.

The crisis came in the winter of 1960. Wedgwood Benn was a promising and ambitious young Labour member of the House of Commons. Then, half-way through a Thursday afternoon, like a prince in a fairy story transformed into a frog, he suddenly found himself turned into a peer. His father, Viscount Stansgate, had had a heart attack in the Lords while waiting to speak in a debate about the future of East Africa. This made Benn not simply a person of title, but a hereditary senator. He was inhabited by the Stansgate peerage just as a Tibetan baby might be inhabited by the nature of the Dalai Llama. A peerage, Mr Justice Dodderidge had ruled in 1626, was 'fixed in the blood', and could never be shaken off.

Next morning, when Benn arrived at Westminster, pipe confidently clenched between his teeth and brown eyes blazing, he found that his MP's salary had been stopped and his travel warrant cancelled. He was handed his National Insurance cards in an envelope addressed to Lord Stansgate. He was thirty-five and, as a peer, was banned by law from his regular place of work for the rest of his life.

P. G. Wodehouse celebrates the situation in *Much Obliged, Jeeves*. Roderick Spode, who had become the 7th Earl of Sidcup, is considered by Bertie Wooster to be 'one of nature's greatest blunders'. Hearing him described as 'one of those silver-tongued orators you read about, a man with an extraordinary gift of the gab who could get into Parliament without straining a sinew', Wooster asks why he doesn't.

> 'He can't, you poor chump, he's a Lord.'
> 'Don't they allow Lords in?'
> 'No, they don't.'
> 'I see,' I said, rather impressed by this proof that the House of Commons drew the line somewhere.

To ask why peers were excluded was to bring out the witch-doctors, to provoke mystery, magic and theatre. This Benn determined to do. Having alerted the newspapers, he returned to Westminster on the following Monday and tried to take his usual green leather seat in the House of Commons, to which he had been elected by the people of Bristol South East. The response, in dramatic terms, could not have been more satisfactory. Acting on orders from the Speaker, the Sergeant-at-Arms called him 'my lord' and threatened to throw him out, if necessary by force.

Benn received little sympathy from his own party. When he told Hugh Gaitskell the news, the opposition leader seemed pleased, and said that Labour needed bright young peers in the Lords. The Tories, though, were more interested in the principle: R. A. Butler listened to Benn's interpretation of the existing law that he thought might enable him to stay in the Commons and asked him whether that would 'get Quintin back'. Lord Hailsham was a potential rival to Butler for the Conservative Party leadership, but at the time was safely entombed in the Lords. Benn said, 'No.' Hogg had already accepted his letters patent and had been Lord Hailsham for some years. 'Ah, well,' Butler said, 'that's all right.'

The problem of MPs having to leave the Commons when they inherited peerages was by no means unfamiliar to ambitious politicians. In 1893 Labouchère had suggested that any peer should be allowed to extinguish his title at any time, and that if he became a minister it should be compulsory. In 1914 one Liberal MP urged the absolute abolition of all titles on the death of the present holders, making everyone eligible to the Commons. In 1947, under a triumphant Labour government hesitating whether to abolish the House of Lords, the only positive suggestion from the all-party committee was that hereditary peers should be free to renounce their titles and stand for the Commons. None of these proposals had ever become law.

Benn's struggle had really begun when he entered the House of Commons in 1950. As president of the Oxford Union he was known as the Hon. Anthony Wedgwood Benn, and when Sir Stafford Cripps, the Labour Chancellor of the Exchequer, invited him to succeed him as Labour candidate for Bristol South East some of his supporters were already alarmed by the 'Honourable'. Benn confessed it meant that one day he would have to go to the House of Lords, 'unless by then we've done the sensible thing and abolished it', but until then he could see no reason why, 'as an active young Socialist', he should not represent them in the Commons.

He was a popular MP, but as his parliamentary prospects brightened he became less optimistic about the chances of Labour abolishing the Lords, and began to investigate practical means of avoiding the need to go there.

He had found support in surprising places. Churchill backed him, as did Quintin Hogg, who had failed to persuade Clement Attlee, Prime Minister in the 1945–51 Labour administration, to let him stay in the Commons when his own father died, but as a peer. On his own side, he had the support of the eccentric Labour MP for Northampton, Reginald Paget, who frequently dismayed his fellow Socialists by turning up to vote in the Commons in full hunting pink. Paget introduced a Bill under the Ten Minute Rule in 1953, which would have allowed peers to remain in the Commons, but it was rejected. Most of the Labour Party continued to believe that any tinkering with the absurdities of the Upper House would only delay its abolition.

Then Benn drafted a Bill, without any success, the Stansgate Titles Deprivation Bill, based on the Titles Deprivation Act of 1917, which had stripped various German royal relations of their English titles during the First World War, and appeared to prove that under certain circumstances peerages could be shuffled off.

In 1955 he tried again, signing a formal renunciation of the Stansgate peerage which was witnessed by Attlee, Aneurin Bevan, Roy Jenkins and Jo Grimond. His case was heard then before a

Lords' Committee for Privileges. The account of the hearing is preserved in the Official Record, dated like all Lords' proceedings in Latin as *Die Veneris 18 Februari*, Friday 18 February 1955.

Politically, Benn was now in a trap: by birth, upbringing and religious inclination, he was a direct heir of the Puritans. In recommending him as his successor at Bristol South East, Sir Stafford Cripps had told voters that Benn was 'as true a Socialist and as keen a Christian' as he was himself. To argue the Horizonist line, for immediate abolition of the Lords, would have satisfied his own conscience and pleased his party. Realistically he recognized that this was unlikely to happen, and chose to fight his own case. In Horizonist, industrial, rational terms, the argument was simple. Long ago members of the House of Commons, the representatives of the Communities, had made it a rule to prevent their assembly from being infiltrated by powerful magnates and members of the King's Council. Now that the peers had lost their power, the rule was no longer of any use and could be scrapped.

Instead, facing the Ladderist Establishment, Benn chose to use their arguments and their language, which involved paying lip-service to the Shining Ladder.

At a time when Russia was putting the first man into orbit round the earth, Benn provoked debates on the floor of both Houses of an overworked modern Parliament that were entirely metaphysical. One MP asked the Attorney-General what happened to a peerage if a peer died leaving his wife pregnant and with a child who would, if she had not been pregnant, have inherited the title. The Attorney-General, with a leer, said he knew the answer to that, but would not tell them.

However great the confusion, as Michael Foot's brother, Dingle, observed at the time, the arguments had nothing whatever to do with the real world.

Behind closed doors in committee rooms, lawyers invoked obscure cases of *feuda genitalia* and ancient Scottish *tailzies*; others conjured up the ghosts of thirteenth-century peers who had 'denuded themselves of their dignities'. All of them worked themselves into a theological frenzy, swapping insults like black-robed clowns exchanging very mouldy custard pies.

Outside, the argument was seen as a great deal simpler: in the headlines and Osbert Lancaster cartoons, Benn became the Reluctant

Peer, the Persistent Commoner, launched by tribal magic towards the Lords but stuck in orbit, unable to achieve re-entry into the Commons, Britain's Man In Space. Most ordinary people thought he should be allowed to waive his title and continue to represent the electors of Bristol South East in the House of Commons. A minority argued that his place was in the House of Lords. 'Supposing a pygmy from the jungles of Africa unable to speak a word of English', one constituent wrote to the *Bristol Evening Post*, 'wanted to stand as a candidate in the next Parliamentary by-election, would he be allowed to do so? No. Why? Because he is not qualified, and nor is Lord Stansgate.'

What made the dispute even more absurd, evoking as it did the whole panoply of coats-of-arms and medieval writs of summons, was that the hereditary viscountcy of Stansgate was less than twenty years old. Benn's father William, who went with his son to meet the Committee for Privileges in the Moses Room, was a tweedily patrician figure, much loved at Westminster, who on his own admission found the House of Lords 'corruptingly nice'. He had been a Liberal junior whip in the Commons at the time of the Parliament Act. He had served gallantly in the First World War as an air-gunner, winning the DSO and the DFC, had returned to the Commons in the 1920s as a Liberal, and had moved to the Labour benches in middle life. He had been made a peer in 1941, when he was approaching seventy and when his son Anthony was still a schoolboy at Westminster – remembered by his contemporary Peter Ustinov as 'a joyous little gnome'. Downing Street stressed that the peerage was not a 'personal honour or reward'. It was 'a special measure of state policy'. At the outbreak of war in 1939 there were still only twelve Labour peers, and Benn's father had been ennobled specifically to 'strengthen the Labour Party in the Upper House'. He was one of the first Labour 'working peers', men and women sent to the Upper House to do a job rather than as a reward, often hailed as the inspiration of Lord Cledwyn of Penrhos, leader of the Labour opposition in the Lords in the early 1980s.

What was even more ironic was that Benn would never have been troubled by the title if a fitter in the RAF had remembered to take the cover off a Pitot tube airspeed indicator at Tangmere in the last year of the war. His elder brother Michael was killed in the resulting crash, and Benn became the heir.

He approached the House of Lords, as every citizen has the right to do, as a petitioner. The petitioner's request has to be approved by a Lords' Select Committee. If approved, it is heard by another committee and, this being a peerage case, by a Committee for Privileges. His argument was that his case was unique and involved no change in the law or the Constitution.

Others who had inherited peerages when they were members of the Commons, like Hailsham, had asked to remain in the Lower House as peers, and with Viscount Hinchingbrooke and Viscount Lambton both in the Commons no one on the face of it would probably have blinked an eyelid. Hinchingbrooke and Lambton were, confusingly enough, still commoners, using junior or courtesy titles until their fathers, the Earls of Sandwich and Durham, died and catapulted them into the House of Lords.

Attlee had rejected Hailsham's request, on the old-fashioned Shining Ladder argument that peers were a different political breed, hereditary and not elected legislators.

Benn's position was different. He was, he said, still a commoner, and he wanted to stay one. He argued his case with great deference and courtesy, and referred to his petition as a 'prayer'. If his prayer failed he promised he would serve faithfully in their lordships' House.

He had studied the constitutional position, and quoted from the parchment rolls in the Victoria Tower, some of them, he told their lordships, 'several skins long'. This was the language of Zion, as far as Shining Ladderists were concerned: every dried length of brownish-yellow sheepskin membrane, covered with cramped, barely legible handwriting, represented to the committee another mystical rung in the Ladder. Unrolled and joined end to end they led upwards, skin after luminous skin, to Original Truth, and Benn happily genuflected before it. He had been looking for a precedent in which an heir had been relieved of his peerage for a specific reason, and he had found it. In 1549, Lord De La Warr had taken his nephew William West to live with him as his heir. William West proved to be a bad hat, not prepared to wait for the title, and he had poisoned his uncle. Lord De La Warr had survived, petitioned Parliament to have his heir excluded from the peerage, and the Lords had ruled that 'the saide William West be From henceforthe duringe his naturall lyffe onlye, clearlye disabled'. Benn told them he had seen the original document in the Victoria Tower, and had noted that it was marked *Soit fait comme il est desiré,* indicating that it had been a Private Act, as opposed to *Le Roi le veult,* which was the official wording on a Public Act. He therefore asked that his case could be dealt with by a Private Bill, which need not affect the Constitution. 'If you are anxious for me to follow precedent exactly,' he suggested, 'I could always attempt to poison my father.'

The Lords' argument, supported by the thoughts of seventeenth-century lawyers, was that a general principle was at stake. It was a public matter. For Benn to stay in the Commons when his father died they would have to change the law.

His contemporaries in the Labour Party had little sympathy for him, least of all George Brown, who attacked him in the Commons tea room afterwards: 'I'm glad you've lost. You with your middle-class voice. Now you're paying the price and it serves you right. You would never have got anywhere without the advantage of being your father's son and it will do you good to suffer the disadvantages!'

Benn's father now succeeded in getting a Private Bill read in the Lords. It came with as much Horizonist support as could be mustered. The bishops were no longer loyal Ladderists: George Bell, the piping-voiced Bishop of Chichester, had made the single bravest speech against Churchill's bombing of Dresden in the House of Lords, and the bishops now lined up behind Benn. The Bill was introduced, in the absence of the Bishop of Bristol, by the Bishop of Ripon, who brought with him a petition signed by the Lord Mayor, aldermen and burgesses of the City of Bristol.

Lord Saltoun, inheritor of a barony granted in 1445, a passionate Ladderist and an old campaigner for the rights of Scottish hereditary peers, said that he thought it improper for the Lords to receive a petition from any mayor and corporation. Lord Woolton, Chancellor of the Duchy of Lancaster, had his doubts about one bishop sending along another as his understudy, but was advised that the mayor and corporation were in order. This did not satisfy Lord Saltoun: the mayor and corporation might be in order to present a petition, but was the House of Lords obliged to receive it? Lord Jowitt, as a socialist, was firm: it was the foundation of our law that any subject had the right to petition the Crown. It was an immemorial right. The debate was not about whether they received it but whether they acted on it.

Then Stansgate got up to tell them the story. He said he had thought in 1941 that his peerage was a great distinction, and had then been told it was 'a measure of state policy'. He remembered young Anthony, at that time 'rather a chatterbox', already dreaming of a career in the Commons, and how abusive he'd been to his father for taking the title. Now, young Anthony was completing his second term as MP for Bristol South East, and all he wanted was to keep his seat. How could anyone object to that? The Committee for Privileges was worried about creating a precedent, but was it likely that there would be 'a flood of renouncers'? He reminded them that the House of Lords was currently being criticized for the number of peers who failed to appear. Why force someone to attend who was so valuably occupied elsewhere? He appealed to their sense of fair play, and in conclusion read a letter of support from Winston Churchill.

The Horizonist argument seemed unusually clear and found much support. Lord Jowitt could see no infringement of principle and pointed out that if Stansgate died before the Bill was passed it would be too late. The boy would never receive the relief he was asking for. Earl Winterton agreed. Where was the logic? Where was the common sense? They were not living in medieval England or in pre-1914 Austria, with aristocrats bragging about their sixteen quarterings and maintaining a strict demarcation between those who had titles and those who had not. The House of Lords was the senate of a modern state and should behave like one. He begged them not to make fools of themselves in the eyes of those who really counted – the great mass of the population.

The ancient Viscount Samuel had been in Asquith's government at the time of the Parliament Act. If Edward VIII could abdicate his title, he wanted to know, why not Anthony Wedgwood Benn? It was not a question of how many millions were available to stand for Parliament, it was a question of the rights of one man. The present rule was an infringement of the liberties of the individual: to snatch a man from his seat in the Commons was a breach of parliamentary privilege. If this case had come up in the reign of George II and Benn had been allowed to keep his seat, they would all be jumping up and down and praising the wisdom of their ancestors for establishing such a wise precedent. He quoted Tennyson on freedom slowly broadening down from precedent to precedent. Unless someone first created a precedent, there would be nothing to broaden.

Then the Ladderists hit back, arguing in favour of the spiritual relation. Lord Elton said that a man should not run away from 'the situation into which he had been born'. Bernard Shaw might argue that it was courageous in a young man to break out of his family circle, but Chesterton was right: the home circle, with its psychological conflicts and potential dead ends, was the real world in which Providence had called the young man to live. Elton called on young peers 'to do their duty in that state of life into which it shall please God to call them'.

Lord Hastings's peerage dated from 1263, and even his enemies conceded that he was proof that heredity now and then produced competent legislators. His attack on Benn was more subtle. He began by ridiculing his Horizonist supporters outside the Lords. Never mind the bishops, he could think of cities, unlike Bristol, where the spectacle of the Mayor, aldermen and burgesses petitioning the House of Lords on behalf of a member of one political party would produce a howl of rage. Spotting that Benn at that stage wanted to preserve the title for his heirs, Hastings hammered on his weak point: let Benn renounce his peerage by all means, but let it be final. A peerage could not be taken up or rejected by each generation. It was not a convertible commodity. Such a 'jack-in-the-box' system – now-you-see-it-now-you-don't – would increase the powers of hereditary peers: it would give them the choice between a seat in the Lords and a seat in the Commons.

Lord Saltoun quoted P. G. Wodehouse. Benn should bite the bullet.

The Lord Chancellor, Viscount Kilmuir, loyal priest of the Shrine of the Shining Ladder, gave judgment. Lord Samuel might talk about individual liberty but the Lords were more concerned with the Constitution. It had been an unchallenged rule for nearly three hundred years that no peerage could be surrendered. To change that rule would create a new view of the responsibilities and duties of the peerage. In other words, to question the nature of what made a hereditary peer worthy of a seat in the senate was dangerous.

The Bill was defeated by fifty-two votes to twenty-four.

Old Stansgate's final words were poignant. As he listened to the Lord Chancellor reading out the Government line, dictated by the office of the Tory whip, he was reminded of when he had been a young whip himself, in 1911: 'I counted the joyous Members of Parliament who trooped through the lobby in support of the Bill which implied that the reform of your lordships' house would "brook no delay". I wonder if my son will have to wait another forty-four years before he can serve his constituents in the House of Commons.'

The truth of this convinced Benn that his only hope lay in making some minor modification to the rules that governed the Lords; under the Tory government, some such minor modification now seemed possible. He became an unwilling recruit to the side of the Tory reformers. That did not prevent him proclaiming the Horizonist ideal. In a pamphlet for the Fabian Society, with its logo, ironic in the circumstances, of a Red Tortoise raising a clenched fist, symbolizing the 'inevitability of gradualness' he argued that the Lords should be abolished and replaced by an enlarged Privy Council. It did him little good with his own side. Jennie Lee, who had not read it, told him he was being 'very unsocialist': he was encouraging reform, reform would give greater patronage to the leaders of the parties, he was playing the Tory game.

Benn was in a cruel position, and even when the rules were modified he was still left out in the cold.

In 1957 and 1958, as Jennie Lee had predicted, the Tories moved to preserve the Lords by what the Labour Party saw as cosmetic reforms. There was no longer any talk, as there had been fifty years before, of phasing out the hereditary peers: instead, the Upper House would be strengthened, almost a century to the day after Queen Victoria had first written to propose it, with life peers. True to its belief that reforms would only make the Lords respectable, the Labour Party voted against life peers, and an amendment that would have allowed Benn to renounce his title was defeated by the Tories.

When Stansgate died in November 1960, Butler did his best to appear reasonable. At the end of November he agreed to a Commons' Committee for Privileges to re-examine the case, which temporarily stalled a by-election in Benn's constituency.

Benn now launched a double campaign. On one hand he fought a highly ironic guerrilla war behind enemy lines, masquerading as a Ladderist, obediently answering the questions of the Committee for Privileges, finding precedents, investigating loopholes in procedure. On the other he appealed directly to the People, with a long-running, skilful and very effective publicity campaign. It was the dawn of the Sixties, he was more confident as a politician, and he was marginally less respectful to the new committee. Its members began by querying his birth certificate, asking him to produce a witness to prove that he was the person it referred to. Benn said he knew that he had been there and his mother had, but he didn't know if anybody else was.

The committee met eleven times over a period of weeks, and Gaitskell, Dingle Foot and many other intelligent, loyal Horizonists became increasingly enthralled by the mysteries of the Shining Ladder. George Brown, also present, said very little.

This time Benn argued from his rights as a Member of the House of Commons. According to Erskine May, the parliamentary bible, they protected him against the Crown: he could not be hauled out of the Commons by the Monarch in the manner attempted by Charles I; he could not be hauled out by the ordinary courts of law; he could not be hauled out by the Lords.

The Attorney-General, Sir Reginald Manningham-Buller, known satirically as Sir Reginald Bullying-Manner, dismissed this argument. Erskine May had said other things too: Benn was not a Member of the House of Commons any more, he was a peer. If he wasn't a peer, what was he doing before this committee?

Benn's second line of argument was more metaphysical. He had dug up the case of a Mr Scrymgeour-Wedderburn, who had sat in the Commons from 1931 to 1945, when he lost his seat in the Labour landslide. In 1952, with more time on his hands, he had successfully claimed first the title of Earl of Dundee, a Scottish peerage which did not automatically entitle him to a seat in the Lords, and then a United Kingdom barony, which did. Once in the Lords, he reverted to his Scottish title, becoming known, on account of his interest in wildlife, as 'Bunny Dundee'. What excited Benn was Scrymgeour-Wedderburn's claim that he had, in fact, been entitled to a seat in the Lords ever since his father's death in 1924. This meant that he had sat as a peer in the House of Commons, knowingly or unknowingly – Benn was shifty on this point – for fourteen years, and had never even paid the official penalty of £500 a day for sitting in the Chamber under false pretences. If Bunny had done it, why not Benn? Bunny Dundee had been a potential claimant to a peerage who had not claimed it. So was he. Benn would only be a peer when he accepted his writ of summons.

This irritated the Attorney-General. He quoted the law, as laid down by Mr Speaker Onslow, who had been Speaker of the House of Commons in 1760. Lewis Monson–Watson, the MP for Kent, had been summoned to the House of Lords as Lord Sondes, and Speaker Onslow had ruled that the mystical change did not depend on accepting the writ: the instant a peer died was the moment at which his heir became another peer. His seat in the House of Commons was immediately vacant.

Dingle Foot questioned this. Mr Speaker Onslow's words might be quoted in *Hatsell's Precedents* but they formed only part of a conversation in 1760 between Onslow and Lord Egmont. They did not have the authority of a judgment given by the House of Lords as the final court of appeal. What was more, Hatsell himself had writen elsewhere that 'until the King, by writ of summons, called a man up to the House of Peers, he could not lose his right to sit in the House of Commons'. Outside in the real world the Beatles sang, the Sputnik turned in orbit.

Sir Edward Fellowes, the clerk to the committee, was still arguing with Manningham-Buller over a case in 1549 when George Brown woke up. When Fellowes concluded that Benn's status could only be changed by an Act of Parliament, George Brown roared at him. None of the objections to peers sitting in the Commons had been based on an official judgment by the House of Lords. This committee was a Committee for Privileges, and its judgment was as valid as any of the other authorities the Attorney-General had quoted. It was up to them to decide, and now.

Rather surprisingly, Sir Edward thought he was right. Manningham-Buller did not. The committee reported, including the full text of Mr Justice Dodderidge's thoughts in 1626, that a peerage was 'a personal dignity annexed to the posterity and fixed in the blood', and recommended that Benn should wait until there was a change in the law.

Butler, the Home Secretary, then allowed a Private Member's Bill, the Peerage (Renunciation) Bill, supported by five Conservatives, including Gerald Nabarro, five Labour members and two Liberals. The intervention of Nabarro, a self-confessed 'swank-pot', a moustachioed New Tory, was crucial. It represented the first wave, at least on the question of the Lords, of Horizonism in the

Conservative Party. Nabarro had accepted a knighthood, but he did not give a toss for the old Shining Ladder.

Benn, playing to his supporters outside the Chamber, demanded to put his case from the Bar of the House – in Ladderist terms outside the Chamber – and before the debate began he watched from the gallery as this was discussed. Fatuous precedents were hurled to and fro, including Irish Nationalists, atheists and priests of the Church of Ireland, all of whom his champion Hugh Gaitskell claimed had spoken before the Bar. Butler maintained that they had all been MPs, and that Wedgwood Benn was not. The last case he could find of a non-MP speaking at the Bar was that of a barrister who had spoken on behalf of the East India Company during the East India Maritime Officers' Bill in 1837, which he considered too long ago.

George Brown, admitting he was not a lawyer – 'for which I dearly thank God' – said that it was for the House of Commons to decide whether Mr Wedgwood Benn was still an MP.

Gaitskell spoke well. Gladstone, Rosebery, Curzon, Samuel, Winterton and Churchill had all been in favour of peers in politics being able to renounce their peerages and sit in the Commons. Certain other classes, it was true, were excluded from election to the House of Commons – felons, bankrupts, lunatics, clergy of the Church of England – but felons could reform, bankrupts could become solvent, lunatics could be cured and clergy could unfrock themselves. Peers were helpless. As Curzon had put it, the world supposed them to be the fortunate heir of what is called the accident of birth; they were, in reality, the hapless victims of the accident of death.

Butler remained firm: Benn would not be heard. He himself described the debate afterwards as one of the most disagreeable he had witnessed in the whole of his time in Parliament. Manningham-Buller closed the discussion by saying that to allow Benn to speak 'would be a nice thing to do', but he was a peer and it would be creating a precedent. With a two-line whip, Benn's request was rejected by 221 to 152.

Despite the official line, many Tories were in favour of change. Some were directly concerned – like Hinchingbrooke and Lambton, who faced the same fate when they succeeded to their fathers' peerages – and some were lower-middle-class populists like Sir Gerald Nabarro, New Tories in the mould of Heath, Thatcher and Major. Butler was therefore doubly under attack from both sides of the House.

Nabarro, however, was not constrained by high office, and laid into the Ladder. They were all equal. Pointing to his old friend Lord Hinchingbrooke, he roared, 'Would anybody dare to suggest that my blood is less luscious, less rich, less red, coursing through my veins as it is at this moment?' This was greeted with cries of 'It is blue!'

Butler, from the dispatch box, made the classic Shining Ladder defence. Heckled on why, three years before, the Conservative government had introduced life peerages, he argued, on slender historical evidence, that life peerages had been 'a feature of the House of Lords in the past'. He meant the law lords. The Duke of Buckingham's mother had been made a life peeress by James I but she didn't have a seat in the House. There was no precedent for allowing a peer to renounce his peerage. Rattled, he came close to admitting the truth. They were, he said, facing something fundamental: the problem of the hereditary principle of the House of Lords. He refused to amend the Constitution 'by pulling out a brick here and there so as to make the wall collapse without knowing what we are doing'.

Infuriated by Butler's performance, the Labour Party voted in favour of Benn being allowed to renounce his title, but the Tory majority stood. Refusing to go to the Lords, Benn remained in space.

Near the end of the Commons debate, Lord Lambton asked the Attorney-General what seemed a purely hypothetical question, like the rest. Would Mr Wedgwood Benn – or Lord Stansgate, as his right honourable and learned friend had called him – find it impossible to stand again as MP for Bristol South East?

Manningham-Buller replied that he could stand as long as his nomination paper was in order but, even if he were at the top of the poll, he would not be qualified to sit in the House of Commons.

Lambton thought, rightly, that this was absurd. What could be more ridiculous, if Mr Wedgwood Benn returned to Bristol, stood for Parliament and was elected by an overwhelming majority? What could make the House of Commons more absurd than that? How could the House of Lords avoid being seen as a knock-about turn?

Benn did exactly that. His constituency had begun to look for a new candidate but, within five days of his father's death, he was on to them with another scheme, which he now put into effect.

When the by-election was called the Liberals agreed not to oppose him. The Tories put up Malcolm St Clair, whom Benn had beaten in the previous election by just over six thousand votes. To complicate things further, St Clair announced in mid-campaign that he was the heir to a peerage from a Scottish cousin.

Driving a public-relations bandwagon that now filled pages of the national press every day, Benn collected a list of sponsors that included Kenneth Tynan, Augustus John, Benjamin Britten, Henry Moore, Graham Sutherland, the poet laureate Cecil Day-Lewis, Professor A. J. Ayer, Jacob Bronowski and John Osborne, who wrote, saying, 'By all means, you can have my support, for what it's worth. Frankly, I should think it would decrease your majority considerably.' Robin Day sent a telegram from Moscow, apologizing that he could not be there in person. Benn was also supported on the Labour platform by the sinister black-bespectacled figure of Lord Lambton. George Brown joined him too, though with less enthusiasm: 'I may as well tell you, I'm dead against you myself. I didn't want to come down and speak in this by-election, but still I was asked to do it and this is my job.'

Local Ladderist Tories published a pamphlet in old-world script, reminding constituents of the law and warning that anyone who voted for Benn was throwing away their vote. Benn published a reply so offensive that St Clair sued him.

When he got back to his hotel before the result was announced, there was a message telling him to say nothing about the future. Whatever the vote, the Labour Party National Executive had no intention of giving him any more support. He beat St Clair by 13,000 votes, with 70 per cent of the total poll. St Clair took his seat in the House of Commons and a hundred Labour MPs walked out in protest, but the Labour front bench stayed where they were. Benn himself watched from the gallery. When he tried to light his pipe in the corridor outside, he was told that smoking inside the Palace of Westminster was a privilege reserved for MPs.

Benn would probably have spent a lifetime outside Parliament, had it not been for the Tory leadership crisis. Harold Macmillan had virtually promised Hailsham that if he could renounce his peerage he would be prime minister. The thought of such a thing being possible led many Tories to think of their former Foreign Secretary, the 14th Earl of Home.

The following spring, almost exactly two years after Benn's exclusion, the Lords sent a message to inform the Commons that they were ready to meet them at eleven a.m. a week later for a joint committee to consider some scheme of general reform. It took them just under a month to make their recommendations.

Another debate took place. The star turn was the eighty-two-year-old Viscount Esher, who had flown from his home in the South of France to take part, who remembered Gladstone, and who mocked the life peers, from an intellectual standpoint, as a terrible disappointment.

Hailsham had been busy behind the scenes. As originally drafted, the joint committee's report only allowed hereditary peers to renounce their peerages if, as Benn had originally suggested, they had not taken their seats in the Lords. This would have solved Benn's problems but left Hailsham where he was. He had already appealed to Benn to try to swing the Labour Party round to reform, showing little concern for the dignity of the Upper House: 'Tell them, if you really want to weaken the House of Lords, let the able young peers try for the Commons. All the good ones will prefer that and the Lords will be left with the second-rate people.' Now he appeared twice before the committee, arguing the case for those who were already sitting in the Lords, and eventually persuaded the Tory MP Gilbert Mitchison to move an amendment that would allow Hailsham to return to the Commons.

The amendment was opposed by both the chairman of the committee, Lord Kilmuir, and by the Attorney General. The clerks, too, had been told that the object was to erect as many hurdles, no less psychological than practical, to a peer deciding to disclaim his peerage. Then Kilmuir announced that the amendment was vitally important: 'The whole future of the Conservative Party is tied up in this. It's not just Quintin, Alec's in this too.' The Mitchison Amendment was finally passed by a majority of one and Lord Mitchison went to the Upper House in 1964.

The Bill was introduced in the Lords by the Lord Chancellor, Lord Dilhorne, formerly Sir Reginald Manninghorn-Butler, with languid charm. No one listening to him would have suspected the Tories of having just performed a highly undignified moral somersault. He skilfully wrapped up the Mitchison Amendment in a little joke, referring to Hailsham and Home *en passant* as 'sitting peers', saying he hoped the term would not sound unsporting 'to those of us who shoot'.

Lord Kilmuir, the chairman of the committee, restated the case for renunciation, and explained why he was against 'drowning' or 'extinguishing'. To renounce for the lifetime of the holder would give complete freedom of action to each generation: he would still transmit the peerage and leave it to his successor to make up his mind whether or not he wanted it.

This time there was no talk of pulling bricks out of walls: the Tories needed Home, so the constitutional change was justified. Benn, the good Puritan, was back in the House of Commons.

CHAPTER TWENTY

The Theatre of Compromise

If the hereditary principle in the House of Lords survived the Liberals' 1911 death sentence and continued throughout the twentieth century it was thanks to an odd combination of factors. Laziness and complacency certainly played their part: nothing happened because there was insufficient Horizonist passion to make it happen. Big money, too, was happy to prop up any system that ensured stability. But there was also a positive romanticism, a nostalgia, an instinctive love of tradition and continuity.

In the Lords' debate to approve the Hailsham and Home renunciations in 1963, allowing peers to renounce their titles, Lord Esher recalled his anger as a young man with Mr Gladstone for being so slow in going to the rescue of General Gordon at Khartoum, and offered his own thoughts, at eighty-two, on the hereditary principle. Much of the pomp and circumstance that used to surround the aristocratic life, he admitted, had gone with the wind. The Lords all knew that the glories of their blood and state, to quote the poet, were shadows, not substantial things. But even in these unromantic days people preserved many marks of distinction, many badges of inequality. Even democrats seemed happy to accept them. 'As a matter of fact, the philosophic notion that all men are equal has been having rather a bad time. First of all, it is not true; and secondly, we do not want it to be true.' In any case, the English were fortunately not a logical people, and no philosophy was ever carried to its logical conclusion. Drafting new constitutions, Lord Esher went on, was great fun. Any semi-educated sixth-former could do it – he had drawn up a dozen or so himself. He remembered Rousseau, Karl Marx, Hitler, Cromwell and Alexander Hamilton in no particular order. 'Our long experience tells us that under every plan, Right or Left, inspired by God or dictated by Satan, someone is going to govern us and control. The problem is how to limit that power to a bearable minimum. Because it is obvious that the House of Lords has influence without power, it is accepted by everybody who has ever examined the question, and tried to consider how to replace it, as the best Second Chamber in the world. We are fortunate to have an institution which we certainly should never have had the intelligence to create.'

People, it was claimed by some members of the House of Commons, dismissed the peers as incompetent nitwits or as antiquated fuddy-duddies of debased intellect. He had never found that: 'If peers were unpopular, as Communists, for instance, are unpopular, people would sheer away from them. They would be reluctant to meet them in social life. They would not want their daughters to marry them.'

The usual interesting variety of English life, he maintained, was just as conspicuous on the red benches as on the green, and anyone who thought anything else was the victim of a form of inverted snobbery. It was not rank that was unpopular, it was power: 'The holders of power have made such a mess of the world: national power, with its futile and disastrous wars; commercial power, with its expensive vulgarity; Civil Service power, with its ruthless and meticulous severity; trade union power, with its wasteful and unintelligent use of the strike weapon.'

'The House of Lords, from which we receive no form which has to be filled up, that never wants to know how many children we have, or whether we have made a profit out of the sale of last year's overcoat, will remain because it is a popular institution, dignified by time and always ready to give unpaid and useful service to the community.'

But, even in that Lords' debate, there were frustrated progressives, disappointed Horizonists, who wanted reform to move faster. Lord Samuel was also well over eighty, and had been a member of Asquith's government in 1911. He believed, foolishly as it turned out, that he was within sight of the Promised Land. He compared watching Lords reform over the last fifty years to seeing 'a slow-motion film of a prima ballerina, marked by an exhibition of almost languid deliberation'.

But reform had not just been slowed down by the kind of concern for the Lords as a part of our national heritage like red squirrels and ancient monuments preached by Lord Esher. In earlier days that had always been the first line of defence, the need, as Edmund Burke put it, 'to nurse a parent's venerable age'. Paradoxically, in the twentieth century, some of the hereditary peers' most passionate defenders were their enemies. Convinced that they were doomed, like capitalism, to inevitable collapse and that any reform would delay that happy outcome, abolitionists fought tooth and nail to preserve them in what Balfour had called their naked absurdity.

In 1911 Horizonists had certainly led the attack, convinced that they could replace the Lords with a democratically acceptable senate. They threatened mass action, the pressure of a new enlarged electorate, and all the language and imagery used in the attack emphasized the hereditary peers' role in state theatre, their coronets and robes, their ancient titles and country estates, the trappings of the Shining Ladder. If the enthusiasm of the reformers seemed to waver, it was partly because such imagery suddenly became respectable again as part of the patriotic pageantry revived in the First World War and in the eventual victory partly because radicals realized that the theatrical show had been used by Capital, like a bullfighter's cape, to bewilder and distract the suffering victim, the People. But they also became less convinced of their objectives.

Throughout the inter-war years Horizonists continued their advance, steadily increasing the influence of democracy. In 1919 there was finally universal suffrage, the recognition of the rights of the common man and the common woman, even of the common child, at the expense of the hereditary landowner. But from Bryce onwards the same logic wavered in the face of Lords' reform. There was a continuing conviction that hereditary peers were an irrational element in modern government and had to go, but, again and again, there was growing concern and hesitation about who should take their place and how such people ought to be chosen.

By the time Attlee called the all-party conference to reform the Lords in 1948 the Horizonists ruled virtually unchallenged, but there were now serious divisions about the way forward. A majority was still in favour of abolishing the Lords altogether, the Commons should reign supreme.

Others, appreciating the virtues of a second chamber, were prepared to risk gradual reform. The House of Lords immediately after the Second World War was behaving in a remarkably docile way, approving higher and higher taxes on the rich to pay for the new National Health Service, only hesitating over the detail of nationalizing coal and steel. Even though Attlee's all-party conference included old Tory Shining Ladderists still keen to retain the hereditary peers, its final report conceded most of the reformers' demands. As in 1911 hereditary peers would go, to be replaced by life peers known as Lords of Parliament. Constitutionally there would be no objection to hereditary peers becoming life peers, and they would have the ordinary rights enjoyed by any other subject to vote and to stand for Parliament. But the hereditary right to a seat and a vote would be ended. In the new Upper House no party would ever have a permanent majority, though quite how this was to be achieved was not worked out in detail.

What continued to divide the reformers was how these Lords of Parliament should be chosen. Horizonist orthodoxy demanded that they should be chosen by as many people as possible, but an elected second chamber would be seen as a rival to the sovereign power of the elected House of Commons. Bryce's proposal that the Lords of Parliament be elected from geographical regions by groups of MPs had dropped out of favour, so the only alternative seemed to be selection, an extension of the Honours List. They would be appointed by the Prime Minister and the party leaders.

In fact, except for a reduction to six months of the period for which the Lords were allowed to delay Bills, nothing happened. Further reforms were postponed.

In 1958, the life peers arrived and, for the first time since the Norman Conquest, women sat in the House of Lords. As envisaged, they were selected by the Prime Minister, and in order to rebalance party strengths in the Lords, the leaders of the other parties each submitted candidates for the Prime Minister's approval. Life peerages, the Tories argued, represented genuine reform. They were free of hereditary embarrassments and would make recruitment to the Upper House easier for Labour. This was probably true. If Hugh Gaitskell, according to Harold Macmillan, was 'a little embarrassed' about nominating life peers, his successors like Michael Foot were perfectly happy to haggle with a Tory prime minister about how many deserving old Labourites they could find a place for in the retirement home.

In practice, 1958 was also a watershed. The arrival of the more active life peers galvanized the active hereditaries, and the five hundred-odd non-participating hereditary peers were encouraged to suspend their membership. Standing Order 21 on Leave of Absence, while not denying the right of backwoodsmen to appear, obliged them to sign off either for the session or permanently if they had no intention of attending. In 1967 this was tightened up with a letter from the Clerk of the Journals to any peer who had not taken part in the previous session's debates. If he did not reply he was excluded. The Tories were less keen to draw attention to the fact that these reforms left the hereditary peers untouched.

Presenting the Bill, Harold Macmillan was characteristically bland. These might seem to be 'rather exiguous proposals after so many years of waiting', and they were not revolutionary, but they made a modest and, he hoped, fruitful advance along the path of evolution.

Clement Davies, a Liberal who had been in the Commons in 1911 and had served on Attlee's committee in 1948, rejected the whole scheme as 'tinkering'. The entire Labour Party opposed it. Jennie Lee spoke of the 'craft and canniness' of the Tory government in shoring up the hereditary House of Lords. She was even prepared to vote against what the Tory minister Lady Tweedsmuir had ironically called 'the awful decision of having women in the Upper House'. The Lords was a duller place without women, Jennie Lee conceded, but she was perfectly happy for it to remain so. She had nothing against the Lords as 'a historical hangover', a place that did a modest job and knew its place, but she would fight to the death the government's attempts to give the old Tory stronghold a spurious respectability and greater authority.

One Liberal lawyer quoted the paradox that the strength of the House of Lords, constitutionally speaking, lay in its weakness, and the fear that the Lords might become more powerful made even moderate Horizonists, like Gaitskell, cautious about grasping the nettle.

Gaitskell believed in a Second Chamber, but any reformed Second

Chamber would presumably contain higher calibre members who would command greater press attention and more influence. Even without, in Horizonist eyes, the sanctifying effect of election, they would challenge the Commons. The alternative, critics of the Upper House now began to realize, was almost worse. An appointed House of Lords would be a bran-tub of patronage. With junior ministries 'breeding like rabbits', already offering more and more jobs to be dangled in front of MPs to ensure their loyalty, retirement posts in the Lords would extend even further the range of rewards available for any prime minister to hand out in exchange for political services.

Later in the same debate Gaitskell later found himself in even deeper trouble when he touched on the inconsistencies or constitutional loose ends in the Upper House: the hereditary peeresses who were excluded by reason of their sex, the Scottish peers who, even when they were not elected to the Lords, were unable to vote in a general election.

These debating points of Gaitskell's were taken up with a great show of serious concern by the Tories during the 1963 Peerage Renunciation debate that released Tony Benn and allowed Hailsham and Home to perform their giddy bungee-jump into the Commons and back into the Lords. The debate in the Upper House was less bitter, but infinitely more mystical, concealing the shoddy party manoeuvrings under much heraldic mumbo-jumbo.

Lord Longford made a long and typically batty speech all about himself, uncharacteristically apologizing for his 'egocentric observations'. In a nutshell his problem was that he had more than one title and didn't know which to renounce. As he apparently had no intention of renouncing any, he might have been accused of wasting their lordships' time and money. He suffered, he thought almost uniquely, from a kind of *embarras de richesses*. Just after the war Attlee had made him a peer as Lord Pakenham. He admitted that the fact that he was heir to a peerage might have influenced Attlee's decision. He was, he boasted, the youngest peer ever created, except for Lord Beaverbrook, and Lord Beaverbrook was a law unto himself. Since then he had inherited an Irish peerage and had become the Earl of Longford, which did not under the present arrangements entitle him to a seat in the Lords, as well as a United Kingdom barony as Lord Silchester, which did. Now there was a clause in the Renunciation Bill forbidding anyone to renounce a first-creation peerage, or personal honour, so could he renounce one of his inherited titles instead?

Lord Rathcavan got up and asked him what his name was. He called himself the Earl of Longford, but did he sit there by virtue of being Lord Pakenham or Lord Silchester?

This confused poor Lord Longford terribly. He said he had never been quite clear. 'It is Silchester, so to speak, that presents the problem.' It was only later in the debate that he rose to his feet again, dome gleaming, to explain that he had made a mistake: it was not Silchester that was the problem, it was Pakenham.

Winding up, Hailsham enjoyed himself at Longford's expense. The noble earl, Lord Longford, had wrung their hearts with his personal and complicated story, but he felt it his duty to confess that he himself had been the innocent occasion of Longford's having accepted the first of his three titles, when Hailsham had beaten him in the 1945 general election at Oxford.

What the public and even the Commons failed to notice at the time, intrigued as they were by the Benn case and the drama of the Tory leadership, was that various other 'loose ends' to do with the composition of the Upper House were tied up, and these included the anomalies pointed out by Gaitskell. The right of hereditary peers to a seat in the Upper House was not deemed a 'loose end', and was once again passed over, but in the course of the other tidying-up Lord Hailsham almost certainly cut through its legal taproot.

It is necessary here to go slowly and consider the historical arguments that had produced the various loose ends. The first was the position of hereditary peeresses, women whose peerages were expressly laid down as passing through the female line, whose titles had never brought with them any right to sit in the Lords. After Lady Rhondda's failed attempt to introduce sexual equality into the Upper House in the 1920s, hereditary peers had come under a certain amount of pressure from those in search of a Feminist Bright Horizon. Baroness Wootton, hesitant about accepting a life peerage, admitted that it was 'hard to resist blitzing such an all-male institution'.

Like many other gentlemen's clubs, the Lords had resisted it. Their argument, as in a gentleman's club, was broadly Ladderist: tradition did not allow the presence of women. Then, with the Tories introducing life peerages, they saw themselves invaded. Of the first three life peeresses one, by a happy touch, happened to be an hereditary peeress. Lady Ravensdale was the daughter of Lord Curzon, another man, like Hailsham, who had tested the elasticity of the arrangements. Returning from his job as Viceroy of India, he was rewarded at his own request with an Irish peerage, which would have allowed him to fulfil his ambitions of attaining high office in the House of Commons. This was not to be, and the Tory Party then shamelessly pushed his name to the top of the list of representative Irish peers waiting to be elected to the Lords, and he took his seat in 1908. This created bad feeling among the Irish peerage, and he annoyed them even more by taking, in addition to an earldom in George V's Coronation honours in 1911, a limited United Kingdom barony he chose should pass, in the absence of a male heir, to his daughter.

But now that Curzon's daughter had taken her seat in the Lords, with Lady Elliott, Lady Swanborough and all the life peeresses who followed, Gaitskell and others found themselves in a dilemma. Feminist Horizonism demanded a world in which women sat in the Lords; Shining Ladderism was all too ready to provide them. Gaitskell had found himself arguing for the rights of hereditary peeresses.

There were then nineteen potential claimants, twelve from England and seven from Scotland. Numbers were complicated by the Dowager Viscountess St Davids, who had inherited three other baronies by writ, one dating from 1299, which made her simultaneously Baroness Strange of Knokin, Baroness Hungerford and Baroness de Moleyns, entitling her to four red-leather seats.

Lord Strabolgi, as Labour's spokesman in the Lords, found himself in a tricky position. He owed his presence there, though he made no reference to this, to a cunning peerage lawyer called Cozens-Hardy in 1877 who had based his case on a highly dubious 'membrane' found in a medieval roll of summonses. Cokayne's *Complete Peerage* was critical of the decision of the Committee for Privileges in accepting it. 'That an individual who represents an unknown fraction of a barony which never existed, a barony which even on the most favourable representation had been unheard of for 547 years, should be given the precedence of 1318, at the expense of most of the barons of the realm, is an outrage which the House of Lords may be expected to resent.' But the Labour Party, Strabolgi said, could not accept any extension of the hereditary principle. Like many things in this country, it might be indefensible in theory but work in practice. But the reality was that as the twentieth century progressed it was becoming less and less defensible. He admitted that he could see advantages, and had to declare an interest. His peerage would be inherited by one of his nieces, and he thought in these days of sexual equality that she should be allowed to take his place.

He could have kept his pangs of conscience to himself. The Tories won the vote, and all the women, by reason of their birth, became members of the Upper House. Strabolgi's niece would succeed him there. It represented an extraordinary late victory for the Shining Ladder.

The second loose end was the case of the Scottish representative peers. The joint committee that met before the 1963 debate found themselves drawn into some extraordinary discussions about the history of the Scottish peerage. Under the clans, a far more ancient system existed than primogeniture, which allowed a clan chieftain to choose and appoint his successor from anyone in the immediate family whom he thought best suited to the job. This was a smack in the face for primogeniture and, according to Ladderist lawyers, amounted to surrendering and regranting the peerage. They smelt Horizonist heresy, merit rather than blind chance. What, they asked, would happen to the English peerage if such a system was found 'good in law' south of the border? They were reassured that it would not, and moved on to the question of the Scottish peers' election to Westminster.

The political theology that justified both their presence in the Lords and that of the Irish peers had a certain constitutional beauty. It was a rare blend of Ladder and Horizon that could have provided a valuable precedent for subsequent reformers. The Scottish peers, as we have seen, sat in the House of Lords by reason of their birth as elder sons. This was the Ladder. But their numbers were limited by election, and there was even an exclusion clause which ruled out a son being elected in place of his father. That was the Horizon.

Since the Union, the eighteen elected at the beginning of every new Parliament served in the Lords, while those not elected remained disqualified from either standing for the Lower House or, like lunatics, from voting in a general election. Many Scottish peers had since taken seats at Westminster by being created peers of Great Britain, and after the Union with Ireland as peers of the

United Kingdom. Many had become extinct. By 1962 the number of pure glen-grown peers with no other entitlement to sit in the Lords had sunk to thirty-one. With sixteen elected, this left only fifteen disenfranchized and disqualified from standing for the Commons. In 1963, therefore, as part of the same exercise in tidying up the loose ends, they, too, became Members of Parliament in the Upper House – another remarkable victory for the Ladder. Where the trouble came was with their noble cousins from Ireland.

Since 1801 the Irish peerage had elected twenty-eight of their number to serve at Westminster for life. Those not elected had the right to sit on the steps of the Throne in the Parliament Chamber and even to stand for election to the House of Commons – Lord Palmerston, for instance, was an Irish peer – though not for constituencies in the North of Ireland. If they won a seat at Westminster they were also given the right to vote as honorary commoners in any general election.

This had changed after the First World War. Until 1922, Ireland was in heraldic terms as British as England or Scotland, with the Knights of the Order of St Patrick rivalling the Order of the Garter and the Order of the Thistle. Whenever an Irish representative peer died, a writ of summons was issued to the Lord Chancellor of Ireland, who instructed the clerk of the Crown and Hanaper – from the Low Latin *hanaperium* meaning Treasury – to write to the Irish peers who would elect a new one by postal ballot.

With Ireland in open rebellion, the work of the Lord Chancellor of Ireland was taken over by the Lord Lieutenant, and before he could call any election of representative peers, Dublin had thrown out the Lord Lieutenant, together with the Crown and even the Hanaper. In principle, the machinery could have been reconstructed on British soil north of the border in Ulster. In practice it was not, and no more Irish peers were elected. As part of their job of tidying up the loose ends the committee preparing the ground for the 1963 debate was asked to clear up this question too.

Rumour in the 1920s suggested a deal had been done to keep the Irish peers quiet, and their leader, Lord Oranmore and Browne, was certainly granted a United Kingdom peerage in 1926, becoming Lord Mereworth.

The question now, in 1963, was whether the old machinery should be rebuilt in Ulster to allow Irish representative peers to return to the Lords. If so, should they be elected for life as before, or for one parliament like the Scottish peers? Should those not elected now be allowed to sit in the House of Commons for constituencies in Northern Ireland?

There were now no Irish representative peers left to argue their case. Their last survivor, the Earl of Kilmorey, had died in 1961. It was therefore left to other Irish-born peers, entitled to a seat there through a peerage of Great Britain or of the United Kingdom.

Lord Rathcavan spoke with nostalgia of the Order of St Patrick, which would die with its last Knight, the elderly and eccentric Duke of Gloucester. He made the apparently obvious point that peers who had been born and lived in Northern Ireland had just as much right to a seat as Lord Hailsham. In the North the Act of Union had not been repealed. The only clue to their position he could find in the committee's report was the line 'It should be noted that there is no Peerage of Northern Ireland as such.'

Lord Longford could hardly have been less sympathetic. Even though he sat in the House calling himself by his Irish title and his heart was with the Irish peers, he was sorry to say that he had no intention of supporting them: 'If they feel I have betrayed them, it will not be the first time that Irish peers have been betrayed, and they are accustomed to taking it in good part.' They had to. Hailsham had virtually dictated terms to the committee, and he showed no respect either for peerage law or the Ladder. His argument was based on nothing but political expediency. Relations with Dublin were strained, it would not do to offend the Irish government. The presence of peers from Ulster in the House of Lords would 'tend to spoil our relations with the Republic of Ireland'.

The Lord Chancellor, Lord Kilmuir, supported Hailsham by a manoeuvre known in military circles as 'laying down smoke'. Some Irish peers, he told the House, lived in the Republic of Ireland. Before the Act of Union in 1801, they would have been entitled to seats in the Irish House of Lords in Dublin, and that institution had now been replaced by the Irish Senate. This, clearly, had nothing to do with the position of Northern Irish peers, who as British subjects had the same rights as any other peer, unchanged by events in the South, and only modified, like the Scots, by the old rules of election.

If, like the Scots, their numbers were so reduced as to make them no threat, they should have taken their seats, and Lord Dunboyne now demanded this.

Here Kilmuir quoted what he thought was an admirably witty answer by Lord Hailsham, that 'It would be weird if the title to sit in the Upper House depended upon the location North or South of the Border of a territorial title conferred before there was a Border to be north or south of.'

However thick the smoke, the rights of hereditary peers were now irretrievably damaged. The precedent existed. Thanks to that decision, though no one drew attention to it at the time, no British citizen would in future be entitled by reason of a hereditary peerage to a seat in the House of Lords. As an act of political expediency it was typical of the remodelling of the Upper House by Tory reformers. As long as the old aristocracy seemed to have some value in maintaining public order and security, lip-service continued to be paid to the Shining Ladder, and this was true both in the Ampthill and Benn cases.

In the Ampthill story, the legal charade had been biological. Blood tests were not yet admissible as evidence, but everything else – questions about the ejaculation of semen, the unruptured female hymen, the physical opportunities for sexual intimacy – was pored over in court and in the press with the unspoken assumption that something more than a name was being transmitted. Even though old Lord Ampthill was a rare visitor to the Upper House, even though his family was known not to be rich, some mysterious gift was being conferred on the child by being acknowledged as his grandson and Stilts's heir. It made the child different: it was associated with membership of a ruling caste. Much of the press interest, the scandal and the moralizing stemmed from that assumption.

In Benn's case, the analysis, beginning with the need to verify that he was the person named in his own birth certificate, was almost exclusively to do with peerage law. Precedent was seen as sacred: a man's right to represent his constituents in the House of Commons was taken away from him by witnesses who had been skeletons for centuries.

Both represented deference to the Shining Ladder: the sap running down the organic channels of the Ampthills' inverted family tree; the truth as to the right of Benn to renounce his peerage only to be derived from the authority of the remote past.

As long as it suited the Tory Party to shore up the social order, the official line held. Garter King Arms, wheeled out during the debates on whether Benn should be allowed to renounce his peerage, talked of the 'social demolition' that would be suffered by a peer's wife if renunciation was made possible. He saw the peerage as part of the monarchy's lustre and support. Anything that harmed it was 'kicking away the props'.

In the Commons debate that refused Benn the right to defend himself at the Bar, R. A. Butler conjured up a vision, first popularized by the constitutional lawyer Blackstone in his *Commentaries* in 1760, of the constitution as a great house incorporating the gradual accretions of the centuries. It was a sacred edifice essential to the maintenance of social order. The impulsive removal of a few bricks would bring about its collapse, with disastrous consequences for the future.

Then, with the slow realization that aristocratic figureheads like the unbelted Earl of Home were no longer necessary to hold the Tory Party together, that the Jimmy Diddlers and City sharks could maintain the structure of society unassisted and manage things to the Party's greater advantage, the mood changed. The façade of the House of Lords would be preserved, but its internal structure would be scrapped. That even the façade was preserved was almost entirely the achievement of the Horizonists. The early 1960s was an era during which much-loved architectural landmarks all over Britain were being bulldozed to make way for steel and glass, and in what looked like the final assault it was only the violent quarrels that broke out among the demolition team that spared the herditary peers once again.

In the Queen's Speech in October 1967, the Labour government announced that legislation would be introduced 'to reduce the present powers of the House of Lords and to eliminate its present hereditary basis', but that it was ready 'to enter into consultations appropriate to a constitutional change of such importance'. By the spring of 1968 an all-party group had agreed to what seemed a relatively simple reform of the composition of the Upper House. What was called a 'two-tier system' would take away the hereditary peers' right to vote, but would allow them, subject to further discussions, the possibility of asking questions and even sitting on committees. Life peers would be appointed to ensure that the Government in power would always have a small working majority, and any who attended less than a third of the debates would forfeit their voting rights. There would also be a general retirement age of seventy-five, to be reduced in time to seventy-two. The Lords' powers of delay would be reduced to allow any Bill to go through, whether they liked it or not, in a single session or in a so-called 'carry-over' session at the start of the next. Almost everyone seemed happy.

Then, in the summer of that year, the Rhodesia crisis polarized the parties. Ian Smith made his Unilateral Declaration of Independence, the United Nations imposed sanctions on his white supremacist regime, and the House of Commons passed the so-called Rhodesia Order approving the UN action.

In the Upper House feelings ran very high. With the capital of Rhodesia still named after his ancestor, Lord Salisbury and other Tory peers determined to make a stand against what they saw as international interference in a former British colony. The Labour government seemed on its last legs, losing at one point in that year three by-elections in a single week, and it seemed an ideal moment for the Lords to make its constitutional power felt, perhaps for the last time. Lord Carrington, Tory leader in the Upper House, urged restraint. Roy Jenkins, who was then Labour Home Secretary, warned them in a public speech that if they made trouble they could expect no mercy in the forthcoming reforms, but the Tory peers made a symbolic stand.

Having satisfied themselves that the Order, if they vetoed it, could go back to the Commons, be redrafted and become law within the UN deadline, they voted 193 to 184 against, and threw it out. Harold Wilson was furious, announced that the all-party talks on Lords' reform were off, and the Labour government would draw up its own White Paper for the reform of the Lords.

In fact the White Paper coincided almost exactly with the all-party proposals of the spring. Despite a fiery speech from Lord Milford, again pleading for immediate abolition, the Lords approved reform as outlined in the White Paper by 251 to 56.

In the Commons the Horizonists sounded dangerous. One Labour MP, David Marquand, urged the final destruction of the Ladder in the clearest possible terms. 'The values symbolized by the Other

Place – by the whole apparatus of medieval pageantry and mysticism that surrounds the Other Place – are values that we on this side of the House find abhorrent. Indeed they are deeply opposed to the values of the liberal enlightenment on which the Western World has been based since the French Revolution.'

Another talked of the need to 'strike a blow at the whole class system by ripping the peerage system in pieces'. A third Labour member quoted a tract from the turn of the century: 'Dissolve the halo of divinity that surrounds the hereditary title, let people clearly understand that our present House of Lords is composed largely of successful pirates and rogues. Do these things and you shatter the romance that keeps a nation numb and spellbound while privilege picks its pockets.' It sounded like the knell of doom.

Richard Crossman, who opened the debate for the Government, was hot for reform. Labour and the Liberals hoped to see the new House of Lords ready for the Queen's Speech at the beginning of the next Parliament in 1969. The Tories wanted more time.

Crossman began by offering what the Tory Norman St John-Stevas satirically described as an *apologia pro vita sua*, an account of his 'spiritual journey from the outer darkness of a newspaper office to the inner light of the Cabinet Room'. As a don and a journalist, Crossman told the Commons, he had always been in favour of abolition. Then, when he came to know more about Parliament as a Labour MP, he had begun to think that an obviously ridiculous collection of peers was serving a useful Socialist purpose. They ensured that Britain had the weakest and most ineffectual Second Chamber in the world. Now, as a minister in a Labour government, he had come to the conclusion that a Second Chamber was needed, and that it should be more efficient.

Few men have been more mocked in the House of Commons than Crossman during the two days of the debate. What attracted the most derision was the scheme for achieving party balance by appointing thirty cross-benchers who would form a permanent block of 'independents'.

Sir Hugh Fraser, the booming aristocratic husband of Lady Antonia, asked, to roars of laughter, whether they would be appointed as stooges by the Tory front bench or the Labour front bench. What would happen to the Government's working majority if they changed their spots or their minds and voted for one of the main parties? Another Tory called them 'political vestal virgins'.

'What sort of men and women are they to be,' asked Enoch Powell, 'who would submit to be nominated to another Chamber upon condition that they will be mere dummies, automatic parts of a voting machine?'

There was also widespread ridicule of the idea of all these new peers being 'appointed'. A Labour MP, Maurice Edelman, had written an article in the *Daily Express* on the day before the debate headed 'Government by Patronage', in which he predicted that MPs, 'already tamed by the whips, would wait in supine deference and expectancy for their elevation'.

This theme was more broadly developed by Eric Heffer, on the extreme left of the Labour Party, who said they were all familiar with the patronage system as it at present existed. A man came up to you in the Commons corridor when your vote was needed and said, 'Look here, you are ministerial calibre.' Did they want the same man to come up and say, 'Look here, the next time you lose your seat you will end up in Another Place'?

Other speakers dwelt on the rewards. Whatever the salary, a peerage need not involve more than forty-five days' work a year, with a title for life and all the social advantages that entailed.

Enemies of an elected rather than a selected second chamber were even more derisive. Those who remembered Bryce recalled the best option, of peers elected from the regions by the local MPs, but any chamber directly elected by the people, even by proportional representation, would challenge the sovereign power of the Commons.

The old constitutional language of the seventeenth century reappeared, unrecognized, when the Tory Tom Iremonger read out a phrase from the White Paper that the work of the two Houses 'should become more closely *co-ordinated* and integrated'. That, he shouted, was a constitutional indignity. 'The function of the Second House is not to be co-ordinated with this one. It is the very opposite.' However great the pressure of business in the last year of a parliament, the Lords must be allowed to answer back. 'I do not believe this House will necessarily be always absolutely right, and I do not want to "co-ordinate" and compound the error by having a lot of stooges up there in the Other House saying "Hear,

hear! Quite right!"' Parliament was never meant to be 'efficient' in the concept of government. That was heresy. Parliament had been established from time immemorial to be a confounded nuisance to governments. He despised the idea that they had to trot upstairs with bulging briefcases and empty minds, 'helping governments in dirty little committees, doing their dirty little work'. Iremonger even advanced a rare defence of the old Shining Ladder, offering as an alternative to prime ministerial patronage the random choice obtained by genetics. Xenophon had been selected by lottery and had been a perfectly adequate commander of the Greek Army.

It was a long time since such extreme ideas had been heard in the Commons, but the most astonishing alliance was that evolved between Michael Foot and Enoch Powell.

Talking about it thirty years later, Michael Foot's eyes still lit up with admiration as he remembered Enoch's arguments: 'I didn't know the fellow at all, but as I listened I realized, my goodness, this man knows more about the history of the place than anyone else in the building. He's a highly intelligent man – and you had to admire that!'

Enoch's arguments shot the platform from under the reformers: 'Reform is commended to us on two distinct and contradictory grounds. One is in order to prevent the Upper House from frustrating or unduly delaying the decisions and wishes of this House. The other ground, which is contradictory to it, is to enable the Upper House to be a more effective check upon the proceedings of this House and to hold a more convincing balance against it.' The idea that the House of Lords had ever in recent times, he said, frustrated or delayed the decisions of the House of Commons was 'a chimera'. The need for greater powers was 'a mirage'.

It was T. G. D. Galbraith, heir to a peerage as the son of Lord Strathclyde and the Tory Member for Glasgow Hillhead, who put the most elegant case for the hereditary peers, paraphrasing the general confession in the Church of England's Book of Common Prayer: 'What are these grounds for change? It is not as though the members of the House of Lords were incompetent; nobody has suggested that. It is not that the Lords have abused their powers; it is not that they have failed to do something which they ought to have done, or done something which they ought not to have done. The objection to the House of Lords is not practical; it is not against the way in which the House of Lords has acted or has worked; it is an entirely hypothetical and theoretical objection to the way in which it might work, because it might do something objectionable to the government.'

In all these speeches there was clear evidence of members of the House of Commons' resentment at being used as lobby-fodder, even an implicit envy of the political independence of Members of the Upper House. It was Willie Hamilton, Socialist MP and lifelong scourge of the monarchy, who introduced the amendment that the White Paper should be rejected. The proposals would turn Parliament into an 'elective bureaucracy', and he was prepared to 'soil himself ' by entering the same lobby as Enoch Powell to support it. He and Michael Foot, who had ridiculed his own party's 'Front Bench Mafia', were the tellers, and they collected 159 votes from all parties against the Government's 270.

The Labour cabinet made minor changes – an earlier idea to pay life peers a salary was dropped – and the Bill was introduced in January 1969. Both Harold Wilson and the opposition leader, now Sir Alec Douglas-Home, spoke in its favour, it passed its Second Reading, and then became hopelessly bogged down at the Committee Stage. Feelings between the two parties were unusually hostile, there was no co-operation between the whips, notions like the 'working majority' for the Government in power, the role of the cross-benchers and the threat of patronage were picked over and ridiculed, the debate dragged on through February and into March, and in April the Labour government dropped it. It was to be a long time before anyone again suggested reforming the House of Lords.

POSTSCRIPT:

Business as Usual

It was nearly ten o'clock on a summer night in 1993, and a crowded House of Lords was listening to the inheritor of the last-created hereditary peerage, the Earl of Stockton. A publisher with a thick black beard, he owed his seat in the Upper House to the fact that he was Harold Macmillan's grandson. He was talking about the more recently ennobled life peer Norman Tebbit, bald, sinister and hollow-eyed, who was expected to arrive later that night to make a widely trailed speech on Europe. Had their lordships noticed, Lord Stockton asked, that Lord Tebbit only ever appeared in the Parliament Chamber after dark? Should someone tell him that Transylvania had not yet applied for membership of the European Community? This got a very satisfactory laugh.

The House of Lords was unquestionably doing its job. It was the second long day of one of many debates about the terms of the treaty of Maastricht, and the Thatcher–Tebbit Europhobes, three clear years before the irruption of Sir James Goldsmith and his Referendum Party, had put down an amendment demanding a referendum on whether the Maastricht treaty should be ratified. Their lordships had been speaking without interruption for more than eight hours, and the cast, complete with traditional Tory backwoodsmen stumbling about, bewildered by the architecture and strange smells, had at one point approached seven hundred.

During the afternoon and early evening there were peers squatting in a low semi-circle on the steps of the Throne, peers squashed uncomfortably together on the red leather benches, peers on the Bench of Bishops with the Bishop of Chelmsford representing the lords spiritual crammed up at one end in his cassock and surplice, even quite elderly peers crouched in the gangways. The messengers in their white ties, black tail coats and dangling silver medallions found their way through the crush with the usual excessive deference, but otherwise there was a mood of gently bored fascination as the senators of the unreformed House listened to a sequence of speeches for or against closer integration with Europe. The sense of theatre was as intense as ever, and there was a comforting historical familiarity in listening to their lordships wriggling their way grumpily into Europe in much the same way as they had wriggled their way grumpily out in the Reformation Parliament of 1531. There was the same outrage at the expense the country had been drawn into by signing the treaty of Rome, the same music-hall edge on the jokes about foreigners, particularly the French.

Lord Beloff, populist right-wing academic, had stood there pugnaciously in the Tory benches like some plump pro-Reformation bishop, hands in pockets, talking without notes. Look what the Common Agricultural Policy had done to our farmers. French protectionism had been in operation since Louis XIV and Colbert. Nothing would change it now, the French were all hypocrites. He also insulted the current Euro-Pope. Douglas Hurd's motto, he said, seemed to be 'Delors is my Shepherd.' This got a more moderate laugh, but there was a louder and crueller guffaw when he, apparently in all innocence, suggested a 'neutral' form of words as the question in the referendum: 'Do you want to be governed by a bunch of foreigners in Brussels?'

Lord Carrington, hereditary peer and a distinguished former Foreign Secretary, who had spent years of his political life wrestling with European milk quotas, took the opposite line. As a farmer he admitted that the last six months had been hell, whether because of bureaucrats in Brussels or the over-zealous enforcement of their directives by our own Ministry of Agriculture, but he was still in favour of Europe. He was calm, a smooth old statesman to his fingertips, arguing for common sense and tolerance. He drew a distinction between the conceptualists and the pragmatists, those who were terrified by the abstract idea and those who were prepared to work within the real system. Most of what was threatened would not happen. His reasoned reassurance was actually no more honest than Beloff's scaremongering, but it suited the mood of the House of Lords. The Lords were the priests of order and law, hierarchy and authority, and as Ladderists the dream of re-creating a Holy European Empire was irresistible, even if its pettier regulations drove them mad and played into the hands of the Horizonists, the reformers and Protestants.

The sets and lighting for this timeless charade remained impeccable. In the afternoon the sunshine had slanted in through the stained-glass windows on a scene of stockbroker-Tudor dignity, lighting the Lord Chancellor in his wig and black robe with the golden facings, dominant on the scarlet Woolsack, still stuffed with all that Commonwealth wool. As evening came the canopy above the Throne glowed into a dim golden splendour, its massive early-Victorian tiered brass candlestands on either side, electric candles blazing in three diminishing circles.

All that was missing was the audience. The public galleries were empty, and so was the press gallery, except for a man in an off-the-peg charcoal-grey suit and a military haircut whose job was to operate the sound system. In front of him was a board with several rows of little green indicator lights, one of which was always lit. He had a puzzle book open beside it, and as each lone voice droned on below he quietly joined up letters to form words, or dots to make pictures. When the tone of the amplified voice changed to indicate that a speech was coming to an end, he glanced over the edge of the press gallery, and as soon as another peer had established himself, punched a button. A new light glowed on the board, the appropriate microphone hanging over the red-leather benches came on, the peer's voice assumed new clarity and focus, and the sound man returned to his puzzle book.

This would all change when Lord Tebbit appeared. He had spent the past week stumping round the country with a busload of journalists drumming up press interest, snarling at radio interviewers, twisting the arms of newspaper editors and television producers. But it was worth brooding for a moment on the more ordinary routine of the House.

In the 1920s Asquith had compared the Lords to a second-rate rural district council, and even that night there were some extraordinarily bad speeches. Lord Harmar-Nichols emptied the red leather benches within seconds. He stood there swaying, ending every line on the same rising inflection, hand sawing the air. He recalled the great days when as a promising young minister he had resigned from Macmillan's government. When I asked one of the doorkeepers if he was always as boring as that, he said simply, out of the corner of his mouth, 'He's barmy!'

Another hereditary peer, Lord Selsdon, there thanks to his grandfather having been Postmaster General in 1924, got up to tell the House he had meant to read out a speech he had made twenty years before but that he had left his glasses at home. He couldn't really make up his mind about Europe, but he thought it was a very tedious debate, and offered a humorous contribution. Did their lordships know that the word 'Maas' in Afrikaans meant sour milk? He also reminded them of a hugely amusing postcard he had once seen, showing a little girl looking down a little boy's swimming trunks and saying, 'Vive la différence.'

The silence was audible, the Lord Chancellor on the Woolsack remained impassive, the *Hansard* writers tapped silently away, the television cameras winked, every word and gesture was recorded.

What was almost more terrible was the silence and the emptiness of the press gallery when peers of intellect and experience were talking. Lord Blake reminded the Lords of four occasions in the 1970s when there had been a referendum. Lord Ezra, former head of the National Coal Board, regretted the missed opportunities of the Messina conference of 1955. Lord Alexander of Weedon, chairman of the National Westminster Bank, explained in simple terms the economic advantages of a single currency. Lord Ardwick counted the cost of European lorries to English roads at £5 million. Lord Simon of Glaisdale, suffering from the after-effects of a stroke, argued powerfully that a single currency did not mean a single government, witness the Latin Union of the last century, the parity of the Irish punt and the pound sterling irrespective of Irish independence. Lord Reay talked with energy and clarity about the insularity of England since the death of Castlereagh. He said it was not an assault by Europe but an embrace.

Not a word of these speeches would ever appear in the newspapers. They had not been meant for a mass audience. A word or two might have been broadcast in *Today in Parliament* on the

BBC, but any reasonable-sized fire would have squeezed them off the television news. The arguments, perhaps naïvely in the presence of the Government whip, were intended to influence opinion in the Parliament Chamber. When they did influence opinion, it admittedly came as a shock. The newly ennobled Lord Skidelsky's confession that the debate had made him change his mind about Europe was received with the same slight writhing of embarrassment that would have greeted a story of religious conversion.

Peers in private conversation beforehand had talked about their chances of 'getting into the debate', of making a particular point. They spoke as individuals, not as representatives of the People. Baroness Blackstone, a recently created lifer, glittered by reason of her comparative youth, but the senility and vacancy of other life peers more than matched that of the feeblest hereditaries. At their worst, they were not so much local councillors as bores in a saloon bar. At their best they might have been a colossally expensive committee of senior management, the CBI, the National Trust.

But it was when they were at their best that their theatrical dignity contrasted so cruelly with the lack of public attention, and that was unquestionably to do with their own lack of real political power. That did not stop individuals like Baroness Thatcher from trying to use the House of Lords as a public platform. But where Brougham had succeeded in talking to the people over the heads of the peers, the Noble Baroness failed.

Earlier that day she had an effective warm-up man in Viscount Tonypandy, who as George Thomas had been one of the most popular Speakers of the Commons. He was now a peer on the cross-benches and the survivor of nearly ten years of throat cancer. It was partly his poor cracked voice, partly the tragic simplicity of his appeal for retaining the sovereignty of what he called in his strained Welsh accent 'Britaine', but he had a powerful effect. Everywhere he looked, peers looked back at him with sorrowful, encouraging smiles and he went for them like a dying evangelist: 'The Suvve-reign-tee uv our countree is at steyake!' he croaked to the sympathetically smiling faces. 'Weeyar deecidin' for those 'oo are yet unborn. Britaine wants this ref-fur-en-dum, an' shee deeserves it!'

After that the Noble Baroness should have had an easy ride, but Lord Tonypandy was followed by Lord Jenkins of Hillhead, the urbane Chancellor of Oxford University. He rose from the Liberal benches on the left of the Throne in highly jocular mood. Twenty years earlier, in 1975, he gleefully recalled, revelling in his inability to pronounce his rs and the mood of general *bonhomie* that welcomed his remarks, the Noble Baroness had not only been all in favour of Europe, she had been against the idea of a referendum: 'In speaking against the Referendum Bill,' Jenkins remembered, standing with his legs well apart, his hands by his sides, and giving his wrists a kind of backward flip to emphasize particular words like a diver propelling himself off the top board, 'the Noble Baroness quoted with approval a 1945 statement of Lord Attlee, which said that the referendum was a device "alien to our traditions which had only too often been the instrument of Nazism and Fascism".'

This produced a roar of laughter, and the Noble Baroness, not a frequent visitor to the House of Lords since her entombment there, pressed her lips together and wrote something on the speech on her lap.

Jenkins went down extremely well. He was not only popular with the Lords, he gave a strong, confident performance.

That of the Noble Baroness, by contrast, was uncertain. 'My lords,' she began, with a tone of weary irony, and a cold smile at Jenkins, 'when I came to this House it was somehow under the impression that things were less lively here, much more courteous, and much less robust.'

There was a murmur of sympathy from her own side, but Jenkins only beamed more broadly. Beside her on the front bench old Lord Hailsham scratched his head and rearranged his sticks, and she began to read her speech. She flailed away with her spectacles just as she used to do in the Commons; she stood in front of the front bench in the Lords as she used to stand in front of the front bench in the Commons. Somehow it didn't work. The power had gone.

Whether by accident or design, and the latter seemed more likely, Geoffrey Howe was sitting behind her in exactly the same position he had occupied in the Commons on the day he had accused her of sawing the cabinet's cricket bats in half behind the pavilion. Any actress in her position would have realized that she was losing her audience. Except, as she made it very clear, they were not her real audience, simply extras in her television studio. When she reached her key line, 'It surely is time to heed Kipling's warning – "And the burned Fool's bandaged finger goes wobbling back to the Fire", she slowed down, focused on the discreet little black camera fixed under the gallery opposite, and enunciated every syllable of her sixty-second soundbite for the world's television news. Brougham would have done the same, but Brougham understood the Lords and could charm them. The Noble Baroness could not.

In the corridor outside was Nicholas Soames, one of her loyal lieutenants in the old days. He had been watching her performance, as a Government minister, from the steps of the Throne, and even he was shaking his head. 'It's the same with Ted Heath. His whole style is based on being very rude to people and people being very rude back. He knows his act would never work in the Lords. What she used to flourish on was interruptions. In the Lords no one interrupts, she has nothing to play off.'

Jo Grimond blamed her unpopularity on the fact that she didn't flatter them enough: 'The peers like to be made to feel tremendously important.' They did, but as an institution, not as individual politicians.

As the defenders of liberty, of the structure of law, of the Ladder itself, they were by nature and religious conviction conservative. They were not aggressive. They were not democratically elected, they could never be demagogues. If their strength lay in their weakness, it was a collective strength in a collective weakness. The purpose of their meeting was to discuss and consider collectively, to revise and approve.

If the Noble Baroness failed to understand this, the Noble Lord Tebbit understood it even less. He appeared in the Chamber at 1.25 a.m., lingering near the Throne, gold-rimmed half-moons glinting, a lean figure on thin legs, one hand hovering over his mouth.

Lord Butterfield, a doctor, had been telling their lordships about a recent trip he had made to Brussels to discuss diabetes and obesity. This produced spasms of mirth from the overweight Baroness Trumpington, who waved her arms, pointed to herself, and rocked to and fro with vast mirth. No one could hear the rest of what Lord Butterfield had to say. Then, as Lord Morris made a mercifully brief attack on the middle-class intellectuals who were ruining Europe, there was a scramble of heavy feet into the press gallery: wooden flaps were banged down, notebooks flipped open, reporters crammed in shoulder to shoulder, whisky fumes were in the air, the sound man punched his diagrammatic board and a new green button glowed. Lord Tebbit was on his feet.

What was so chilling about Lord Tebbit was hard to define. The semi-housetrained polecat, as he was affectionately described in the House of Commons, was still there, but it was something more than that: a kind of deep-toned, snarling contempt for the very institution of the House of Lords: the Noble Baroness's private bouncer standing up to sneer at them, inviting them if they didn't agree with him to come outside. Again and again he referred to members of the House of Lords as his 'Honourable Friends'. The first couple of times there were pained interventions of 'the noble Lord', but Tebbit wasn't interested. He was interested in power. The steps in front of the Throne had filled up again, the hacks were scribbling in their notebooks with a fervour entirely absent when the Noble Baroness had been speaking, and at nearly two o'clock in the morning the atmosphere was more electric than it had been at any time during the last two days.

The Maastricht treaty was Bad for Britain, Bad for the Other Eleven Members, Bad for the Rest of Europe.

Above the heads of the opposition peers the black remote-controlled eye of the television camera glinted. From his style of speaking, Lord Tebbit could have been addressing a mass rally and probably was.

There had been Dirty Dealing Behind Closed Doors. Delors was Another Bonaparte. He Feared for the Fate of the Fragile Democracies of Eastern Europe, Excluded from the Prosperous Club, Ready to Release their Starving Millions into Germany and Engulf Us All.

It was a terrifying performance, slow, deliberate, brutal. It may even have terrified the Noble Baroness, though she gave no sign of terror. It clearly thrilled the hacks, who stroked Magic Marker across key passages of their shorthand, threw up their desk-flaps and scrambled for the press room.

Then the peace of the Lords returned. Lord Bonham-Carter, a life peer and Asquith's grandson, got up from the Liberal Democrat benches to answer him. He was, he said, perfectly in agreement with the noble lord, Lord Tebbit, in his concern for the fragile democracies of Eastern Europe, but disagreed with him as to the means of helping them. He believed, on the contrary, that a strong and united European Community would be the best safeguard of their future.

The Noble Baroness listened.

Lord Hesketh sat through the debate to the end, a pink carnation in his buttonhole, legs stretched out to reveal matching pale pink socks in well-polished black slip-on shoes. In private, he had continued to be highly satirical about Europe and the treaty. As Government chief whip it was his duty to shepherd his Tory peers through the Lobby, rod and clicker in hand, urging them to ratify Maastricht.

The Referendum Amendment was defeated by 445 votes to 176. Lord Hesketh resigned some time later.

In 1996 one of the more excitable ladies in Sir James Goldsmith's Referendum Party condemned that debate as a notorious and shameful retreat. Now, she had been a supporter of the House of Lords. The peers, she told their conference, they were 'a pack of craven good-for-nothings incapable of rising to the call of duty to defend this nation, probably the only time in their lives that they have been asked to do so, and they failed! I no longer defend the House of Lords.'

Coupled with the rage of Margaret Thatcher as her government was defeated there on no fewer than one hundred and thirty-seven separate occasions, and the Law Lords' relentless muzzling of the Home Secretary, Michael Howard, the evidence suggests that the Upper House was still providing what Charles I called 'a screen or bank' between the tyrant and the people that it was doing its job.

Whether or not membership of the House was in itself 'a job', remained more difficult to answer. In the absence of the old hereditary peers, would anyone be interested in doing it?

At the time this book goes to press the 1997 Labour Government has pledged itself, like so many of its predecessors, to reform the Lords. It seems unlikely that there will be much demand for an increase in its powers. But if the largely impotent Second Chamber painstakingly engineered by a near-sovereign House of Commons continues to command so little public interest, will senators of any calibre, even in a reformed Upper Chamber, be prepared to give up their time to do glorified voluntary work?

As now, retired politicians and the elderly unemployed entitled to membership will continue to turn up, relishing the experience of being fawned over by the doorkeepers, of eating at the club, meeting their old cronies and being allowed to hold forth uninterrupted on their favourite subjects. Their numbers have been strengthened until now by the hereditary peerage, a few of them still young and relatively energetic. A few of them, too, grew up with an old-fashioned sense of public duty and the habit of taking on voluntary committee work. A few of them benefited from having been brought up to manage large estates, with a traditional sense of responsibility for their tenants, for preserving farmland and forests for their sons and grandsons. It could even be argued that their random selection by birth provided the Upper Chamber with specimen unambitious human beings who would have been cut to pieces in the struggle for democratic election to the House of Commons.

Against that, Tony Blair, in announcing his plans for reform, based his argument on three generations of Brockets. The first Lord Brocket bought his title from Lloyd George, the second was a Nazi sympathiser, the third, Blair told a delighted House of Commons, was a jailbird who had first attended the House of Lords to plead for a tougher line on crime.

But if the right of the hereditary peerage to a seat in the Upper House is indefensible against such Horizonist attacks in an age when Horizonism might appear to reign unchallenged, it is perhaps worth offering, in conclusion, the Ladderist defence. Ladderism, after all, has an extraordinarily large underground following, beginning in the tunnels dug by protestors trying to stop roads and airports, and extending through that part of society that believes in continuity and prefers things as they used to be: middle-class subscribers to the National Trust, those who dress up in funny costumes to re-enact the battles of the Civil War, those who try to save the red squirrel. Hereditary legislators are, after all, an endangered species on the brink of extinction.

Lord Salisbury's mid-nineteenth-century argument about 'wealth, in some countries birth, in all countries intellectual power and culture' giving an aristocracy 'every right that superior fitness can confer' looks even more threadbare today. It might at a pinch be applied to some of the life peers, but hardly to the old hereditaries. Salisbury made the mistake of defending his order in purely Horizonist terms. His descendant, Viscount Cranborne, as Tory leader in the Lords in

1996, moved into more spiritual and Ladderist realms. Summarized in a leading article in the *Daily Telegraph* by his close friend the editor, Charles Moore, his line was that 'the rights of inheritance, whether of property or citizenship, have deeper roots in people's minds than the rights of the ballot box.'

This reference to 'roots in people's minds' would have appealed to Richard Trench. As Christian Socialists with a romantic passion for hereditary peers remaining in the Upper House, Trench and F. D. Maurice and the other Cambridge Apostles had an odd hero and spokesman in Thomas Carlyle.

In *Heroes and Hero Worship*, he presents the most compelling image of the spiritual relation: not of a ladder, but more dynamically of a kind of universal family tree with roots. He found it in the Icelandic sagas.

> Igdrasil, the Ash Tree of Existence, has its roots deep down in the Kingdom of Hela or Death; its trunk reaches up heaven-high, spreads its boughs over the whole Universe . . . At the foot of it, in the Death-Kingdom, sit three *Normas*, Fates: the Past, Present, Future; watering its roots from the Sacred Well. Its 'boughs' with their buddings and disleafings – events, things suffered, things done, catastrophes – stretch through all lands and times. Is not every leaf a biography, every fibre there an act or word?

Carlyle mocked the Apostles for their 'Christianism', he asked his readers in *Sartor Resartus* to imagine 'a naked House of Lords, he dismissed the Crown as 'a piece of bent metal', and has the distinction of being one of the last authors Goebbels read aloud to Hitler in the Berlin bunker. The image of the Tree Igdrasil could be used as a Fascist text: the dark, irresistable forces of destiny shaping our lives, individual resistance being useless. But that is not what Trench and the Apostles saw in it. They saw what Burke saw: dynamic continuity, Christian love governing creation, the human family united by its common roots, part of the same tradition. It was essentially optimistic, with every individual playing a part in one vast and significant soap opera that had been growing and developing for thousands of years, was doing so still, and would continue to do so for thousands of years to come. We were subject to the Fates, to the Will of God: we could suddenly be written out of the script or our role could be thrillingly and unexpectedly extended, but we were responsible actors maintaining a long-running series, links in a living chain. We were consciously creating the future as conscious heirs of the past.

This demanded humility. On the industrial principle we could forget the past, concrete it over. Considering the spiritual relation, we were obliged to remember it, to recognise that we would soon be part of the past ourselves, that we were responsible for the future. In such a picture of the world the hereditary peerage took on real importance, like a theatrical dynasty descended from the soap stars of the past, what Edmund Burke called 'the chain that connects the ages of a nation'.

The writer Ben Okri, in a documentary he made about the British punitive expedition that destroyed and looted the palace of the Oba of Benin, wrote that to disperse the sacred Benin Bronzes to museums all over the world was to disperse the nation's soul. The same might be said of the dispersal of hereditary peers from the House of Lords.

But the hereditary peerage also provided a reminder of the half-forgotten Shining Ladder in dignifying the scale of honours. Honours, as Dom Pedro Gastao Orleans y Braganza, great-grandson of the last Emperor of Brazil and claimant to the throne, explained in an interview in 1992 at the age of eighty, had a point. Brazilian presidential elections, he said, were held every five years and cost about two million dollars in bribes. The annual cost to the country in everyday corruption was ten times that.

'If you did away with the Presidency and I was Emperor instead, I would not need to make my friends and allies heads of state companies. I could offer them all titles.'

He was talking about titles not only as rewards but as inducements. In the old Prussian *Herrenhaus*, or House of Lords, individual industrialists or magnates could be appointed to sit in the chamber for life, but without being ennobled. England being England, fewer busy lawyers, businessmen and academics would accept nomination for such unpaid committee work without the inducement of a title. Even with a title, membership of a House of Lords emptied of aristocratic eccentrics and obsequious doormen might not carry the same clout. One disgruntled life peer complained to me that since his ennoblement he had probably used his credit card two hundred times, everyone could see from it that he was a lord, and no one had ever asked him what he had done to deserve it. The Wodehousian mystique, gilt on the gingerbread by association with the old Dukes and Earls, was a more powerful social aphrodisiac than mere merit.

There is also the question of money. The idea of the old magnates, local kings and mafia bosses of their day, being 'summoned' by the central power is in itself an anachronism. No other country on earth sees attendance at the senate as voluntary work even in return for a title. Senators abroad, like any other politicians, are paid.

The United States Senate has a hundred members, required only to be over the age of 30 and to have been resident in the country for nine years, all directly elected and paid. France has three hundred and twenty-one, with a lower age-limit of 35, all elected by proportional representation and paid. Japan has two hundred and fifty-two, all elected by the same system, also paid, and meets three afternoons a week. Modern Germany probably offers the most insulting comparison. Its *Bundesrat* has no members as such, being made up of ninety-six elected members of parliament from the various states of the German Federation, nominated by their colleagues. It meets only once a month.

Such countries, of course, do not understand the mysteries of state theatre, and it is in that context that the hereditary peers have always been of the greatest constitutional value. Lord Saye and Sele, criticising Cromwell's House of Lords, longed for the good old days when the red benches were filled with hereditary peers, who 'as steps and stairs upheld the Crown from falling and being cast down upon the floor by the insolence of the multitude'.

As part of the dignified side, the hereditary peers not only lent glamour to the new lifers, they shored up the monarchy as the only other institution built on heredity in the light of the Shining Ladder. They were as much a part of the ritual magic as the Woolsack and the Throne itself. Over the centuries the real power of the monarchy and the aristocracy evaporated in the increasingly corrosive Horizonist atmosphere. What was left was something very close to Peter Horsfall's Vacuum behind the Throne, and it became a valuable part of the mechanical operation of government.

In civil war and revolution the Throne, the central power, was challenged with bombs and bullets. But there were always less violent and potentially more dangerous threats. New claimants to power, armed with money or economic resources, national or international, were constantly surging up the financial hierarchy, keen to control markets, to make money, to adapt the law to make it easier for them to do so, and the best place to do that from was from the top.

If the system worked, the climbing interlopers encountered the Vacuum. They were beaten back by the law, certainly, but also by phantoms: by Her Majesty, by members of the House of Lords summoned by her Especial Grace and Mere Motion to be personally present at her Parliament, to treat and give her counsel. In that invisible world at the top of the Ladder, the Queen had already bagged a place that could be taken by a corrupt or politically ambitious president. The hereditary peers filled a few hundred slots that might have contained as many yes-men appointed by a prime minister with a vastly expanded source of patronage. In an elected Second Chamber the slots could have been filled by the same number of ambitious elected senators bent on challenging the House of Commons. In the United States the President could avoid deadlock between the two Houses by using his Veto. The last 'single person' who had the Veto in England was Oliver Cromwell, and it didn't work.

Social and economic hierarchies will always exist, many of them overlapping. Aspirants scamper up them like angels up Jacob's Ladder, an upsurge as fast-moving as water up an ornamental fountain, where cookery experts, pop stars, sportsmen and weather-forecasters are drawn up, glitter for a moment, and then plunge decoratively back into the level pool. Many hierarchies are infinitely more powerful: in material terms, a billionaire with houses all over the world is in a position to patronize members of the House of Lords, the Royal Family, even the Prime Minister himself.

The Shining Ladder represented the idealised form of all those other hierarchies, still and immutable. The vacuum at the top, the 'dignified' part of government, may have been an illusion, but in terms of political theatre, it worked.

SELECT BIBLIOGRAPHY

Direct quotes from speeches in the House of Lords are from *Parliamentary Debates (Hansard)* or from contemporary records. Other quotations, apart from my own interviews, are from published biographies, diaries and correspondence. The following is a short list of specialist sources I have also drawn on:

Allyn, Emily, *Lords versus Commons 1830–1930*, 1931

Bagehot, Walter, ed. R. H. S. Crossman, *The English Constitution*, 1964

Bence-Jones, Mark, and Montgomery-Massingberd, Hugh, *The British Aristocracy*, 1979

Bouissou, Michel, *La Chambre des Lords au XXme Siecle (1911–1949)*, 1957

Braham, Stuart, *A Hard Core of Wind*, 1986

Cannadine, David, *The Decline and Fall of the British Aristocracy*, 1990

Cockayne, G. E. (ed.) and others, *The Complete Peerage 1910–59*

Colvin, H. M., *The History of the King's Works*, 1963–82

Foster, Elizabeth R., *The House of Lords 1603–1649*, 1983

Heuston, R. F. V., *Lives of the Lord Chancellors 1940–1970*, 1987

Jenkins, Roy, *Mr Balfour's Poodle*, 1954

Jones, David L., *Peers, Politics and Power: the House of Lords 1603–1911*, 1986

Lehmburg, Stanford E., *The Reformation Parliament 1529–1536*, 1970

Lindsay, Martin A., *Shall We Reform the Lords?*, 1948

Mackenzie, A., *The Peers and the Franchise*, 1884

Macmillan, Gerald, *Honours for Sale. The Strange Story of Maundy Gregory*, 1954

Morgan, Janet P., *The House of Lords and the Labour Government 1964–1970*, 1975

Pike, Luke Owen, *A Constitutional History of the House of Lords*, 1894

Powell J. Enoch, and Wallis, Keith, *The House of Lords in the Middle Ages*, 1968

Prochaska, Frank, *Royal Bounty: The Making of a Welfare Monarchy*, 1995

Roth, Andrew, *Lord on the Board*, 1972

Round, J. H., *Peerage and Pedigree*, 1910

Sayles, G. O., *The Functions of the Medieval Parliament of England*, 1988

Schoenfeld, Maxwell P., *The Restored House of Lords*, 1967

Stanworth, Philip G., and Giddins, A., *Elites and Power in British Society*, 1974

Smith, Robert (ed.), *The House of Lords, a Thousand Years of British Tradition*, 1994

Turberville, A. S., *The House of Lords in the Reign of William III*, 1913

Turberville, A. S., *The House of Lords in the Eighteenth Century*, 1927

Turberville, A. S., *The House of Lords in the Age of Reform 1784–1837*, 1958

Weston, Corinne Comstock, *English Constitutional Theory and the House of Lords 1556–1832*, 1965

Weston, Corinne Comstock, and Greenberg, J. R., *Subjects and Sovereigns: The Grand Controversy over Legal Sovereignty in Stuart England*, 1981

Winchester, Simon, *Their Noble Lordships: The Hereditary Peerage Today*, 1981

INDEX

Aberdeen, Earl of, 201
Act Restoring the Temporal Power of the Clergy (1661), 131
Act for the Union of England and Scotland (1707), 136
Act of Union of Great Britain and Ireland (1801), 263, 265
Acton, Maud, 224
Advisory Council, 120
Albemarle, 9th Earl of, xv
Albert, Prince Consort, 188, 189
Alexander of Weedon, Lord, 276
Alfred, King, 50, 51
Allen, Dr, Bishop of Bristol, 171, 172
American War of Independence, 155–6, 175
Ampthill, Lady (née Christabel Hart), 217, 218–28, 232–5
Ampthill, Lady ('Stilts'' mother), 220, 221, 226, 233
Ampthill, Lord (Geoffrey Russell), 88, 141, 143–6, 148–52, 217, 221, 227, 228, 233–4, 237, 266
Ampthill, Lord ('Stilts'' father), 234, 266
Ampthill, Lord ('Stilts' Russell), 217, 218–27, 266
Anglican Church, see Church of England
Anglo-Saxon Chronicle, 17, 40
Annandale, Marquess of, 136
Anne, Queen, 136, 138, 139–40
Anselm, Archbishop of Canterbury, 39–42, 44
Anyone for Denis?, 27
Appeal Court, 229
Appellate Jurisdiction Act (1876), 58
Ardwick, Lord, 276
Aristotle, 70, 97
Army Council, 115, 120

'Army of God', 65, 67
Arran, Earl of, 32
Ashburnham, Lord, 157
Asquith, Cyril, 53
Asquith, Herbert, 1st Earl of Oxford and Asquith, 210, 212, 230, 244, 256, 275, 280
Astor, 1st Viscount, 212
Athequa, Jorge de, Bishop of Llandaff, 98–9
Attlee, Clement, 1st Earl, 53, 239, 242, 257–60, 278
Attorney General, 240, 248, 250, 252
Attwood, Thomas, 169
Audley, Lord Chancellor, 100
Augustine, St, 36
Ayer, Professor A.J., 251
Aykroyd, Dan, 183, 184, 193, 196

Bacon, Francis (Lord Verulam) xviii, 31, 53
Bagehot, Walter, 11, 12, 200
Bahauder, Nabob Wallajh Cawn, 175
Balfour, 1st Earl of, 206–7, 208, 211–12, 214, 257
Balfour of Burleigh, Lord, 210
Bancroft, Richard, Archbishop of Canterbury, 106, 110
Banqueting House, 7, 126
Bar of the House, 4, 10, 108, 112, 114, 118, 148, 150, 249, 267
Barons of the Exchequer, 105
Barry, Sir Charles, 28, 91, 184, 188
Barry Room, House of Lords, 144
Bartholomew Fair (Jonson), 105
Bartlett, Lord, 114
Bathurst, Lord, 174, 178
The Battle of Maldon, 13, 15
B.B.C., 54, 88, 277
Beaufort, Duke of, 209
Beaumarchais, Pierre Caron de, 156

Beaumont, Lord de, 42
Beaverbrook, Lord, 231, 260
Becket, St Thomas à xviii, 39, 40, 43–7, 53, 93, 95, 96
Bedford, Duke of, 221
Beefsteak Club, 32
Bell, George, Bishop of Chichester, 243
Beloff, Lord, 274, 275
Bench of Bishops, 2–3, 50, 110–11, 130, 131, 274
Benn, Anthony Wedgwood, 146, 237–53, 260, 261, 266–7
Bennard, the Hon. Mrs Edith Ellen xiv
Benoit, Thomas, 96
Bentham, Jeremy, 165
Berkeley, Lord, 134
Berkshire, Earl of, 108
Bernstein, Leonard, 143
Bevan, Aneurin, 239
Bibbiani, Mr (catering manager), 144
Bigge, Sir Arthur (George V's private secretary), 213
Bigod, Hugh, 9
Bill of Rights, 131
Bills, 11, 125, 147, 191, 258; amendments, 149–50, 203; committee stage, 148; Commons, 11, 148; First Reading, 148; Lords, 11, 150; money, 125, 202–3, 208, 210; private, 125, 148, 243, 248; public, 125, 146; reasoned amendments, 149; report stage, 149; Second Reading, 148, 149; Third Reading, 149, 150
Birch, Colonel, 136
Birkenhead, Frederick Edwin Smith, 1st Earl of, 53, 207, 231
Birmingham Constitutional Society, 164
Birmingham Political Union, 169, 170, 171, 180, 202
Birthday Honours List, 230
'Bishops' Boy', 82
Bishops' Exclusion Bill, 110, 201–2
Black Prince see Edward III
Black Rod, 10, 29, 79–81, 84, 85, 88, 106, 126
Blackstone, Baroness, 277–81
Blackstone, Sir William, 139, 154, 267
Blake, Lord, 276
Blue Rod, 79
Blyton, Lord, 21
Bonham-Carter, Lord, 280–81
Boniface, Archbishop of Canterbury, 69
Book of Common Prayer, 271
'Borough mongers', 157
Boston, Lord, 157
Boyd-Carpenter, Lord, 30
Bradlaugh, Charles, 57
Bradley, 'Flick', 218–21, 223, 225
Braham, Stuart xv
Brigade of Guards, 84
Bristol, Bishop of, 243

Bristol, Earl of, 130
Britten, Benjamin, 251
Bronowski, Jacob, 251
Brougham and Vaux, Henry Brougham, 1st Baron, 59, 167–71, 173–80, 184, 199, 201, 202, 279
Brown, George, 243, 247, 248, 249, 251
Browning, Giles, 107
Bryce, Lord, 228, 231, 257, 258, 270
Buckhurst, Lord, 124
Buckingham, Duke of, 250
Buckingham, Earl of, 31
Buckingham Palace, 53, 84, 187
Bundesrat xix
Burke, Edmund xix–xx, xxi, 79, 103, 105, 159, 257
Burnet, Bishop, 108
Bury St Edmunds, Abbot of, 62
Butler, R.A., 238, 246, 248, 250, 267
Butterfield, Lord, 279
Byrhtnoth, 13–17, 43, 61, 64, 121, 153

Cairns, Lord, 55
Calvin, John, 104
Camden, Lord, 154–5
Candide (Bernstein), 143–4
Canning, George, 53
Canterbury Cathedral, 45, 93, 94
Carnarvon, Earl of, 171
Caroline, Queen, 170, 171
Carrington, Lord, 268, 274–5
Carrington family, 9
Carson, Sir Edward, 209
Castle, Barbara, 89
Castlehaven, Mervyn Gay, Lord, 107
Castlereagh, Lord, 276
Catherine of Aragon, 96, 98
Catholic Order of the Knights of Malta, 22
Cawdor, Earl, 211
Caws, Genevra xiv
Celtic Church, 36
Chaff Wax, 59
Chancery Courts, 185
Charles, HRH the Prince of Wales, 21–2, 193
Charles I, King, 5, 26, 106–12, 114, 115, 119, 121, 122, 126, 130, 131, 135–6, 139, 232, 247
Charles II, King, 7, 126, 127, 130–31, 133, 134
Charnwood, Lord, 232
Chartists, 204
Chatham, Earl of, 154
Chaucer, Geoffrey, 94
Chelmsford, Bishop of, 264
Chesterton, G.K., 245
Cholmondeley, Marquess of, 9, 197
Cholmondeley Castle, 88
Cholmondeley family, 9
Christian Socialists xxi
Church of England, 96, 101, 104–5, 131, 137, 207, 210, 249, 271

Church of Ireland, 249
Churchill, Sir Winston Spencer, 53, 54, 59, 199–200, 207, 209, 239, 243, 244, 249
Clancarty, Earl of, 193–4, 195
Clarenceux King of Arms, 96
Clarendon, Earl of, 130, 131
Clarendon, hunting lodge near Salisbury, 44, 61, 65
Cledwyn of Penrhos, Lord, 241
Clerk of the Crown, 125
Clerk of the Crown and Hanaper, 264
Clerk of the Journals, 259
Clerk of the Parliaments, 85
Clerks' Table, 148, 168
Cloth of Estate, 124
Coal Mines Act, 207
Cobbett, William, 171
Cogidubnus of Chichester, 18, 61
Colbert, Jean Baptiste, 274
Cole, Sir Colin, Garter King at Arms, 21–2
Colepeper, Lord, 112
Coleridge, Samuel Taylor, 162
Colet, John, 93, 94, 95
College of Arms xviii, 19, 21
Columba, St, 36
Commentaries on the Laws of England (Blackstone), 267
Committee for Privileges, 18, 39, 107, 231, 234, 240, 241, 242, 244, 246, 247, 248, 262
Committee of Public Safety, 66
Committee Stage, 7
Common Agricultural Policy, 274
Common Sense (Paine), 162
Commons' Clerks, 148
Commonwealth, 101, 120, 124
Commonwealth of Oceania (Harrington), 118–20
Complete Peerage, The, 39, 61, 262
Constantine, Emperor, 36
Constitutions of Clarendon, 44, 46
Convention Commons, 133, 135
Convocation, 72
Conyers, Lord, 100
Cook, Peter, 32
Corn Laws, 204
Coronets, 7–8
Corresponding Societies, 159
Court of Appeal, Lords as a, 55, 56, 57
Court of Bankruptcy, 186
Court of Exchequer, 186
Cozens-Hardy (peerage lawyer), 262
Cranborne, Viscount xiii
Cranmer, Archbishop, 100
Crewe, Earl of, 212, 232
Cripps, Sir Stafford, 239, 240
Criterion Theatre, London, 32
Croker, John Wilson, 169
Cromwell, Oliver, 114, 115–16, 119–26, 191, 256
Cromwell, Richard, 126

Cross, Captain, 220, 221, 222, 223, 225
Crossman, Richard, 269
Cumberland, Duke of, 173
Curzon, Lord, 211, 214, 249, 262

Danby, Earl of, 131
Danegeld, 15, 183
Dante Alighieri, 37
d'Aumale, Lord, 62
Davies, Clement, 259
Davies of Leek, Lord, 194–5
Day, Sir Robin, 251
Day-Lewis, Cecil, 251
De La Warr, Lord, 100–101, 242
de Vere family, 9
Deedes, Lord, 21
Delamer, Lord, 134
Delors, Jacques, 274, 280
Denbigh, Earl of, 130
Denham, Lord, ('Bertie'), 2
Denman, Lord, 57
Derby, Earl of, 106
Devonshire, Duke of, 171, 172
Devonshire, Earl of, 131
Diana, Princess of Wales, 193
Dilhorne, Lord, 252–3
Director of Works, 85
Discourse on Inequality (Rousseau), 160
Division Bell, 192
Dodderidge, Mr Justice, 107, 137, 237, 248
Dod's Parliamentary Companion, 83
Domesday Book, 72
Donaldson of Lymington, Lord, 52, 230
Donovan, Terence, 32–3
Dorset, Earl of, 110
Dunboyne, Lord, 266
Dundee, Earl of (Mr Scrymgeour-Wedderburn), 247
Dunraven, Lord, 210
Durham, Bishop of, 201
Durham, Earl of, 242
Dyce, William, *The Baptism of St Ethelbert*, 189

Eadmer (Archbishop Anselm's chaplain), 41
Earldred, 38
East India Company, 154, 249
Ede and Ravenscroft, Chancery Lane, 6, 7, 27, 29, 49
Edelman, Maurice, 270
Education Bill, 207
The Education of a Christian Prince (Erasmus), 97
Edward, Brother, 46
Edward the Confessor, King, 38, 51, 65, 67, 75
Edward I, King, 71, 74
Edward III, King, 8, 19, 73, 74, 76–7, 188
Edward IV, King, 4
Edward VII, King, 55, 212, 213
Edward VIII, King, 244

Egmont, Lord, 248
Eldon, Lord, 52–3, 163, 173
Elliott, Baroness xvii, 184, 262
Elizabeth I, Queen, 104–5, 106, 109, 200, 283
Elizabeth II, Queen; and Denis Thatcher, 84;
    and the Great Seal, 59; Queen's Speech, 4,
    10, 81, 267, 269; and the State Opening of
    Parliament, 8, 9, 10, 12, 51
Elton, Lord, 245
Ely cathedral, 13
Embryology Bill, 148
Émile (Rousseau), 159
English Civil War, 110, 112, 114, 128, 130, 284
Erasmus, Desiderius, 93, 94–5, 97, 98, 101
Erskine, Thomas, lst Baron, 163
Esher, Viscount, 252, 255–6, 257
Essay on the First Principles of Government
    (Priestley), 161
Essex, Earl of, 101
Ethelred, King, 14–15, 16, 17
Eure, Lord, 123
European Parliament, 146
Evelyn, John, 7
Evelyn, Sir John, 114
Evesham, battle of, 71
Ezra, Lord, 276

Fabian Society, 246
Fauconberg, Lord, 123
Fauconbridge, Lord, 107
Fawkes, Guy, 1, 78
Fellowes, Sir Edward, 248
Fiennes, Lord, 121, 124
Fifth Monarchy Men, 117
Fisher, John, Bishop of Rochester, 99, 100,
    101, 104
Fitz Patrick, Mervyn, 107
Fitzurse, 45, 46
F.M. Kirby Foundation, 19
Foliot, Gilbert, Bishop of London, 44, 45
Foot, Dingle, 240, 247, 248
Foot, Michael xiii, 33, 240, 259, 271, 272
Fortescue, Sir John, 97
Foster, Sir John, 234
Francis of Assisi, St, 70
Franklin, Benjamin, 156, 160
Fraser, Lady Antonia, 269
Fraser, Sir Hugh, 269
French Revolution xix, xx, 79, 103, 117, 159,
    163, 164, 170, 188, 269
Friends of the People, 171
Frost, Sir David, 9
Fuchs, Dr, 189

Gage, General, 155
Gaitskell, Hugh, 238, 247, 249, 258–62
Galbraith, T.G.D., 271–2
Galloway, Joseph, 156
Gardiner, Lord, 55

Garrick, David, 51, 157
Garter King at Arms, 18, 29, 30, 267
Gentlemen-at-Arms, 10
George I, King, 139–40
George II, King, 244
George III, King, 8, 155, 163
George IV, King, 7, 176–7
George V, King, 212, 213, 214, 234, 262
George VI, King, 234
Gieves and Hawkes, Savile Row, 8
Gladstone, William Ewart, 204–5, 206, 230,
    249, 252, 255
Gladwyn, Lord, 195
Glanusk, Lord xvi
Glorious Revolution, 128, 131
Gloucester, Duke of (Charles I's son), 121
Gloucester, Duke of, 265
Godwin, William, 161–3, 165
Goldsmith, Sir James, 273
Gordon, General Charles, 255
Gordon Riots (1780), 157, 179, 233
Gower, Earl, 155
Gowrie, 2nd Earl of xv
Grand Orange Lodge, 171
Granville, 2nd Earl of, 206
Greal Seal, 53, 55, 58, 59, 66, 133
Great councils xix, 61, 127
Great Reform Bill (1832) xx
Green Rod, 79
Greenpeace, 85
Greville, Charles, 173, 203–4
Grey, Charles, 2nd Earl, 168, 171–2, 180,
    181, 204
Grey, Lord (1680), 192
Grey, Lord, of Rotherfield, 77
Grey of Wark, Lord, 130
Griffin, Lord, 134
Grimond, Lord, 2, 79, 143, 239, 279
Grosseteste, Robert, Bishop of Lincoln, 70
Guildford, Bishop of, 28
Gulliver's Travels (Swift), 129–30, 132, 138, 139
Gundulf, Bishop of Rochester, 41
Gwynne-Jones, Peter Llewellyn, Garter King at
    Arms, 20

Hailsham of St Marylebone, Lord, 32, 50, 59,
    81, 238, 239, 242, 251, 252–3, 255, 260, 261,
    262, 265, 266, 278
Halifax, Lord, 134
Hall, Richard, 99
Hallam, Arthur, 188
Halsbury, 1st Earl of, 52, 55, 196, 199, 206, 214
Hamilton, Alexander, 256
Hamilton, Willie, 272
Hampden, 5th Viscount, xvi, xvii
Hampton Court Palace, 105, 106
Hansard xiv, 29, 83, 173, 193, 195, 276
Hardie, Keir, 206
Hardy, Thomas, 163

Harmar-Nichols, Lord, 276
Harrington, James, 118–20
Harris, Lord, 230
Hastings, Lord, 245
Hastings, Patrick, K.C., 221–5, 226
Hatsell's Precedents, 248
Hay, Lord, 31
Haydon, Benjamin Robert, 188–9
Heads of the Proposals of the Army (Ireton), 114
Heath, Sir Edward, 249, 279
Heffer, Eric, 270
Henderson, Sir Peter, 90
Henn Collins, Lord Justice, 52
Henry II, King, 39, 40, 43, 45, 46–7, 58, 63, 66, 95
Henry III, King, 67, 69, 70, 71, 74
Henry IV, King, 136
Henry V, King, 19, 31
Henry VI, King, 97
Henry VIII, King, 95–6, 97, 99, 101, 103–4, 108, 109, 115
Heraldry/heralds, 18–23, 96, 106
Hesilrige, Sir Arthur, 126
Hesketh, Lord, 9–10, 183, 184, 185, 190–93, 196, 197, 281
Hewlett, Lord, 193, 196
Hill, Mr Justice, 225, 228
Hillsborough, Lord, 157
Hinchingbrooke, Viscount, 242, 249, 250
His Majesty's Answer to the Nineteen Propositions of both Houses of Parliament (Charles I), 111
History of the Four Last Years of Queen Anne's Reign (Swift), 138–9
Hitler, Adolf, 256
Hogg, Sir Douglas (1st Lord Hailsham of St Marylebone), 233
Holland, Henry Fox, 3rd Baron, 171
Home, Earl of, (1707), 136
Home of the Hirsel, Baron Alexander Douglas-Home, 252–3, 255, 260, 267, 272
Honourable Corps of Gentlemen-at-Arms, 9
Honours List, 230, 258
Horsfall, Major Peter, 2, 3, 6, 8, 80, 82–92, 141, 144
House of Commons, catering, 144; and destruction of the HoL xxi; formed, 71; role, 3; running costs, 146
Household Cavalry, 1, 82
Howe, Lord, 278
Hugh, Abbot, 62–3, 66
Hugh of Horsea, 46
Hume-Williams, Sir Ellis, 222
Hunsdone, Lord, 114, 130
Hurd, Douglas, 274

Iddesleigh, Earls of, 22
Ignatius, St, 104
Inchcape, Lord, 230
Ingrams, Richard, 32

International Brigade xii
Iolanthe (Gilbert and Sullivan), 10
Iremonger, Tom, 270–71
Ireton, Henry, 114, 115
Irish Home Rule Bills, 204, 205, 206, 215
Irish Nationalists, 249
Irish Republican Army (IRA), 1, 137

James, Henry, 205–6
James I, King of England xv, 5, 31, 105, 106, 107, 109, 127, 128, 131, 134, 136, 230, 250
James II, King of England, 59, 131–5, 137
Jay, Lord, 193
Jellicoe, Earl, 146
Jenkins of Hillhead, Lord, 81, 151, 239, 268, 277–8
Jewel Tower, Palace of Westminster, 74, 188
John, Augustus, 218, 251
John, King, 4, 61–6, 69, 211
John, St, 35
Jonson, Ben, 105
Joseph, Lord, 29
Jowitt, Earl, 53, 243, 244
Joynson-Hicks, William, 209
The Just Man in Bonds (tract), 113
Justices of the Courts of Common Pleas and King's Bench, 105

Keeper of the Great Seal, 55, 58, 59
Keeper of the Queen's Conscience, 51, 52
Keppel, Arnold Van, xv
Kilmorey, Lord, 265
Kilmuir, Viscount, 245, 252, 253, 265, 266
Kimberley, Earl of, 194
King's House, Greenwich, 31
King's Bench, 185
King's Council, 240
King's Counsels, 98
Kings Norton, Lord, 195
Kinnoull, Lord, 136
Kipling, Rudyard, 278–9
Knights of the Order of the Garter, 8
Knollys, Sir Francis, 213
'Kremlin' (bar), 90, 91–92

Labouchère, Henry, 238
Labour Leader, 215, 230
Lambton, Lord, 242, 249, 250, 251
Lancaster, Osbert, 240
Langton, Stephen, Archbishop of Canterbury, 62, 65, 67
Lansdowne, Marquess of, 164–5, 207, 208, 212, 213, 228
Laud, Archbishop, 110
Law, Harry, 234
Law lords, and the Appeal Court, 229; the first, 57
Law-clerks, 65, 73

League of Nations, 231
Lee, Bishop, 100
Lee, Jennie, Baroness Lee of Ashridge, 246, 259
Legitimacy Act (1924), 233, 234
Lehmann, Rosamund (later Lady Milford) xii
Leinster, Duke of, 8
Lennox, Duke of, 106
A Letter to a Friend Concerning the Ruptures of the Commonwealth (Milton), 128
Letters on a Regicide Peace (Burke) xix
Levellers, 112, 113, 161
Leverhulme, Lord, 230
Lewes, battle of, 71
Lewis, C.S., 196
Liberal Democrat peers, 150, 151
Liberal Unionists, 206, 207
Licensing Bill, 208
Lilburne, John, 112, 113
Lincoln, Bishop of, 157
Lincoln, Earl of, 114, 130
Lisle, Lord, 101
Littlewood, Joan, 32
Liverpool, Earl of, 159
Llewelyn-Davies of Hastoe, Baroness, 9
Lloyd George, Gwillym, 53
Lloyd-George of Dwyfor, David Lloyd George, lst Earl, 53, 205, 207–10, 215, 230
London, Bishop of, 110, 131, 201
London Corresponding Society, 159
London Working Men's Association, 204
Londonderry, Marquess of, 172, 202, 214
Londonderry House, Park Lane, London, 180
Long, Sir Lislebone, 125
Longford, Earl of, 146, 260–61, 265
Lorby, Thomas, 106
Lord Chairman of Committees, 143, 149
Lord Chancellor, 5, 10, 11, 27–31, 49–59, 82, 86, 98, 100, 108, 124, 148, 149, 150, 167, 170, 174–5, 206, 245, 252, 265, 275, 276
Lord Chancellor of Ireland, 264
Lord Chief Justice, 105, 124, 157, 172
Lord Great Chamberlain, 9, 197
Lord Lieutenant of Ireland, 264
Lord Treasurer, 124
Lords of Appeal in Ordinary, 58
Lords' Clerks, 98, 148
Louis IX, King of France, 67
Louis XIV, King, 274
Lovejoy, Lord, 107
Lovelace, Lord, 107, 134
Lumley, Lord, 131
Lyndhurst, Lord, 180

Maastricht Treaty, 32, 183, 273, 280
MacDonald, Ramsay xiv
Mace, 5, 27, 59, 84, 180
Mackay of Clashfern, Lord xviii, 27, 50, 56
Maclise, Daniel, *Alfred in the Danish Camp*, 183, 189, 191; *The Spirit of Chivalry*, 189
Macmillan, Sir Harold, lst Earl of Stockton, 251, 258–9, 276
Magna Carta, 63, 65, 66–7, 69
Maidstone, John, 122, 124
Major, John, 250
Mallalieu, Baroness, 89
Manchester, Earl of, 112, 114, 115, 123, 130
Manners, Lord John, 206
Manningham-Buller, Sir Reginald, 247–50
Manorial Society, 20
Mansfield, Earl of, 51, 157, 172, 233
Marie Antoinette xix
Marlborough, first Earl of, 124
Marquand, David, 268–9
Married Love (Stopes), 219
Marshall Hall, Sir Edward, 225, 227, 228
Martin, George, 81
Marx, Karl, 256
Mary II, Queen, 131, 136
Master of the Rolls, 232, 233
Masters of Chancery, 98, 105
Masters of Requests, 105
Maurice, F.D. xxi
Maxwell Fyfe, Sir David, 59
May, Erskine, 247
Mayer, Edgar, 223–4, 225, 226, 228
Maynard, Lord, 114, 130
Melbourne, Lord, 188
Memoirs (Greville), 173, 203–4
Mereworth, Lord, 264
Messel, Oliver, 144
Messina Conference (1955), 276
Middlesex, Earl of, 114
Milford Haven, Marquess of, 226
Milford, Lord (Wogan Philipps) xi–xii, 268
Miller, Jonathan, 143
Milton, John, 128
Mitchison, Lord, 252
Mitchison Amendment, 252
Monck, General 126, 127
Monkswell, Lord, 83
Monson-Watson, Lewis (Lord Sondes), 248
Monteagle of Brandon, Anne, Lady xvi
Monteagle of Brandon, Lord xvi–xvii
Montfort, Simon de, Earl of Leicester, 9, 69, 70, 71
Moore, Henry, 251
More, St Thomas xviii, 101
Morley, Earl of, 214
Morrelet, Abbé, 165
Morris, Lord, 279
Morris, William, 229
Motion for Papers, 147
Motion for Resolution, 147
Motion to Take Note, 147
Mowbray, Roger de, 38, 39
Mrs Wilson's Diary, 32

Much Obliged, Jeeves (Wodehouse), 237–8
Mulgrave, Earl of, 123

Nabarro, Sir Gerald, 248, 249, 250
Naismith, Mrs (clairvoyant), 222
National Health Service, 258
Naylor, James, 122
Neave, Airey, 1
Newton, Lord, 58, 211
Norfolk, Dukes of, 7, 9, 39, 100, 130, 171, 172
Norreys, Lord, 192
North, Lord, 124
Northampton Castle, 45
Northumberland, Duke of, 130, 157
Norwich, Bishop of, 195
Nottingham Castle, 180
Nottingham, Lord, 131, 134

O'Boyle, Brian, 87
O'Connell, Daniel, 57
Old Age Pensions Act, 207–8
On the Treasons of Becket (play), 95
Onslow, Mr Speaker, 248
Oranmore and Browne, Lord, 264
Order of the Garter, 8, 19, 264
Order of St Patrick, 264, 265
Order of the Thistle, 79, 264
ordo, 18, 61
Osborne, John, 251
Oswald, Richard, 156
'Other House' (under Cromwell), 122–4, 125, 126
Oxford, Earl of, 139

Paget, Reginald, 239
Paine, Tom xx, 159, 161, 162, 164, 165
Palace of Westminster, 1, 14, 26, 43, 69, 71, 74, 75, 76, 77, 85, 88, 98, 108, 124, 130, 138, 157, 167, 171, 184, 185, 187–90, 251
Palmerston, Lord, 264
Il Paradiso (Dante), 37
Parke, Sir James, 57–8
Parker-Bowles, Camilla, 10
Parkes, Joseph, 202
Parliament Act (1911), 3, 149, 199, 212–15, 229, 232
Parliament Act (1949), 149
Parliamentary Roll of Arms, 19
Partridge, Frances xii
Pass Office, Palace of Westminster, 85–6
Passfield, Lord, 229
Peel, Sir Robert, 203
Peerage and Landed Gentry (Debrett), 21
Peerage Bill (1719), 139
Peerage (Renunciation) Bill, 248, 260–61
Pepys, Samuel xv, 127, 130
Percival, Sir John (later Lord Egmont), 137
Peter, St, 38, 74, 104

Philip, HRH Prince, the Duke of Edinburgh, 9, 21–2, 80
Philipps, Richard xi
Pirrie, Lord, 230
Pitt, William, the Younger, 157, 162, 169, 175–6
A Plea for the Lords (Prynne), 113
'Plod's Café', Palace of Westminster, 86
Police, 2, 84
Political Justice (Godwin), 162
Polybius, 97
Portland, Duke of, 209
The Portrait of a Lady (James), 205–6
Poursuivants at Arms, 105
Powell, Enoch, 61, 270, 271, 272
Presbyterians, 104, 105, 113
Pride, Colonel, 115
Priestley, Joseph, 160–61, 162, 164, 165
Private Notice Questions, 147
Privy councillors, 105
Prophetess of Abingdon, 115
Provisions of Oxford (1258), 70
Prynne, William, 109–10, 113–14, 115, 127
Pugin, August Welby Northmore, 1, 2, 27, 32, 61, 86, 90, 183, 188, 192
Puritans, 105, 106, 108, 109
Purple Rod, 79

Queen's Speech, 4, 10, 81, 267, 269
Quibell, Lord, of Scunthorpe xiv
Quilley, Denis, 144

Ralph Luffa, Bishop of Chichester, 41
Rankeillour, Lord, 196
Rathcavan, Lord, 261, 265
Ravensdale, Lady, 262
Rawlinson, Lord, 51–2
Readie and Easie Way to Establish a Free Commonwealth (Milton), 128
Reay, Lord, 276
Redcoats, 82, 141
Referendum Amendment, 281
Referendum Bill, 278
Referendum Party, 273, 281
Reflections on the French Revolution (Burke) xix
Reform Bill, (1832), 52, 84, 169–70, 176, 177, 179–81, 186, 201
Reformation Parliament, 96, 274
Reith, Lord, 54, 162
The Relapse (Vanbrugh), 153
Remonstrance of Many Thousand Citizens (Overton), 113
Restoration, 128, 134
Reynolds, Sir Joshua, 51
Rhodesia Order, 268
Rhondda, Viscountess, 231, 261
Ribblesdale, Lord, 200
Richard I, King, 63, 127
Richard II, King, 136

Richard III, King, 39
Rights of Man (Paine), 159, 161
Ripon, Bishop of, 243
Rix, Lord, 19, 22
Robinson, Sir Joseph, Bt, 230
Rockingham Castle,
  Northamptonshire, 40, 61, 65
Roman Catholic Church, 35, 36, 58, 69, 94,
  130–31, 137
Roman Empire, 36, 37
Roose, Richard, 101
Roper, Christopher, 106–7
Rose, Kenneth, 21
Rosebery, Lord, 206, 211, 249
Rothermere, Lord, 231
Rothschild, Lord, 209, 230
Rotten boroughs, 168, 175
Rousseau, Jean Jacques xxi, 67, 159–60, 256
Royal Assent, 11, 125, 149
Royal councils xix, 61
Rump Parliament, 120
Runcie, Lord, Archbishop of Canterbury, 89
Runnymede, 61–4, 67, 70, 211
Russell, Hon. John, 227, 234
Russell, 4th Earl xiv
Rust, Tamara (later Lady Milford) xii

St Calais, William de, Bishop of Durham, 41–2
St Clair, Malcolm, 251
St David's, Bishop of, 134
St David's, Viscountess, 262
St George's Chapel, 230
St James's Palace, 6, 7
St John, Oliver, 121
St John, Lord, of Fawsley, 269
St Leonard's, Lord, 53
St Stephen's Chapel, Palace of Westminster,
  74, 75, 76, 102, 108, 116, 122, 125, 133, 167,
  176, 184–7
Salisbury, 3rd Marquess of, 52, 200, 201, 202,
  204, 268, 282
Saltoun, Lord, 243, 245
Samuel, Viscount, 244, 245, 249, 256–7
Samuelson, Pauline xvi
Sandwich, Earl of, 242
Sankey, Lord, 53
Sartor Resartus (Carlyle), 284
Saye and Sele, Lord, 107, 123, 130
Schiller, Johann Christoph Friedrich von, 11
Scobele, Henry, 124
Secombe, Harry, 23
Second Reform Bill (1867), 200, 204
Seditious Practices Act, 171
Selsdon, Lord, 276
Sergeant-at-Arms, 238
Service with a Smile (Wodehouse), 6
Sex Discrimination Act xiv
Sex Disqualification (Removal) Act, 231
Seymour, Sir Edward, 133

Shand, Bruce, 10
Shaw, George Bernard, 245
Shelburne, 2nd Earl of, 154, 160
Shelley, Percy Bysshe, 162
Shinwell, Lord, 2, 148
Shrewsbury, Earl of, 106, 131
Simon, Sir John, 221–2, 225
Simon of Glaisdale, Lord, 276
Simonds, Lord, 54, 55, 59
Skidelsky, Lord, 277
Skinner, Dennis, 10
Smith, Ian, 268
Snowdon, Earl of, 144
Soames, Nicholas, 279
Soane, Sir John, 187
Society for Commemorating the English
  Revolution, 164
Society for Constitutional Information, 159
Solicitors' Journal, 52
Spender, Stephen xi
Speaker of the House of Commons, 55, 148,
  229, 238, 248, 277
Spens, Lord, 142
Standing Orders, 108; on Leave of Absence,
  259
Stanhope, 3rd Earl of, 164
Stansgate, Viscount, 146, 237, 241, 243–6, 251
Starred questions, 147
State Opening of Parliament, 3, 8–12, 51, 78,
  84, 92, 98, 105–6, 163, 184
Stewart, Prince James Francis Edward, 133,
  135, 139
Stigand, Archbishop of Canterbury, 38
Stockton, 3rd Earl of, 273
Stopes, Marie, 219
Stormont, Lord, 156, 157
Strabolgi, Lord, 262–3
Strange of Knokin, Baroness, 262
Strathclyde, Lord, 271
Strawberry Hill, Twickenham, 153, 188
Suffolk, Earl of, 106, 130
Suggia, Guilhermina, 218
Sutherland, Graham, 251
Swan, Conrad, Garter King at Arms, 22
Swanborough, Lady, 262
Swaythling, Lord, 230
Swift, Jonathan, 129–30, 132, 137–9, 168, 176
Swithin, St xviii
Synod of Whitby (664), 36

Tacitus, 17
Taff Vale case (1901), 206, 207
Tawney, R.H. xiv
Taylor of Blackburn, Lord, on insanity in
  HoL xiv–xv
Tebbit, Lord, 273, 275, 279, 280
Television, 4, 145, 278–9
Tennyson, Alfred, Lord, 50, 244
Teynham, Lord, 107, 173

Thatcher, Carol, 27
Thatcher, Denis, 21, 26–7, 28, 29, 32, 84
Thatcher, of Kesteven, Baroness, 51, 84, 85, 90, 137, 151, 249, 273; her government xv; made a peer, 25, 29–32, 33
Thatcher, Mark, 27
The Theatre Considered as a Moral Institution (Schiller), 11
Thomas, Celia, 151
Thomas, J.H., 228–9
Thomas, Admiral Sir Richard, Black Rod, 79
Thorney Island, River Thames, 74
Thorneycroft, Lord, 32
Throne, Parliament Chamber, 2, 3, 4, 10, 11, 28, 59, 61, 77, 88, 89, 98, 108, 131, 135, 167, 168, 180, 184, 189, 191, 273, 279, 282, 283
Titles Deprivations Bill (1917), 239
Today in Parliament (television programme), 276–7
Tonypandy, Lord, 277
Tories, origin of the name, 137
Tower of London, 127
Townshend, Lord, 155, 157
Trade Boards Act, 207
Trade Disputes Bill, 207
Treasonable and Seditious Practices Act, 163–4
Treasury xiv
Treatise concerning Civil Government (Tucker), 156
Tredenham, Sir Joseph, 136
Tree Igdrasil, 283
Trefgarne, Lord, 194, 195
Trench, Richard xx, xxi, 68, 103, 190
Trumpington, Lady, 88, 279
Tucker, Josiah, Dean of Gloucester, 156
Turner, J.M.W., 187
Tweedsmuir, Lady, 259
Tyburn, 74
Tynan, Kenneth, 251

United Nations, 268
United States Senate xix
Ussher, Bishop, 128
Ustinov, Peter, 241
Utrecht, Treaty of (1712), 138

Vanbrugh, Sir John, 153
Vestey, Lord, 230
Victoria, Queen, 57, 197, 203, 246
Victoria Tower xix, 8, 74, 85, 91, 185, 191, 242, 243
Villiers, George, Duke of Buckingham, 106
Voltaire, (François-Marie Arouer) François de xxi

Walker, Sir Edward, 107
Walpole, Horace, 153, 157, 188
Walpole, Sir Robert, 139, 153, 188
Walsingham, 93

Waltheof, 64
Walton of Detchant, Lord, 148
The Wanderer, 16, 17
War Crimes Bill, 149
Warham, Archbishop, 99
Warwick, Earl of, 123
Webb, Beatrice, 229
Webb, Sidney, 229
Wedgwood Benn, Michael, 241
Wellington, 1st Duke of, 172, 174, 175, 180–81, 203, 204
Welsh nationalists, 207
Wesley, Charles, 158
Wesley, John, 158
West, William, 242
Westminster Abbey, 74, 77, 88, 187
Wharncliffe, Lord, 57, 176
Wharton, Lord, 123, 130
Whigs, origin of the name, 137
White, Dr, Bishop of Oxford, 133–4
White Paper on reform on HoL reform, 268, 270, 272
Whitehall Theatre, London, 27
Whitelaw, Lord, 10
Whitelocke, Bulstrode, 116
Wilberforce, Lord, 234
William the Conqueror, 38, 39, 40, 112–13, 209
William III, King, 131, 133, 136
William IV, King, 180, 181, 187
William Rufus, 41, 42, 43, 74
Williams, Marcia, 55
Willoughby de Broke, Lord, 214
Willoughby of Parham, Lord, 114
Wilson, A.N. xiii–xiv
Wilson, of Rievaulx, Baron xvii, 32, 55, 194, 268, 272
Wilson, Lady, 32, 33
Winchester, Bishop of, 202
Windsor Castle, 63
Winterton, Earl of, 244, 249
Witanagemot (Assembly of Wise Men), 14, 18, 38, 39, 40, 43–6, 51, 62, 71, 72, 127, 231
Wodehouse, P.G., 6, 221, 237–8, 245
Wollstonecraft, Mary xx
Wood, Anthony, 127
Woolavington, Lord, 230
Woolsack, 3, 4, 5–6, 11, 28, 29, 50, 52, 53, 54, 56, 59, 89, 98, 148, 157, 168, 172, 173, 174, 180, 275, 276, 282
Woolton, Earl of, 243
Wootton of Abinger, Baroness, 261
Worcester, Bishop of, 38
Workmen's Compensation Act, 207
Wren, Sir Christopher, 187, 191
Wright, Mrs (housekeeper at the Old Palace), 186
Wulfstan, Archbishop of York, 16
Wyatt, James, 185–6, 187
Wynford, 1st Baron, 171, 173

Xenophon, 271

Yeoman Usher, 27, 84, 87
Yeomen of the Guard, 10
York, Archbishops of, 148, 201, 213

Zouche of Ashby, Lord , 77